FOREWORD

This report was discussed and commented upon by Working Party No. 1 of the OECD Economic Policy Committee (EPC) in October 1994 and subsequently revised. The EPC Working Party No. 1 has dealt with the issue of global warming twice before, at its Spring meetings of 1991 and 1992. On these occasions the focus was on the macroeconomic impacts and means of reducing carbon emissions. In particular, the Delegates discussed the modelling tools designed to assess the costs of different policies to cut carbon emissions. Other Directorates and the International Energy Agency have also dealt with different aspects of the global warming issue which have been reported in several OECD publications. Building on this previous work, this study aims to inform the process of developing an appropriate policy response to the risk of global warming, given the commitments taken by signatory parties of the Framework Convention on Climate Change.

The report was prepared in the Resource Allocation Division of the Economics Department of the OECD. The opinions expressed here do not necessarily reflect the views of the OECD Member countries. This report is published on the responsibility of the Secretary-General of the OECD.

76, 79

TABLE OF CONTENTS

Economic Dimensions and Policy Responses 7

1. Background and Main Policy Considerations 7
   1.1. Background and summary 7
   1.2. Policy response 8

2. The Current State of the Debate 11
   2.1. The UN Framework Convention on Climate Change: summary and interpretation 11
   2.2. Uncertainty surrounding the climate change issue: a summary 14
   2.3. Gains from international co-operation 14
   2.4. The carbon leakage problem 17

X 3. Possible Measures to Prevent Climate Change 21
   3.1. Overview 21
   3.2. Emission mitigation options 22
       3.2.1. Raising energy efficiency 23
    ↘ 3.2.2. Fuel substitution 23
       3.2.3. Mitigating emissions of other greenhouse gases 26
   3.3. GHG sequestration and removal 28
       3.3.1. Carbon sequestration through biomass use 28
       3.3.2. CO_2 removal 29
   3.4. The link to policy levers 30

4. Elements of an Appropriate Policy Response 31
   4.1. No-regrets policies 31
   4.2. Climate research and energy-related R&D 32
       4.2.1. Basic climate research 32
       4.2.2. R&D on mitigation and sequestration 32
   4.3. Policy making under uncertainty 33
       4.3.1. The insurance approach to global warming 33
       4.3.2. Uncertainty about policy effectiveness 34
       4.3.3. Building institutions 34
   4.4. Optimal emission abatement over time 35
   4.5. Establishing a level playing field 37

5. The Fiscal Implications of a Carbon Tax 39
   5.1. Estimates of carbon tax revenues 39
   5.2. The use of carbon tax revenues 39
       5.2.1. Earmarking revenues 40
       5.2.2. Increase government spending 40
       5.2.3. Reduce budget deficits 40
       5.2.4. Revenue switching 41
   5.3. Wider public finance implications 44

6. Joint Implementation 47
   6.1. From cost efficiency to joint implementation 47
   6.2. Joint implementation: negotiating side payments 47
   6.3. Joint implementation: partial schemes 47
   6.4. Joint implementation: taxes or quotas? 49
   6.5. Distribution implications of comprehensive joint implementation schemes 49
       6.5.1. Quota allocation principles 49
       6.5.2. Gains and losses from emission quota allocation rules 50
   6.6. Global carbon tax fund 51

Notes 56

Bibliography 60

Appendix: Glossary of Terms/Abbreviations 63

Annex A: Technical background information 67

Annex B: Unilateral emission control, energy-intensive industries and carbon leakages 105

Annex C: Carbon sequestration through biomass use 125

Annex D: Uncertainties in climate policy design 139

Economic Dimensions and Policy Responses

1.   Background and Main Policy Considerations[1]

1.1.   Background and summary

It is widely believed that the rising atmospheric concentration of greenhouse gases (GHG) related to economic activity could result in a change in the global as well as regional climate, entailing severe detrimental economic and ecological effects. There is considerable uncertainty about the extent to – and speed at – which such climate change is likely to occur, what its overall effects and their regional distribution might be, and the cost and effectiveness of efforts to prevent, slow down, or adapt to this process. Despite this uncertainty, the magnitude of potential damage from global warming led 157 governments in Rio de Janeiro in June 1992 to sign a treaty on the issue, the Framework Convention on Climate Change (FCCC), which commits parties to immediate action. The FCCC outlines the main considerations based on which GHG abatement, absorption and adaptation policies towards reducing the threat of global warming should be developed, but provides little precise guidance as to how these objectives are to be achieved and hardly any assessment of the benefits of the suggested actions compared with the costs they will entail.

The OECD has dealt with the issue of global warming on several occasions. The Delegates of Working Party No. 1 of the Economic Policy Committee discussed, at the Spring 1992 meeting, the OECD's GREEN model, a tool designed to evaluate the costs of different policies to cut carbon emissions (OECD, 1992). The results of the GREEN model were systematically compared with five other global models (OECD, 1993); this project was designed to assess the range and causes explaining the different estimates of taxes and economic costs across models for a given set of emission reduction scenarios. The OECD Environment Directorate and the International Energy Agency have also dealt with the issue of global warming: immediately following the 1992 United Nations Conference on Environment and Development in Rio de Janeiro, the OECD published the results of two workshops dealing with the practical implementation of economic instruments such as GHG taxes and tradeable emission permit schemes (OECD, 1992a, 1992b). The aspects more directly related to the energy dimension of GHG emissions were discussed in IEA (1991) and the scope for energy efficiency improvements and their potential for reducing carbon dioxide emissions has been analysed in IEA (1991a). In the follow-up to the Rio Conference, the OECD and the IEA jointly organised a Conference in June 1993, analysing and discussing key economic aspects of the climate change issue (OECD, 1994).

Building on this previous work, this paper aims to inform the process of developing an appropriate policy response to the risk of climate change, given the commitments taken by signing the FCCC. The major problem facing policy makers is that of taking far-reaching policy decisions under conditions of significant uncertainty: how to choose sensible policy targets and suitable instruments to achieve them, with limited knowledge of both the likely costs and the resulting benefits.

Since CO_2 remains the principal GHG, accounting for well over half of the global warming effect from the accumulation of man-made GHGs (mainly from fossil fuel combustion), much attention centres on the level and distribution of costs entailed by policies designed to limit CO_2 emissions.

The paper begins (Part 2) with a brief introduction to, and interpretation of, the FCCC, followed by a summary of the uncertainties surrounding the climate change issue, an assessment of how extending the geographical coverage of efforts to achieve the abatement target implied by the FCCC can reduce total cost, and an introduction to the ''carbon leakage'' problem. Possible policy responses to the risk of global warming are reviewed in Part 3: three main generic classes of response measures are covered – emission curtailment (preventive action); GHG sequestration (offsetting action); and adaptation (adjustment action). The basic problems and possibilities for an efficient overall policy response, including the role of research and development, are discussed in Part 4. Given the crucial role of a carbon tax in both the theoretical discussion as well as the actual policy debate concerning climate change, the fiscal implications of a carbon tax are discussed in some detail in Part 5. Recognising the global scope and public good aspects of the problem, Part 6 of the paper is focused on the need for international co-operation and discusses various key issues pertinent to joint implementation.

1.2. Policy response

The costs of counter-measures to respond to the risk of climate change are shrouded in considerable uncertainty and controversy. Estimates range from negative cost (''no-regrets'') measures, exploiting un-utilised potential for energy saving, to gradually accumulating costs reaching several per cent of GDP. Even after standardising for the degree of policy action and various differences in assumptions on exogenous variables (*e.g.* future output and population growth), considerable differences in cost estimates remain, which can be traced to differing views on the adaptive capacity characterising future economic developments and on the penetration of new technologies, *e.g.* carbon-free ''backstop'' options.

A first uncontroversial step in a comprehensive and efficient policy approach is the exploitation of no-regrets policy potential, *i.e.* the implementation of all measures which will lead to a reduction in GHG emissions without causing any loss in output. No-regret potential arises from inefficient regulations and/or ''natural'' market imperfections and barriers, like imperfect information, which the government can partly or fully compensate for by de- or re-regulation, providing pertinent information on profitable energy saving measures and – in some situations – setting of efficiency standards. Such measures should be implemented whether or not the risk of climate change is real, as by definition they imply net benefits for the economy, even excluding their mitigating effect on global warming. Though no-regret potential is often overestimated by ignoring hidden costs of implementing such measures (*e.g.* in the form of losses in consumer surplus), some opportunities no doubt exist, to various degrees in different countries. And the case for no-regret measures is often strengthened by additional positive external effects (*i.e.* reduced air pollution, less traffic congestion, etc.).

Because uncertainty considerably complicates policy design in this area, investment in R&D to reduce this uncertainty would contribute to better policy making. Two types of R&D appear to be relevant in the context of the climate change issue. The first is basic research on the science of climate change, aiming directly at increasing knowledge about the causal links in the relationship between economic activity and detrimental effects of resulting GHG emissions on output and the environment. This basic research has largely a global public goods character and should therefore be sponsored by governments, preferably co-operating on a global scale.

The second type of climate change related R&D concerns the development of new technologies to raise energy efficiency (and thus reduce the GHG emissions per unit of output) and/or to develop carbon-free or carbon neutral energy sources. This sort of R&D is basically similar to other industrial applied R&D. Hence, the argument for government support to this type of research is much weaker than in the previous case of basic climate research where public goods characteristics dominate. Only to the extent that social benefits have not been – or cannot be – internalised, is government support justified in this area.

While climate research may help to reduce uncertainty, it is unlikely to come up with definite answers to many of the relevant questions in the near future. In any case, the very nature of the risk of climate change may imply that more immediate action is required to reduce the risk: there may not be enough time to wait for research results before acting. Furthermore, some experimental action may actually form part of the research agenda, by providing relevant data on the cost side of the problem, thus speeding up the availability of crucial results for (improved) policy making. The strict dichotomy between alternative policy approaches of ''learning by doing'' and ''first learning, then doing'' sometimes posited in the literature seems artificial in the context of a process of gradual policy refinement.

Policy action beyond no-regret measures and relevant R&D is likely to work best through economic (market) instruments, in particular when the processes generating the external effects are highly decentralised and widely dispersed across the economy in both the areas of production and consumption. In such circumstances, given the large number of possible actions to pursue, and detailed information required to make rational choices, it is practically impossible for the government to meet efficiency conditions through generalised command and control policies. Because the negative externalities – if they exist – exert their effect through the increase of GHG concentrations in the atmosphere, the most effective way of correcting for the externality is to adjust the price of economic activities that contribute to the externalities, to tax the emission of GHG and to subsidise activities that remove GHG permanently from the atmosphere.

To the extent that taxation of GHG compensates for a negative externality, it increases economic efficiency rather than decreasing it, in contrast to the case of (most) other taxes imposed for the purpose of raising revenue to finance public expenditure. This provides an opportunity to finance a larger part of government expenditure from (non-distorting) carbon taxes, allowing a reduction of the most distorting taxes on output and/or production factors. Whether such a tax switch can also be expected to lead to net increases in employment can, however, only be determined by a careful investigation of existing tax systems and their interaction with prevailing labour market distortions, on a case by case basis. In any case, a carbon tax is likely to stimulate no-regrets measures and relevant R&D projects by strengthening the incentives to develop and implement energy-saving technologies.

The arguments in favour of R&D and of a carbon tax say little about their "correct" levels: the optimal level of public support for R&D related to climate change and the "correct" price for GHG emissions (*i.e.* emission tax rates) may be difficult to pin down precisely for some time to come. Nonetheless, some action on both accounts can be defended on the basis of the "precautionary" (or insurance) principle: incurring some certain cost at present in order to reduce the likelihood of uncertain damage in the future. How much it is reasonable to spend on this account will depend on the size and probability of future damage and on the degree of risk aversion. The timing of the possible damage in combination with the social rate of discount also play a major role in determining the appropriate "insurance premium" (expenditure on reducing risk). The choice of the "correct" social rate of discount is partly a value judgement, involving – among other things – intergenerational equity considerations.

Different countries may thus respond with different intensity to the risk of climate change and these differential responses include different desired levels of emission taxes. However, to the extent that marginal abatement costs differ greatly between countries, a common emission tax that tends to equalise marginal emission curtailment costs across different regions may reduce significantly the global costs of achieving a given emission curtailment target. Such a common emission tax will nonetheless distribute the total costs of that control very unevenly, concentrating it on those countries where marginal curtailment cost are low. These are typically less developed countries with a heavy reliance on coal in their energy supply. While the benefits of emission control are mainly global (or very uncertain in their regional distribution), emission control costs are local. This discrepancy between the accrual of benefits and incidence of costs will require that a common emission tax be accompanied by transfers to induce the low abatement cost countries to incur the cost of abatement for the benefit of the global community at large.

A frequently evoked additional argument for aiming at the global harmonisation of emission tax rates across countries is the effect of differential carbon tax rates on the competitive position of carbon-emission-intensive industries. If carbon tax rates differ greatly between countries, energy-intensive industries may relocate to countries with low emission taxes, leading to the phenomenon of "carbon leakage" (or "offshore effects"). This may, in principle, reduce the effectiveness of unilateral action to curtail carbon emissions through a carbon tax and entail an inefficient international reallocation of resources. Empirical analysis suggests that the unilateral imposition of a carbon tax may indeed entail non-negligible changes in sectoral trade balances, but that the overall amount of carbon leakage is more difficult to ascertain as the carbon leakage from changes in trade flows is (partly) offset by negative carbon leakage arising from induced real income changes and inter-fuel substitution.

The equalisation of abatement cost across countries could also be achieved through tradeable emission quotas (TEQ). This instrument differs from a common carbon tax in that TEQs create certainty about the emission level, rather than the emission price, while the opposite holds for emission taxes. On this basis the choice between TEQs and emission taxes will depend on whether price or quantity deviations from the target level cause greater damage to the economy. In addition, TEQs make transparent the policy link between equity and efficiency issues in global emission control, by requiring an explicit decision on their allocation. TEQs also facilitate the development of derivative markets (futures and options) for emission rights, which in turn facilitates risk management by private agents facing climate change uncertainty and related policies.

Implementation of global schemes like a common carbon tax or TEQs require substantial preparations and negotiations between countries to sort out not only the equity issues involved, but also relevant matters of implementation, monitoring and control. Such negotiations, which involve delicate issues of national sovereignty, will become more complicated the more parties participate. It might be easier to reach agreement among a subset of countries, and it would be a major step towards a global agreement if this subset accounted for a high enough share of world emissions to assure global policy effectiveness. A group comprising the OECD countries, countries of the former Soviet Union and eastern Europe, and China and India (the group of "Major emitters") accounted for 84 per cent of global emissions in 1990 and is projected to account for 75 per cent in the middle of the next century.

Agreeing on, and implementing, a global carbon tax or TEQ system, which *inter alia* requires agreement on the transfers required to achieve participation is likely to take time; and this is true even if coverage is limited to the smaller group of Major emitters. Smaller scale measures might be implemented in the short term, pending a more comprehensive multilateral agreement. There are currently various bilateral initiatives between OECD countries and non-OECD countries, involving both governments and private agents in both regions, combining the technical know-how of the OECD partners with the low cost emission reduction potential of the other partner country in order to reduce GHG emissions. And the Global Environmental Facility (GEF) is using grants from the World Bank and industrialised countries to finance – among other things – the incremental cost of add-on investments to curtail emissions from energy generation projects in LDCs. Through learning by doing, these partial schemes can generate valuable information for the subsequent creation of more comprehensive and multilateral schemes.

2. The Current State of the Debate

2.1. The UN Framework Convention on Climate Change: summary and interpretation

The United Nation's Framework Convention on Climate Change (FCCC) signed at the Earth Summit in Rio de Janeiro in the summer of 1992 defines a comprehensive framework within which greenhouse gas abatement, absorption ("sink enhancement" in the terminology of the FCCC) and adaptation policies towards reducing the risk of global warming can develop.[2] In keeping with the notion of a framework convention, the FCCC lays out the main considerations that should govern future policy and specifies – if not very precisely – the obligations of signatory nations, but leaves details on choice of policy instruments, implementation strategies, monitoring, enforcement and adequacy of the commitments to be determined in future protocols to the convention.

The FCCC objective is to achieve a "... stabilisation of greenhouse gas concentrations in the atmosphere at a level that would prevent dangerous anthropogenic interference with the climate system" (Article 2). Given that many uncertainties remain about the prediction of climate change, rigid targets are deliberately avoided. Rather, a precautionary approach is employed, embracing immediate, but modest measures which provide a kind of insurance against the risk of adverse climate changes and which can – if and when necessary – evolve in response to new scientific and economic information. Initially, Annex 1 countries commit themselves to a serious effort to stabilise anthropogenic GHG emissions at 1990 levels by the end of the current decade, while all other countries pledge to provide comprehensive information on anthropogenic GHG emissions in their territories.

Several general principles and ways of achieving the Convention's objective are suggested in the FCCC itself. Two fundamental elements are economic efficiency (Principle 3, Article 3) and equity (Principles 1 and 2, Article 3). The balanced observation of these principles is intended to make effective co-operation and global policy co-ordination possible, recognising that unilateral responses to the threat of climate change would be unlikely to prove effective. Without being specific, the FCCC provides scope to comply with these two principles via a provision known as joint implementation. Joint implementation alludes to policies which allow Parties to achieve the commitments of the convention among a wider coalition of countries and through allowing a re-distribution of abatement costs so as to make participation attractive (relative to an uncoordinated approach) and reduce the global cost of policies designed to reduce the risk of climate change.

Realistically, no agreement is likely to achieve a perfect balance of efficient abatement commitments combined with "ideal" side-payments and attract universal participation from the outset; but the FCCC does establish a foundation upon which to build and refine present commitments which, in principle, promote efficient and equitable climate change policies. Within this framework, it is possible to envisage many different types of agreement employing a variety of policy instruments. The GREEN model has been used to simulate the impact of implementing the FCCC commitments on CO_2 emissions and real income under four different scenarios about the specific form future agreements might take: in all scenarios, global baseline emissions are reduced by an amount equivalent to the stabilisation of emissions in Annex 1 countries at their 1990 level, implying a 26 per cent reduction in global emissions from their baseline (no policy action) level by the year 2050. This target is achieved by successively larger country coalitions:

 i) OECD;
 ii) Annex 1 countries (OECD, eastern Europe, former Soviet Union);
 iii) Major emitters (same group as under *ii)*, plus China and India);
 iv) All countries (global participation).

In each case, it is assumed emissions are stabilised by the year 2000 and beyond, to the period 2050 (the time horizon of GREEN). Section 2.3 analyses these kinds of targets in order to focus on the issues of how design of agreements and the choice of policy instruments influence the effectiveness and efficiency of CO_2 abatement policies. The results presented below suggest a considerable cost-saving potential for the achievement of a given emission target by extending geographical coverage of participating nations.

Table 2.1. **IPCC greenhouse gas scenarios**
Panel A: Selected results

Scenario[1]	Period	Decline in TPER/GNP (average annual change)	Decline in carbon intensity (average annual change)	Year	Emissions for selected years				
					CO_2 (GtC)	CH_4 (Tg)	N_2O (Tg N)	CFCs (kt)	SO_x (Tg S)
IS92a	1990-2025	0.8%	0.4%	2025	12.2	659	15.8	217	141
	1990-2100	1.0%	0.2%	2100	20.3	917	17.0	3	169
IS92b	1990-2025	0.9%	0.4%	2025	11.8	659	15.7	36	140
	1990-2100	1.0%	0.2%	2100	19.1	917	16.9	0	164
IS92c	1990-2025	0.6%	0.7%	2025	8.8	589	15.0	217	115
	1990-2100	0.7%	0.6%	2100	4.6	546	13.7	3	77
IS92d	1990-2025	0.8%	0.9%	2025	9.3	584	15.1	24	104
	1990-2100	0.8%	0.7%	2100	10.3	567	14.5	0	87
IS92e	1990-2025	1.0%	0.2%	2025	15.1	692	16.3	24	163
	1990-2100	1.1%	0.2%	2100	35.8	1 072	19.1	0	254
IS92f	1990-2025	0.8%	0.1%	2025	14.4	697	16.2	217	151
	1990-2100	1.0%	0.1%	2100	26.6	1 168	19.0	3	204
Memorandum item:				*1990*	*7.4*	*506*	*12.9*	*827*	*98*

TPER = total primary energy requirement.
Carbon intensity is defined as units of carbon per unit of TPER.
CFCs include CFC-11, CFC-12, CFC-113, CFC-114 and CFC-115.
Units of mass are: GtC – gigatons of carbon; Tg – teragrams; TgN – teragrams of nitrogen; TgS – teragrams of sulphur.
1. A detailed description of the assumptions underlying each scenario is given in Panel B.
Source: IPCC (1992).

Table 2.1. Panel B: Summary of assumptions (cont'd)

Scenario	Population in 2100	Average annual output growth		Energy supplies	Other	CFCs
IS92a	World Bank 1991 11.3 billion	1990-2025 1990-2100	2.9% 2.3%	12 000 EJ conventional oil, 13 000 EJ natural gas. Costs of solar energy fall to $0.075/kWh. 191 EJ of biofuels available at $70/barrel.[1]	Legally enacted and internationally agreed controls on SO_x, and NO_x and NMVOC emissions. Efforts to reduce emissions of SO_x, NO_x and CO in developing countries by middle of next century.	Partial compliance with Montreal Protocol. Technological transfer results in gradual phase out of CFCs in non-signatory countries by 2075.
IS92b	World Bank 1991 11.3 billion	1990-2025 1990-2100	2.9% 2.3%	Same as "a".	Same as "a" plus commitments by many OECD countries to stabilize or reduce CO_2 emissions.	Global compliance with scheduled phase out of CFCs.
IS92c	UN Medium-Low Case 6.4 billion	1990-2025 1990-2100	2.0% 1.2%	8 000 EJ conventional oil, 7 300 EJ natural gas. Costs of nuclear energy decline by 0.4% annually.	Same as "a".	Same as "a".
IS92d	UN Medium-Low Case 6.4 billion	1990-2025 1990-2100	2.7% 2.0%	Oil and gas same as "c". Solar costs fall to $0.065/kWh. 272 EJ of biofuels available at $50/barrel.	Emission controls extended worldwide for CO, NO, NMVOC and SOx. Halt deforestation. Capture and use of emissions from coal mining and gas production and use.	CFC production phased out by 1997 for industrialized countries. Phase out of HCFCs.
IS92e	World Bank 1991 11.3 billion	1990-2025 1990-2100	3.5% 3.0%	18 400 EJ conventional oil Gas same as "a". Phase out nuclear energy by 2075.	Emission controls which increase fossil energy costs by 30%.	Same as "d".
IS92f	UN Medium-High Case 17.6 billion	1990-2025 1990-2100	2.9% 2.3%	Oil and gas same as "c". Costs of solar energy fall to $0.083/kWh. Nuclear costs increase to $0.09/kWh.	Same as "a".	Same as "a".

1. Approximate conversion factor. 1 barrel = 6 GJ.
Source: IPCC (1992).

2.2. Uncertainty surrounding the climate change issue: a summary[3]

FCCC commitments were accepted in order to modify long term trends of anthropogenic GHG emissions and thereby reduce the risks of global climate change. These commitments, however, are not based on an explicit analysis of costs and benefits, because of substantial uncertainty characterising each step in the causal link between economic activity and damage from climate change; in particular:

i) uncertainty concerning current and future GHG emissions;
ii) uncertainty concerning the link between GHG emissions and concentrations of GHG in the atmosphere;
iii) uncertainty concerning the link between atmospheric GHG concentrations and climate change;
iv) uncertainty concerning economic and ecological damage resulting from climate change.

And the results of any policy action aimed at influencing the risk of climate change by intervening at any stage in this causal chain are also subject to great uncertainty.

Current GHG emissions are measured with varying degrees of precision. Measurement of CO_2 emissions from the use of fossil fuels are relatively precise, since they are directly related to fuel consumption. But measurement of emissions from land use changes (mainly deforestation) is not as straightforward. More uncertainty surrounds emissions of methane and N_2O, which have a wide range of natural as well as man-made (anthropogenic) sources. Future GHG emissions are even less certain, since they depend on the rate of economic growth, structural change, technological innovations and substitution possibilities between fuels as well as between energy and other inputs, which cannot be predicted with accuracy. The IPCC has prepared six scenarios of global GHG emissions under various economic, policy and technical assumptions.[4] Among the major GHGs, the range of projected CO_2 emissions is largest, running from just under 5 to some 35 gigatons of carbon annually by the year 2100 (Table 2.1).[5]

The relation between GHG emissions (flows) and changing concentrations (stock) of GHGs in the atmosphere is not straightforward either. The major uncertainties concern the limited understanding of GHG removal processes (the operation of "sinks"), as well as the complicated interactions between gases in the atmosphere: there is uncertainty about the atmospheric residence time of different GHG gases, which influences the rate of change in concentrations.

The link between atmospheric GHG concentrations and climate change is also far from being fully understood. Complicating matters is the difficulty of determining whether the climate is actually changing, because the climate has a high rate of natural variability over short to medium term periods. It is therefore difficult to differentiate between signals (climate is changing) and "noise" (natural/random disturbances). An unequivocal confirmation of global warming can still not be given, despite the already significant increase in atmospheric GHG concentrations.

Finally, little is known about the effects of climate change on the economy and ecological systems, although areas where climate change could lead to damage can be identified. The problem, however, is obtaining precise quantification and valuation of the potential impacts on a regional basis.

Despite many uncertainties attaching to key linkages, there is a distinct possibility that an unfettered increase in GHG emissions will have serious consequences, and that many of the likely impacts of climate change are irreversible. Policy choices must be made in the light of this.

2.3. Gains from international co-operation[6]

Since CO_2 remains the principal GHG, accounting for well over half of the global warming effect from the accumulation of man-made GHGs (mainly from fossil fuel combustion), much of policy makers' attention centres on the level and distribution of costs entailed by policies designed to limit CO_2 emissions.

The carbon emission obligations implicit in the FCCC will not halt the rise of global carbon emissions in the medium run. Though Annex 1 countries accounted for roughly 71 per cent of global carbon emissions in 1990, their share in global emissions is projected to fall, declining to 51 per cent of baseline emissions by the year 2050 (Figure 2.1). Even when assuming that emissions by Annex 1 countries are stabilised at their 1990 level from the year 2000 onward, annual global emissions will still be 12.6 billion tons of carbon by the year 2050, more than twice their level in 1990.

The limited impact of current FCCC targets becomes even more evident when analysing their effect on the concentration of carbon in the atmosphere – the relevant variable in the transmission mechanism from economic activity to potential climate change (Annex D). The estimated time paths of atmospheric carbon concentrations

Figure 2.1. **Annual carbon emissions in the GREEN baseline scenario**

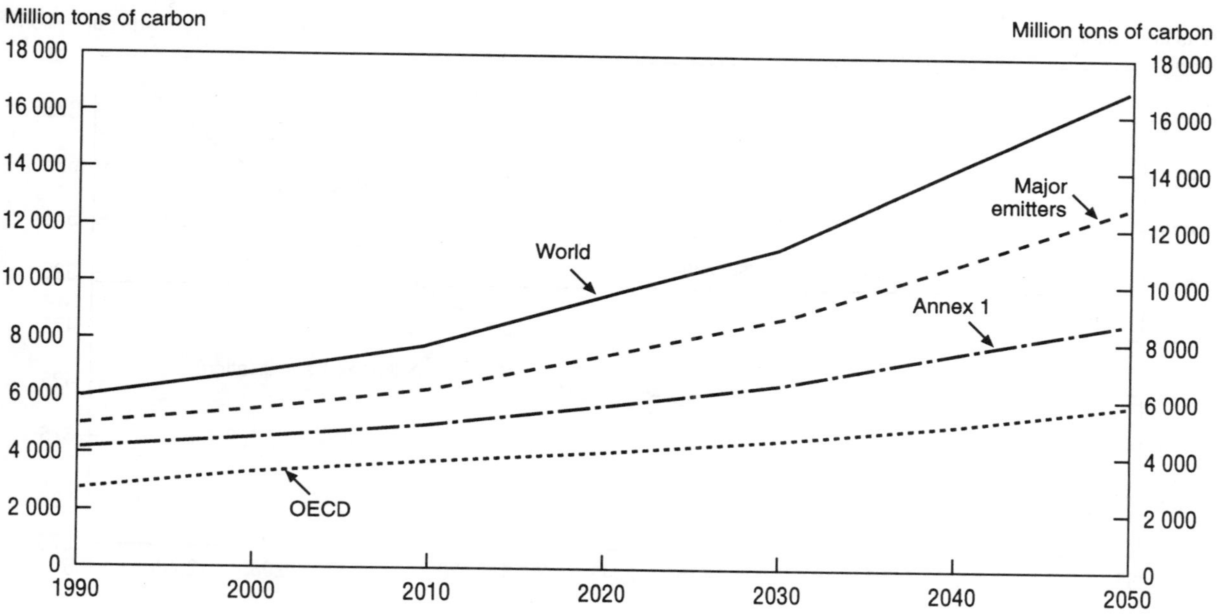

Million tons of carbon

Source: OECD GREEN model simulations.

based on baseline emissions and emissions under the assumption of emission stabilisation in Annex 1 countries are presented in Figure 2.2. In both cases concentrations keep rising steadily; achieving current FCCC emission targets merely delays the increase in concentrations.[7] The implication is that stabilising GHG concentrations through emission curtailment would require much greater emission abatement efforts than envisaged in the preceding interpretation of the FCCC. In practice, such massive emission cuts would only be feasible with the participation of non-Annex 1 countries.[8]

Extending geographical coverage of abatement policies will not only make major emission reductions and/or stabilisation of concentrations at low levels feasible, but can also greatly improve the cost efficiency of abatement. Expanding participation among a wider coalition of countries can lower the global costs of attaining a given emission target, by allowing abatement to take place at the lowest cost location. To actually achieve emission cuts cost efficiently requires a mechanism which allows marginal abatement costs to be equalised across countries.[9] In theory, this requirement is achieved if all countries participating in the agreement are subject to a common price signal – a situation achieved by a uniform carbon tax or a system of tradeable emission quotas. Other considerations which are important for implementing efficient climate change policies, including practical issues such as monitoring and enforcement, are discussed in more detail in Chichilnisky and Heal (1995).[10] Part 6, below, on joint implementation, provides an assessment of some of the distributional implications and more generally, of the kind of transfers needed to secure broader country coalitions.

From a global perspective, cost-effective FCCC type agreements offer substantial potential to reduce real world income losses, compared with individual country pursuit of FCCC targets. An indication of the potential gains can be obtained by simulating a suite of agreements with a common emission target, starting with OECD participation and then successively incorporating larger country coalitions, eventually encompassing global participation.[11] The target is a reduction in world CO_2 emissions from their baseline level by the same amount as that resulting from stabilisation of emissions in Annex 1 countries at 1990 levels from the year 2000 onward. This is equivalent to reducing growth in Annex 1 baseline emissions by almost 1 percentage point per annum and represents a 26 per cent cut from global baseline emissions in 2050.

The results, summarised in Annex A, Note 2, demonstrate the wide range of abatement costs, varying between 1.1 and 0.2 per cent of global real income,[12] depending on the extent of country participation (Table 2.2).

Figure 2.2. CO$_2$ concentrations: baseline and stabilisation of 1990 Annex 1 emission scenarios[1]

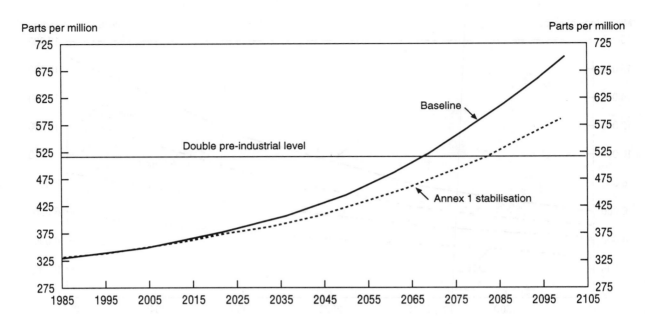

1. After 2050, the emissions were extrapolated from the 2030-2050 trend.
Source: OECD GREEN model simulations.

When OECD countries stabilise the equivalent of Annex 1 emissions at 1990 levels (Scenario 1), average global real incomes are 1.1 per cent below baseline. If the same target is achieved with global participation, average real incomes (1995-2050) are 0.2 per cent below baseline. In other words, the potential savings could be 0.9 per cent of global income per annum, equivalent to $120 billion in 1990 (at 1985 prices and exchange rates).[13]

Cost savings arise via an increased flexibility to meet the emission target in low cost countries. If participation is confined to OECD economies, the gains from co-operation are relatively small, since the differences in marginal abatement costs are less pronounced than between OECD and non-OECD countries. If country participation is extended to include non-OECD countries, the magnitude of cost savings increases, reaching a maximum when carbon taxes are uniform and imposed at a global level (Scenario 5, Table 2.2). It is not, however, only OECD countries which benefit from expanded co-operation. Most notably, real income changes in energy-exporting countries improve by 3.7 percentage points (from –3.6 to 0.1 compared with baseline) when co-operation increases from OECD countries to involve the Major emitters (Scenario 1 vs. Scenario 4). The reason energy-exporting countries benefit from an agreement which secures this broader coverage is linked to the greater efficiency of achieving emission cuts by curbing coal rather than oil demand: reduced oil demand weakens their exports, both on account of lower prices and a fall in volumes, reducing their real income.

Not all countries, however, reduce their welfare losses under the implementation of cost-effective agreements: such agreements achieve lower costs of abatement by shifting the burden of emission curtailment to countries with low marginal abatement costs. While global costs decline, the distribution of output and real income losses across regions is uneven. Relative losses tend to shift towards, and are concentrated among, the coal intensive developing countries. Relative real income losses in India and China from cost efficient policies are about four times larger than the OECD average. Thus, the likelihood of securing the co-operation of Non-Annex 1 countries depends critically on the level and form of compensation side-payments. This issue is explored further in Part 6, where several relevant simulations are presented.

The simulation results reported above depend on both model structure and on specific model parameter values. Sensitivity of these results to assumptions on GDP growth rates, "autonomous energy efficiency improvement" (energy-saving technical progress), backstop energy prices, inter-fuel elasticities of substitution and fossil fuel supply elasticities are provided in Annex A, Note 3. Differences can be important, although

Table 2.2. **Gains from international co-operation**

Summary of simulation results

Region	OECD region-specific tax (S.1)	OECD uniform tax (S.2)	Annex 1 uniform tax (S.3)	Major emitters uniform tax (S.4)	Global uniform tax (S.5)
	CO$_2$ emissions cut in 2050 (% relative to baseline)				
OECD [1]	−77.3	−77.3	−46.7	−26.4	−21.0
Annex 1	−53.6	−53.6	−51.9	−30.1	−23.8
Major emitters	−37.0	−37.0	−35.2	−35.5	−28.4
World [2]	−28.7	−28.7	−25.8	−26.2	−26.7
	Carbon tax in 2050 ($ per ton of carbon)				
OECD [1]	397 [3]	397	130	41	28
Annex 1	..	..	130	41	28
Major emitters	..	..	..	41	28
World [2]	..	..	..	..	28
	Average real income over the period 1990-2050 [4] (% relative to baseline)				
OECD [1]	−0.85	−0.76	−0.56	−0.25	−0.15
Annex 1	−0.86	−0.77	−0.57	−0.20	−0.10
Energy exporters	−3.62	−3.32	−0.31	0.07	−0.18
Major emitters	−0.79	−0.71	−0.46	−0.33	−0.19
World [2]	−1.07	−0.97	−0.36	−0.22	−0.22

S.1: Four OECD regions cut emissions in equal proportions (using region/country-specific carbon taxes) to stabilise Annex 1 emissions at 1990 levels.
S.2: OECD regions stabilise Annex 1 emissions at 1990 levels by a uniform carbon tax.
S.3: Annex 1 countries stabilise Annex 1 emissions at 1990 levels by a uniform carbon tax.
S.4: Major emitters countries reduce emissions by an amount equivalent to the stabilisation of Annex 1 emissions at 1990 levels by a uniform carbon tax.
S.5: Global coalition reduce emissions by an amount equivalent to the stabilisation of Annex 1 emissions at 1990 levels by a uniform carbon tax.
1. Excluding Mexico.
2. Since the target is always an *ex ante* reduction of emissions among participating countries the *ex post* level of world emissions varies slightly between scenarios mainly due to different carbon leakage rates.
3. The regional carbon tax is $383 per ton of carbon for the United States, 401 for Japan, 410 for the EC and 426 for the other OECD countries. The average tax rate, weighted by 2050 carbon emissions, is by coincidence, equal to the uniform tax rate in scenario 2.
4. Real income is defined as the sum of domestic household consumption, investment and government net expenditure.
Source: OECD GREEN Model simulations.

modifying GDP growth and AEEI assumptions proportionately for all regions by and large preserves the regional distribution of emissions. However, different regional impacts arise when backstop prices and input substitution elasticities are modified. The conclusion that a larger geographical coverage leads to a lower marginal cost of Annex 1 emission stabilisation is robust and not affected by alternative assumptions or parameter values. However, the size of the uniform carbon tax required to achieve the target is highly sensitive to assumptions on GDP growth and backstop prices, and less sensitive to assumptions on various parameter values.[14]

2.4. The carbon leakage problem

The effectiveness of unilateral action to curb emissions is influenced by a phenomenon called "carbon leakage" or "offshore effects", referring to changes in carbon emissions in non-participating regions induced by abatement efforts in participating regions (See Annex B for a detailed analysis). The scope for leakages is reduced the greater the number of countries participating in an agreement. If participation is global, carbon leakage is not an issue.

There are three major effects determining the size and sign of carbon leakages, involving mechanisms that may work in opposite directions:[15]

  i) Changes in the trade structure; imposing an energy tax changes the comparative advantage in the production of energy intensive goods, entailing changes in the location of their production.
  ii) Changes in world energy prices; imposing a tax on energy will reduce energy demand and thus weaken world prices which may stimulate energy demand in non-participating regions. It could also modify the

Table 2.3. Carbon leakage when Annex 1 countries/regions curtail emissions individually [1]

	1995	2000	2005	2010	2030	2050
	In million tons of carbon					
Emissions in Annex 1: baseline scenario	4 369	4 561	4 802	5 027	6 532	8 769
Stabilisation of emissions in Annex 1 countries/ regions individually:						
Ex-ante reductions in World emissions	−298	−595	−821	−954	−2 315	−4 552
Ex-post reductions in World emissions	−294	−590	−818	−998	−2 356	−4 471
	In percentage of Annex 1 emission reduction					
Leakage rate	1	1	0	−1	−2	2
of which: DAEs, Brazil and RoW	2	3	3	2	0	1
China	−1	−1	−1	−1	−1	0
India	0	0	0	0	0	0
Energy exporters	0	−1	−1	−2	−1	0

1. Annex 1 countries' emissions are stabilised at their 1990 levels.
Note: Figures may not add up due to rounding.
Source: OECD GREEN Model simulations.

Table 2.4. Change in sectoral trade balances when four OECD countries/regions stabilise emissions individually [1]
Deviations relative to baseline in billion 1985 US$

Sector/region	1995	2000	2005	2010	2030	2050
Agriculture						
United States	0	−1	−2	−2	−8	−16
Japan	0	−1	−1	−2	−2	1
European community	−1	−1	−2	−2	−5	−8
Other OECD countries [2]	0	−1	−1	−2	−4	−9
Energy exporting countries	2	4	6	8	15	20
Other non-OECD	0	0	−1	−1	5	13
Energy						
United States	2	4	7	11	44	78
Japan	7	16	27	33	55	67
European community	3	6	10	15	35	82
Other OECD countries [2]	0	0	0	1	10	32
Energy exporting countries	−10	−23	−39	−51	−81	−124
Other non-OECD	−2	−4	−6	−9	−64	−135
Energy intensive goods						
United States	1	1	1	−2	−6	−10
Japan	−4	−9	−14	−7	−20	−29
European community	−1	−2	−3	−6	−21	−41
Other OECD countries [2]	0	1	1	−1	−6	−13
Energy exporting countries	2	3	5	6	13	23
Other non-OECD	3	6	9	10	40	70
Other goods and services						
United States	−2	−4	−7	−7	−30	−53
Japan	−3	−7	−12	−24	−33	−38
European community	−1	−3	−5	−7	−8	−33
Other OECD countries [2]	0	0	0	2	0	−10
Energy exporting countries	7	16	27	36	53	82
Other non-OECD	−1	−2	−3	0	19	53

1. Emissions are stabilised at their 1990 levels.
2. Excluding Mexico.
Source: OECD GREEN Model simulations.

structure of prices among different energy sources, inducing inter-fuel substitution in non-participating countries and thus a change in their emissions.

   iii) Regional terms of trade gains and losses. Relative price changes can alter the terms of trade in each region, causing a change in emissions via induced real income changes. For energy exporting countries, depressed energy prices reduce real incomes and thus consumption and carbon emissions compared with baseline (''negative'' carbon leakage).

An additional negative carbon leakage effect occurs if energy production in energy-exporting countries is reduced in response to carbon abatement efforts in Annex 1 countries, leading to reduced income (and thus consumption and emissions) on the basis of lower resource rents.

Estimates of leakage effects differ considerably across models. The results from GREEN are examined in Annex B. Small leakages, and large changes in trade flows, could occur if the world oil price falls enough, relative to the price of coal (Tables 2.3 and 2.4). The GREEN leakage estimates, though, are very sensitive to parameter values (for example, the supply elasticity of fossil fuels and the elasticity of substitution between capital and energy, see Annex B, Section 3.2). A different model, 12RT, yields leakage estimates that are consistently higher than the GREEN ones (see Manne and Oliveira Martins, 1994 and Figure 2.3), because the production of energy-intensive goods shifts more from Annex 1 countries to China. Neither model treats capital flows explicitly. The overall conclusion is that the leakage issue is still open to debate.

Emission control based on taxation of fossil fuels may also raise concerns for the competitiveness of energy-intensive sectors (EIS). Reflecting such concerns, some policy analysts suggest that EIS products should be exempted from carbon taxation despite the fact that the share of EIS sectors in total emissions is substantial:[16] among OECD countries, energy-intensive industries account for 10-20 per cent of total carbon emissions related to the burning of fossil-fuels. Therefore, the exemption of EIS in pursuit of a given emission target will entail a serious efficiency loss for the rest of the economy which would have to bear the extra burden of emission reduction. In the presence of a carbon tax, the exemption will entail a mis-allocation of resources in favour of energy-intensive goods which is exactly the opposite of the initial policy purpose.

In assessing effects on ''competitiveness'' it is essential to distinguish between competitiveness, which is an absolute concept, and comparative advantage, which is a concept defined in relative terms. It is comparative

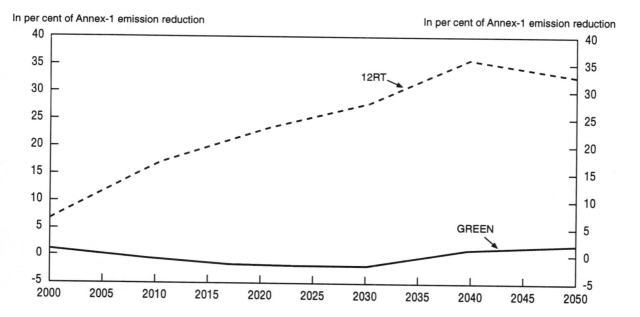

Figure 2.3. **Comparison of carbon leakage rate in two global models**

Note: Stabilisation of emissions in Annex 1 countries.
Source: Manne and Oliveira Martins (1994).

advantage rather than competitiveness that is crucial to the link between trade in energy-intensive products and carbon emission abatement. Imposing a carbon tax shifts the comparative advantage in the country imposing an emission constraint away from energy-intensive industries to other sectors in the economy. One of the objectives of environmental policy might well be a reduction of competitiveness for some products and, in this way, creating the right economic incentives for an overall decrease in environment-damaging activities – although there could be political (as well as economic) concerns if structural rigidities and high adjustment costs make the resulting sectoral adjustment difficult and slow. Indeed, in countries with high unemployment rates the threat of reducing output in the EIS sectors may be a politically sensitive topic, especially if there is uncertainty about the degree of mobility of the industrial labour force.[17] As an indication of the potential importance of the policy problems, it can be noted that, depending on the country, the share of the energy-intensive sectors ranges from 10 to 18 per cent of total manufacturing employment by the end of the 1980s, or well below 3 per cent of total employment.

3. Possible Measures to Prevent Climate Change

3.1. Overview

Measures that might prevent (or slow) climate change fall into several – not mutually exclusive – categories. These are shown in Figure 3.1, presented according to the link (or phase) in the climate-change feedback loop at which they intervene:

- Emission mitigation: measures that reduce the anthropogenic generation of GHG emissions.
- Sequestration and removal: measures that "collect" the GHG emissions either where they occur ("scrubbing") or from the atmosphere in general (GHG "absorption").
- Compensation: if rising GHG concentrations lead to increased global warming through radiative forcing, this process might be compensated by various "geo-engineering measures".[18]
- Adaptation: if climate change does occur, its cost can be reduced by adaptation to the changed climate, either by protecting existing activities and assets or by changing activities to better suit the changed climate.

Among these alternative response categories, the first two – emission mitigation and GHG sequestration – are at present considered the most likely candidates for large-scale application. Most of the compensation measures imply large scale geo-engineering projects with considerable uncertainty about cost and possible

Figure 3.1. Transmission-mechanism of the climate change risk and possible response measures

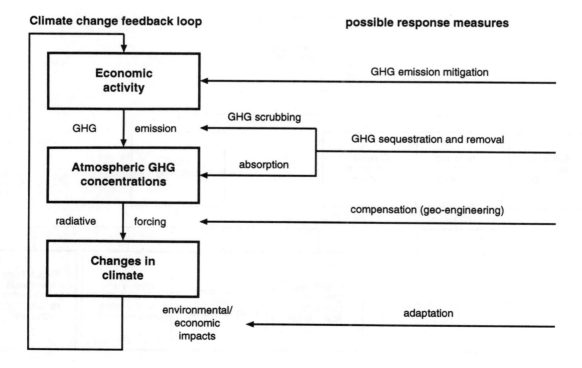

21

environmental side effects, and are therefore currently not considered likely response options. Adaptation could certainly play a role in the future if and when climate change actually occurs:[19] it represents an attractive response option if climate change were to be very gradual and moderate. A further advantage of this option is that adaptation can be problem-and region-specific, and that costs will occur in the future (when the impacts from climate change are manifest) rather than already now. However, the uncertainty about the possible climate change effects is considered too large to rely entirely on adaptation as a response strategy.

3.2. Emission mitigation options

If GHG emissions seem likely to exceed acceptable levels, the most obvious response would seem to curtail these emissions. Given the predominance of CO_2 among total GHG emissions, this section will concentrate on the mitigation of CO_2 emissions, while mitigation of other GHGs is briefly discussed in Section 3.2.3 below. The various possible mitigation options are depicted in Figure 3.2:

- Curtailing output growth: carbon emissions are mostly related to energy use, which is intimately associated with economic activity. Slower economic growth would therefore mitigate emissions.
- Improving energy efficiency: large energy losses occur in primary energy production and energy end-use. Efficiency measures aim to reduce these losses, thus reducing emissions for a given output path.
- Changing consumption and production patterns: the energy (and thus carbon) content per unit of output differs between components. A shift from carbon intensive to carbon poor consumption and production items can thus reduce emissions at constant aggregate output levels.
- Fuel substitution: as most carbon emissions are related to combustion of fossil fuels, a change to low-carbon or carbon-free fuels will reduce CO_2 emissions.

Curtailing output growth is not an efficient option to mitigate carbon emissions, the implicit cost being more than $2 000 per ton of carbon in 1990.[20] Much less costly methods of reducing carbon emissions are available. Some observers (*e.g.* Cline, 1992) have suggested limiting population growth as a policy to curtail GHG

Figure 3.2. **Emission mitigation options**

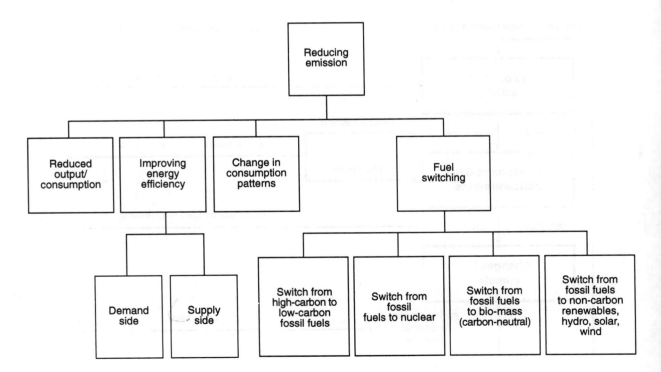

emissions. However, while population control may be desirable for a number of other (environmental and wider) reasons, its effectiveness in curtailing **GHG emissions** is far from obvious. Indeed, the World Bank recommends population control as one of the major instruments to raise per capita incomes. As a reduced number of children increases both the potential supply of and the likely demand for saving (for retirement), investment and thus output are likely to increase in response to curtailing population growth.[21]

Similarly mandating changes in consumption patterns seems unlikely to be an efficient solution. In a market economy, markets provide what consumers demand, and forcing other demand patterns on consumers may lead to a loss of consumer surplus. Where this argument is weakened by market imperfections leading to price distortions and thus sub-optimal composition of final demand, it is preferable to correct the underlying causes of the price distortions and let demand adjust to the new undistorted prices, rather than leaving the distortions in place and trying to compensate for them by mandated changes in final demand patterns.[22] Some aspects of final demand patterns (*e.g.* local transport choices) are strongly influenced by earlier public sector decisions on infrastructure, land zoning and the resulting urban development patterns. To the extent that these long term planning decisions have not taken into account negative externalities from transport related GHG emissions (as well as other externalities), the resulting private choices concerning local transport may be socially inefficient. Reversing these development patterns may be extremely costly or take a very long period during which existing infrastructure is replaced by systems taking due account of the relevant externalities.

As both curtailing output growth and mandated changes in final demand patterns are therefore not likely to be efficient mitigation strategies, this section focuses primarily on gains in energy efficiency and fuel substitution.

3.2.1. *Raising energy efficiency*

In general, technologies capable of substantial improvements in energy efficiency are commercially available. The IEA (in IEA/OECD, 1991*a*) has assessed the scope for potential energy savings for different end-use activities in the residential, commercial, industrial and transport sector, and the extent to which savings are inhibited by market imperfections or other barriers. These results, summarised in Table 3.1 and discussed in more detail in Annex A, Note 6, suggest that reductions of CO_2 emissions of up to 30 per cent can be reached by implementing known energy efficiency measures.

The production of electricity also offers significant opportunities for reduced distribution and generation losses, for co-generation and for retrofitting of existing power plants with more energy-efficient and cost-effective technologies (IEA/OECD, 1993). Compared with current average coal-based power stations, CO_2 emission reductions of 15 to 20 per cent appear to be currently feasible, and additional reductions of 20 to 25 per cent may be available in the medium term as technology in this area improves further (IEA/OECD, 1991).

Energy efficiency improvements are often considered to carry a significant no-regrets potential. This implies that these measures can be introduced at zero or negative net economic cost, *i.e.* the costs of implementing the measures are equal or lower than the value of resulting energy savings. Whether these measures are not implemented because of market imperfections, such as lack of information and price distortions, or because their "true" costs are higher than estimated in the engineering ("bottom-up") studies of potential energy efficiency gains, has been a long-standing bone of contention between (bottom-up) optimists and (top-down) pessimists. Key arguments in the debate about the existence or otherwise of an "energy efficiency gap" are summarised in Box A.

3.2.2. *Fuel substitution*

As most anthropogenic carbon emissions are related to combustion of fossil fuels, a shift to carbon-low or carbon-free fuel sources is an effective measure to curtail emissions. An important option within this category is substitution among fossil fuels: oil has a lower carbon content than coal, and gas has an even lower carbon-content (Table 3.2). These fuels are not perfect substitutes, however. Coal is mainly used in electricity generation and gas mainly for residential heating and cooking, whereas the main use of oil and its liquid derivatives is in the transport sector.

With a given technology, the actual mix of fossil fuels used will depend on their fuel characteristics and their relative prices. How much fuel substitution can be achieved in response to a change in relative fuel prices depends again on available technology, *i.e.* the "ease" with which one fuel can be replaced by another fuel. In the medium to long run, fuel substitution possibilities are also influenced by the relative size of fossil fuel reserves: existing reserves of coal are much larger than those of oil and gas; a substitution to gas (and to a lesser extent oil) can therefore only provide a medium-term contribution to reducing carbon emissions. But as oil and

Table 3.1. **Potential energy savings by end-use component in IEA countries** [1]

	Share in total CO_2 emissions (1)	Potential energy savings (2)	Number of market imperfections [2] (3)	Potential effect on CO_2 emissions [3] (4)	Savings not likely achieved due to existing market imperfections [4] (5)
1. *Residential sector*	21.7%				
Space heating and air-conditioning	11.0%	10-50%	Some/many	1.1-5.5%	0-50%
Water heating	3.6%	0-50%	Some/many	0-1.8%	0-50%
Refrigeration	2.1%	30-50%	Many	0.5-1%	10-30%
Lighting	1.2%	> 50%	Many	> 0.6%	30-50%
2. *Commercial sector*	13.4%				
Space heating and air-conditioning	6.8%	0-50%	Some/many	0-3.4%	0-50%
Lighting	3.4%	10-30%	Some/many	0.3-1%	0-50%
3. *Industrial sector*	34.1%				
Improved motors/drives	9.0%	10-30%	Few/some	0.9-2.7%	0-10%
Steel production	4.6%	15-25%	Few/some	0.7-1.2%	0-15%
Chemical production	5.9%	10-25%	Few/some	0.6-1.5%	0-20%
Pulp and paper industry	1.2%	10-30%	Few/some	0.1-0.4%	0-10%
Cement production	0.9%	10-40%	Few/some	0.1-0.4%	0-10%
4. *Transport*	28.1%				
Passenger cars	13.7%	30-50%	Many	4.1-6.9%	20-30%
Goods vehicles	9.1%	20-40%	Some	1.8-3.6%	10-20%
5. *Other* [5]	2.6%				
Total	100.0%			10.9-30%	

1. The table shows the energy savings which could be reached by a move from average market practice to best market practice, in response to current market forces and government policies. Measures were only considered economic if they offered a real rate of return of 20-30 per cent (IEA/OECD, 1989).
2. This column indicates the incidence of existing market imperfections, which may reduce potential savings. These market imperfections differ between end-use category.
3. Calculated as column (1) times column (2).
4. As percentage of column 2.
5. Agriculture and other uses.

Source: Adapted from IEA/OECD (1991*a*), *Energy Efficiency and the Environment*, Paris (Table IV.31 and Table A1.1), figures refer to all IEA countries; see also IEA/OECD (1989), *Electricity End-Use Efficiency*, Paris.

gas reserves are gradually exhausted, a substitution to carbon-free or carbon-neutral energy might take place, or "carbon-scrubbing" (see below) might become an economically attractive option.

The carbon content of estimated total global reserves of oil and gas is moderate relative to the carbon carrying capacity of the atmosphere, in the sense that even an exhaustion of these reserves by the middle of the next century is compatible with what is currently considered a low-risk increase in atmospheric CO_2 concentrations, especially if oil and gas are used aggressively to replace coal. By the same criteria, global coal reserves are substantial, and one of the major causes of an excessive increase in atmospheric carbon concentrations in many baseline projections (*i.e.* assuming no offsetting policy action) is the replacement of gas and oil by carbon-based synfuels when reserves of the former two fossil fuels approach exhaustion while energy demand continues to expand.

The second major opportunity for a fuel switch is the use of nuclear energy. Nuclear energy is a carbon-free energy source and existing reserves of uranium allow considerable expansion of nuclear energy.[23] The nuclear option is subject to three major concerns, namely:

– nuclear (reactor) safety;
– waste disposal, including decommissioning of reactors;
– military uses of nuclear material.

All three concerns have made nuclear energy a sensitive political issue in many OECD countries, which has limited the expansion of the nuclear industry.

Renewable energy forms an important, but thus far limited, alternative to fossil fuels. Several renewable energy sources (wind, solar, hydro, geothermal,[24] tidal, wave, ocean thermal) have no or very limited emissions of greenhouse gases (Table 3.3). Except for hydro-power, these sources currently provide only a very small

---

Box A. The Energy Efficiency Gap

Studies on the economic costs of CO_2 emission curtailment can be divided into two types, namely those with a top-down, macroeconomic focus and those with a bottom-up, engineering focus. The two approaches generally provide quite different estimates of curtailment costs. Engineering studies suggest a considerable no-regrets potential. In top-down models, this possibility is generally ignored and engineering studies are considered to overstate the economic potential of energy savings. The difference in results is customarily referred to as the ''energy efficiency gap''.

Comparisons of the two approaches suggest that engineering studies often ignore or underestimate the costs associated with the implementation of new technologies, but that, nevertheless, a range of technological options does indeed exist, which often can be implemented at low cost, and sometimes at a net economic benefit. That these measures are currently not being implemented is due to a number of causes, comprising both market imperfections and other barriers (Jaffe and Stavins, 1993).

Market imperfections are defined as any market condition that results in an inefficient allocation of resources, such as (Sanstad, et al., 1993):

- Price distortions. If energy is subsidised, or prices are otherwise distorted, energy users do not have incentives to adopt energy-efficient technologies.
- Externalities. Market signals will not work properly, if there are significant externalities from adoption of energy-efficient technologies, or from energy use.
- Information barriers. Information partly has the character of a public good and the market may therefore not provide it at an optimal level.
- Principal/agents problems. Decisions concerning energy efficiency investments are made by one party, whereas another party pays the energy bills, leading to sub-optimal design.
- Capital market imperfections. Energy consumers use a higher discount rate than energy producers to calculate the present value of investments in energy conservation. This may reflect imperfect capital markets, but also differential appraisal of uncertainty and risk. As a result, producing an additional unit of energy requires a larger investment than saving a unit of energy in final consumption.

In case of market imperfections an appropriate policy response can in principle be formulated and implemented. Other perceived barriers, however, may be the result of an understatement of the costs of implementation of a new technology, or the overstatement of benefits. The main items in this category are (Grubb, et al., 1993):

- Hidden costs. Consumers may face additional costs for investments in new energy conservation systems.
- Average/typical benefits. A technology may appear to have a positive pay-off for the average consumer, but this does not imply that it has a positive pay-off for all consumers.
- Uncertainty. Under uncertainty, the benefits of energy conservation technologies are uncertain as well.
- Trade-off between efficiency and performance. A fuel-conserving technology may provide less performance than a fuel-using technology.
- Sunk costs. The existing capital stock of a company or power plant has a sunk cost character. Many conservation measures which appear attractive on an average-cost basis, are not if they are evaluated on a marginal cost basis.

Bottom-up studies may also overstate energy savings because they often ignore income and substitution effects entailed by the increase in energy efficiency, both of which may partly or wholly offset the initial savings from increased energy efficiency.

---

proportion of global energy production. Hydro-power is a highly competitive alternative to fossil fuels and some room for expansion still exists (World Energy Council, 1992). The other renewable energy technologies are still under development, and are currently only competitive with fossil fuels under favourable natural conditions, or in isolated areas. Market imperfections, such as price distortions, externalities and high discount rates play a similar role as in the case of energy efficiency (see Box A). The most important barrier is due to the fact that renewable energy is not a perfect substitute for conventional types of energy.[25]

Another option for fuel substitution concerns biomass fuels. These are not carbon-free, but can be carbon-neutral if integrated in a closed biomass loop. Biomass could be grown for commercial fuel production, sequestering carbon during its growth. After some time the biomass can be harvested and used as a fuel, for instance for electricity generation. The combustion would release the previously sequestered carbon, making

Table 3.2.   **Carbon content of various fossil fuels**

Kg carbon/Gigajoule

Synthetic fuels (carbon based)	39.0
Solid fuels	25.8
Oil	20.0
Natural gas	15.3

Source: IEA (1991); OECD GREEN Model.

Table 3.3.   **Carbon emissions of electricity generation technologies** [1]

Tons of CO_2/Gigawatthour

Conventional coal plant	964.0
Oil fired plant	726.2
Gas fired plant	484.0
Boiling water reactor (nuclear)	7.8
Geothermal steam	56.8
Large hydropower	3.1
Wind energy	7.4
Photovoltaics	5.4
Wood (sustainable harvest)	−159.9 [2]

1. Carbon emissions include emissions during fuel extraction, plant construction and plant operation.
2. Sustainable biomass may have negative carbon emissions, since roots and other unharvested parts of biomass may remain in place. Carbon emissions from fertilizers, pesticides and fossil fuels during the production stage are included in the analysis (see San Martin, 1989).

Source: IEA (1991).

biomass a carbon-neutral energy source. To the extent that the biomass replaces fossil fuels, the net carbon emissions for a given total amount of energy used drops. This option is further discussed in Section 3.3.1. and Annex C.

3.2.3.   *Mitigating emissions of other greenhouse gases*

Emissions of other GHGs are generally more difficult to mitigate than CO_2 emissions. Except for CFCs and related compounds (*e.g.* HCFCs), the sources of other GHGs are less well known, more diverse and more difficult to control. Table 3.4 shows anthropogenic emissions of GHGs, the direct contribution of 1990 emissions to global warming and the main anthropogenic sources of the gases. Methane (CH_4) and N_2O, in particular, have a very wide range of anthropogenic sources. In this situation, mitigation policies may have to be tailored to specific circumstances and may therefore prove to be quite costly. In contrast to CO_2, a suitable (operational) tax-base for these gases is often difficult to find.

Most efforts to control other GHGs therefore involve regulation. Options to reduce methane emissions focus on improved feed for livestock (to reduce emissions by ruminants), collection for use of methane as a fuel (from animal waste and landfills) and prevention of gas leakages, in particular at gas production sites. As methane has a commercial value, some studies have suggested that there may be some no-regrets potential in this area. Emissions of nitrous oxide can be controlled by improvements in fertilizer use and a change to low-nitrogen fertilizer. In industrial processes, in particular the production of acids, it may also prove possible to control nitrogen emissions. CFCs are already being phased out on a global scale because of their effect on the ozone layer. They have a narrow range of industrial and domestic uses (refrigeration, aerosol propellants, foam blowing agents, solvents) for which innocuous substitutes have been developed.

Emissions of some energy-use related GHGs may fall as a result of the mitigation of CO_2 emissions. For example, a drop in the use of fossil fuels may decrease emissions of methane due to reduced coal mining, oil well venting and flaring, and gas distribution leakages. Emissions of carbon monoxide and nitrous oxides may be reduced if improvements in combustion technologies (*e.g.* better car and power plant designs) are implemented in

Table 3.4. **Characteristics and sources of major greenhouse gases**

	Anthropogenic emissions in 1990 (million tons)	Direct contribution of 1990 emissions to global warming	Main anthropogenic sources of emissions
GHGs with direct effect on radiative forcing			
CO_2	26 000	64.2%	Energy use (80%), deforestation and changing land use (17.3%), cement production (2.7%).
CH_4	300	19.3%	Energy production and use (25.9%), enteric fermentation (23.9%), rice paddies (17%), wastes (7.4%), landfills (10.8%), biomass burning (8%), domestic sewage (7.1%).
N_2O	6	4.0%	Combustion of fossil fuels (8.7%), fertilized soils (47.8%), land clearing (17.4%), acid production (15.2%), biomass burning (10.9%).
CFC-11	0.3	2.5%	Industrial (100%), primarily refrigeration, aerosols, foam blowing, solvents.
CFC-12	0.4	7.0%	Industrial (100%), primarily refrigeration, aerosols, foam blowing, solvents.
Other halo-carbons	1.2	2.9%	Mostly industrial, similar uses as CFCs, also aluminium production.
GHGs with indirect effects on radiative forcing			
CO	200	–	Incomplete combustion of fossil fuels (30.4%), biomass burning (69.6%).
NO_x	66	–	Combustion of fossil fuels (73.5%), biomass burning (26.5%).
Non-methane hydrocarbons	20	–	Biomass burning, solvents and fossil fuel combustion.

Source: Annex D, Table D1.

the context of carbon emission curtailment. In principle, these effects could be taken into account when calculating GHG tax equivalents for different fossil fuels. However, they are quite uncertain and can not be easily related to a typical fossil fuel.

Mitigation of CO_2 emissions has a more direct impact on emissions of NO_x (nitrogen oxides) and SO_x (sulphur oxides). This is because NO_x and SO_x are largely emitted through fossil fuel combustion, and a carbon abatement policy will thus reduce emissions of these gases through its effect on fossil fuel consumption.[26] This creates a potential source of secondary benefits from a CO_2 mitigation strategy (Alfsen, *et al.*, 1994). Increasing concentrations and reactions of NO_x (as well as CO and methane) with OH (hydroxyl radical) are important for the ozone chemistry of the troposphere (see Annex D). Liu (1994) shows that the curtailment of other GHG emissions resulting from a carbon abatement policy can lead to a significant supplementary reduction in radiative forcing and global temperature rise. In addition, while SO_x is not a GHG, its emission levels can significantly affect acid precipitation and local environmental conditions.

Table 3.5 summarises percentage changes in CO_2, NO_x and SO_x emissions relative to the baseline which result from the five Annex 1 stabilisation scenarios discussed in Section 2.3.[27] The results indicate that the percentage reductions in NO_x and SO_x emissions are highly correlated with those in CO_2 emissions and that the total world emissions of these gases depend upon the geographical location of abatement efforts. The latter result is due to fuel and sector-specific NO_x and SO_x emission factors.[28] Since coal generally has the highest emission factors for both gases, inclusion of regions with high consumption shares of coal (*e.g.* China and India) in an abatement coalition leads to a greater reduction of NO_x and SO_x emissions compared with exclusion of these regions (*e.g.* scenarios where only OECD regions stabilise Annex 1 emissions).

Table 3.5. Global CO_2, NO_x and SO_x emission reduction under alternative scenarios

Percentage reduction relative to baseline

Region	OECD region-specific tax (S.1)	OECD uniform tax (S.2)	Annex 1 uniform tax (S.3)	Major emitters uniform tax (S.4)	Global uniform tax (S.5)
	CO_2 emissions cut in 2050				
OECD[1]	−77.3	−77.3	−46.7	−26.4	−21.0
Annex 1	−53.6	−53.6	−51.9	−30.1	−23.8
Major emitters	−37.0	−37.0	−35.2	−35.5	−28.4
World[2]	−28.7	−28.7	−25.8	−26.2	−26.7
	NO_x emissions cut in 2050				
OECD[1]	−53.8	−53.7	−39.6	−24.1	−18.9
Annex 1	−32.7	−32.7	−47.3	−29.0	−23.0
Major emitters	−22.3	−22.3	−32.3	−35.0	−28.2
World[2]	−17.4	−17.3	−25.0	−27.2	−27.4
	SO_x emissions cut in 2050				
OECD[1]	−72.6	−72.5	−54.2	−33.5	−26.6
Annex 1	−39.1	−39.0	−57.5	−35.9	−28.8
Major emitters	−23.9	−23.9	−35.3	−41.1	−33.3
World[2]	−19.8	−19.8	−29.5	−34.4	−32.1

S.1: Four OECD regions cut emissions in equal proportions (using a carbon tax) to stabilise Annex 1 emissions at 1990 levels.
S.2: OECD regions stabilise Annex 1 emissions at 1990 levels by a uniform carbon tax.
S.3: Annex 1 countries stabilise Annex 1 emissions at 1990 levels by a uniform carbon tax.
S.4: Major emitters countries reduce emissions by an amount equivalent to the stabilisation of Annex 1 emissions at 1990 levels by a uniform carbon tax.
S.5: Global coalition reduces emissions by an amount equivalent to the stabilisation of Annex 1 emissions at 1990 levels by a uniform carbon tax.
1. Excluding Mexico.
2. Since the target is always an *ex ante* reduction of emissions among participating countries the *ex post* level of world emissions varies slightly between scenarios mainly due to different carbon leakage rates.
Source: OECD GREEN Model simulations.

3.3. GHG sequestration and removal

The various GHG sequestration and removal options are depicted in Figure 3.3. The sequestration (absorption) potential is almost exclusively related to CO_2, as this is the only greenhouse gas which has large natural sinks. Other GHGs are primarily broken down in the atmosphere and the discussion of absorption options is therefore not relevant for them. Removal of CO_2 (scrubbing) can also occur directly at the point of fossil fuel use, either before or just after the combustion of fossil fuels.

3.3.1. Carbon sequestration through biomass use

The sequestration of carbon from the atmosphere through biomass growth is of immediate policy interest. Biological processes absorb carbon from the atmosphere through the process of photosynthesis. Growing biomass removes carbon dioxide from the atmosphere for many years, in particular if the wood is never harvested at all or if it is eventually harvested and used for building materials or other long-term structural purposes. This option does not arrest growth of gross carbon emissions, however, as it does not replace fossil fuels.

A more effective option is to use biomass (which already provides more than 10 per cent of global energy needs) as a source of fuel to replace fossil fuels. This option is discussed in more detail in Annex C. Key elements in the current debate about the commercial use of biomass are:

- The production choice for biomass, either *a)* conventional timber oriented forestry (medium to long rotation periods); *b)* bio-fuel oriented forestry (short rotation); or *c)* herbaceous cropping for biofuel products. Each technology will make substantial demands for land, competing with other land uses, such

Figure 3.3. **Carbon sequestration and removal options**

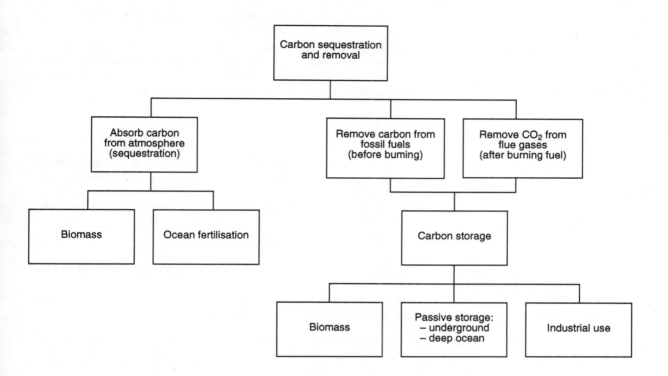

as conventional agriculture, in particular in land-scarce countries or countries with rapid population growth.
- Uncertainty about the economic viability of biomass. Some analysts (Ekins, 1994; Waide and Boyle, 1993) claim that biofuels are already competitive in many areas if all externalities of fossil fuel use are properly taken into account. And as commodity-linked support for agriculture is reduced, profitable opportunities for growing biomass instead of food crops or fibres may emerge.
- Technical (*e.g.* choice of species grown) and environmental concerns (*e.g.* vulnerability of biomass plantations to pests and diseases, long-term soil fertility, possible soil erosion, water pollution due to use of agrochemicals, bio-diversity).

At present, deforestation (and some related land-use changes) are thought to form a major source of anthropogenic emissions of CO_2. In 1990, estimated emissions of carbon from this source were almost 20 per cent of global anthropogenic emissions. Arresting deforestation can therefore also provide an important contribution to an optimal climate policy. Important policy elements in this area include the development of property rights, the removal of logging subsidies and a move to an economic-based pricing of forest resources.

Biomass options do not have to be restricted to terrestrial systems. Some studies (Spencer, 1994) have discussed the potential contribution of marine biomass systems (kelp, algae) to carbon sequestration. Marine biomass could, for instance, be grown to produce synthetic gas. Proposals have also been made to influence the carbon uptake by marine biomass artificially, by fertilizing the oceans with iron.[29] It is uncertain whether iron is really the limiting factor in growth of phytoplankton, however. In addition, the environmental uncertainties of these options are large, and little is known about their cost-effectiveness.

3.3.2. *CO_2 removal*

This technology is directed at large, stationary emitters of carbon dioxide (in particular power plants), where the CO_2 can be captured and subsequently stored or used for other purposes. The CO_2 can be captured directly from the flue (exhaust) gases or, alternatively, in modern IGCC (Integrated Gasified Combined Cycle) power plants from the gasified fossil fuels (Audus, 1994). The captured CO_2 can be used as feedstock in some industrial processes, although the industrial demand for carbon is at present relatively small compared with the volume of annual emissions. It can also be stored in empty oil or gas wells, which have already proven to be able to hold hydrocarbons. The global storage potential of gas wells is estimated at approximately 140 GtC, or about 70 years of current annual CO_2 emissions from power plants. The final option relates to deep ocean storage; the ocean is a large natural carbon sink and could store global carbon emissions for centuries.

All the above options, while technically feasible, are currently not considered likely candidates for large-scale application because of the high cost per unit of carbon prevented from entering the atmosphere. They substantially lower the efficiency of electricity generation and are also faced with some storage costs. The deep ocean storage option in addition faces large uncertainties in respect of other environment issues.

3.4. The link to policy levers

The possible actions to respond to the risk of global warming described above all pertain to activities carried out (actually or potentially) predominantly in the realm of the private sector, in the process of producing and consuming goods and services. For policy makers the relevant question is what instruments are available to influence private sector activity so as to implement the desired amount of mitigation or sequestration effectively and efficiently (*i.e.* achieving the desired result at least cost).

In principle the government has three options to pursue this objective:

- carry out the projects itself (for instance, afforestation of government owned land);
- oblige private sector agents to carry out projects, or behave in a certain manner so that objectives will be achieved (regulatory measures);
- use market instruments, such as taxes and subsidies, which induce private sector agents to behave in a way, or take actions, conducive to the achievement of stated objectives.

As noted earlier, there is general agreement among economists that indirect (market) instruments are usually preferable as they leave decentralised decision making to those agents with most knowledge about technical details. Market prices are the essential signal inducing private agents to achieve efficient allocation of resources by equalising marginal costs and benefits.

In the case of GHG emissions, however, the negative externalities (the effect of emissions on the climate) and the subsequent impact on the economy and the environment are not taken into account in market pricing, so that all emission generating activities are underpriced, while activities accompanied by the (permanent) absorption of GHG from the atmosphere are overpriced, *i.e.* they generate a benefit not remunerated by the market. Market instruments (*e.g.* a carbon tax and subsidies for carbon sequestration) can correct for this externality, inducing all carbon emitting/absorbing activities to be re-adjusted to levels taking into account the negative externality.[30]

In practice, there are many complications which make optimal policy design much more complicated than limiting it to the simple introduction of a comprehensive and uniform carbon tax. Market imperfections of various types, all-pervasive uncertainty, and bounded rationality of consumers open a much wider range of policy measures for useful government action, to be discussed in the next part.

4. Elements of an Appropriate Policy Response

An optimal climate change policy can in the abstract be defined as a policy that equalizes the discounted present values of the marginal (net) damages caused by climate change and the marginal (net) cost of policies aimed at preventing climate change damage. However, there is uncertainty about: the extent and timing of future damages resulting from cumulative anthropogenic GHG emissions;[31] the costs entailed by efforts to curtail such emissions; and the social discount rate to apply to the time path of both damages and costs.[32] This makes a policy design based on simple marginal cost benefit calculus impossible in practice.

Another major complication for the efficient implementation of climate change policy arises from the fact that both GHG emissions and their curtailment have a global public good character: most GHG disperse rapidly in the global atmosphere, creating identical GHG concentrations everywhere. In addition, the costs of climate change are unevenly distributed among nations. This leads to two complications: first countries can "free ride" on the abatement efforts of other countries; and second conflicts of interest can arise about how much abatement is required and who should bear the costs of policy actions.

4.1. No-regrets policies

Irrespective of the fundamental difficulties in designing an appropriate policy response to the risk of global warming, no-regrets measures should be implemented regardless of the size (or even existence) of such a risk, as they provide a net benefit to the economy over and above the potential benefits from emission reduction. The largest potential in this area probably consists of improvements in energy efficiency.[33] For several OECD member countries, assessments of no-regrets potential have been made (IEA/OECD, 1991a; Krause, et al., 1994), and most suggest considerable possible energy savings from various efficiency measures. The exact potential of efficiency measures in reducing carbon emissions remains controversial. They may have considerable hidden costs attached (see Box A in Part 3), and the net emission reductions may be less than expected, as the measures can have substantial take-back effects.[34]

It is puzzling that even though no-regrets measures lead to net savings, consumers and firms do not immediately implement these measures on their own account. Market imperfections can form a barrier to their implementation, implying a constructive role for government policy. Such policies should primarily be addressed at these market imperfections, by providing information to consumers, removing price and regulatory distortions, and the provision of low-cost access to efficient technologies and appliances.[35]

It is, however, important that a realistic cost assessment be made of the efficiency measures considered. The provision of information by governments or utility companies is not costless. Inappropriate government intervention can turn a potential no-regrets measure into a costly policy failure. Demand side management (DSM) programmes[36] can be burdened with significant implementation costs and have not always been as effective as anticipated (Joskow and Marron, 1992). In addition, care needs to be taken to evaluate whether or not the proposed measures have hidden (implementation) costs attached to consumers, or if they trade off efficiency against other desirable characteristics, leading to a loss in consumer utility not accounted for in the initial cost-benefit analysis.

A mix of policy instruments can be used to implement efficiency measures (IEA/OECD, 1991a). Although in theory economic instruments are superior to regulatory measures, in the presence of market imperfections the latter can be cost-effective if they are carefully designed and used flexibly. For instance, standards for energy-efficient appliances can expand markets for such technologies, help to reduce information barriers and can lower consumer's decision costs. Similar arguments apply to energy efficiency standards in public and private construction. Standards can also provide incentives to private research and development (R&D), by reducing uncertainty in the market. Flexibility in standards is important, however, as they must be economically feasible for firms, while standards which are set too low may lead to underachievement compared with technological potential and reduce incentives for further efforts.

The removal of existing price distortions, such as energy subsidies or price regulations, can also be a no-regrets measure. Price distortions result in excessive and inefficient energy use and in a non-optimal composition of energy supply. Energy is still subsidised in many, especially developing, countries (Hoeller and Coppel, 1992; Shah and Larsen, 1992), although price distortions also persist in OECD countries, in particular with respect to coal production. In eastern Europe, the former Soviet Union and China, more realistic pricing policies are now gradually being implemented.

Some no-regrets potential may be available for other GHGs. As methane has a commercial value as a fuel, gathering of methane at landfills, oil wells and the reduction of gas leakages may prove a cost-effective measure. For other sources of methane emissions, such as rice fields or ruminants, emission control is more difficult and is less likely to be no-regrets.

Some measures may be justified even if they are not completely no-regrets: if an anthropogenic activity resulting in GHG emissions has other strong negative externalities attached, mitigation of this activity may be justified, even though it is not costless to society. For instance, CFCs are phased out because of their effect on the ozone layer, not because of their effect on global warming. Another important policy measure in this context is arresting deforestation, which also has significant negative externalities attached, not directly related to global warming. Other environmental measures, such as control of local air pollution and/or traffic congestion resulting from road transport may also be justified from this point of view, leading to reduced carbon emissions as a welcome by-product.

No-regrets measures may help countries in reaching their targets under the FCCC. However, they only lead to a once-and-for-all step decline in emissions, but do not help to arrest the growth in energy demand and concomitant GHG emissions. In general, a further mitigation of emissions will require the implementation of measures which do carry some costs. The following sections look at policy actions which may be taken, additional to no-regrets measures, to insure against the risks of global warming.

4.2. Climate research and energy-related R&D

Since uncertainty is a major obstacle to designing an appropriate policy response, it would seem appropriate to invest in pertinent research to reduce this uncertainty.[37] To implement a climate-related R&D policy efficiently, it is necessary to decide how much should be spent on such R&D, on which projects it should be spent, and how it should be financed. R&D often has a partial public goods character which may require (some) government involvement through tax credits, subsidies or direct funding to achieve efficiency: private investors generally have only a limited ability to appropriate the benefits of many specific kinds of R&D, which leads to sub-optimal private investment in these activities.

4.2.1. Basic climate research

If pervasive uncertainty is a significant obstacle to policy making, gathering and analysing relevant information to reduce uncertainty, *i.e.* basic climate research, is a necessary part of an effective policy approach. Ideally uncertainty should be reduced substantially before deciding on costly policy actions, but the character of the uncertainties is such that many are likely to remain unresolved for some time to come (Annex D).

Most basic climate R&D will have to be carried out on the basis of government funding, as it has few commercial applications. The annual funding requirements for the main global research programmes in this area are estimated to amount to $700 to $800 million at current prices (OECD, 1994a). International co-operation, which is already emerging in this area, should increase the effectiveness of this expenditure by preventing duplication and should be strengthened. In addition there may be tangible side benefits from this type of research in the form of improved (short-term) weather forecasts.

Climate change is a global problem which has regional and local aspects. This implies that there is a need for both global and country-specific research, including local monitoring of climate change and anthropogenic emissions. The need for local research can create a problem for countries with poorly developed research capabilities, and strengthens the argument for international co-operation.

4.2.2. R&D on mitigation and sequestration

R&D on mitigation and sequestration[38] is much more market-driven and mostly takes place in the energy sector. The aim of this type of R&D is primarily to develop low-cost mitigation technologies. Private industry can take a much larger stake in funding this type of R&D, as much of the R&D has commercial applications, and the benefits are appropriable. Private industry is generally more aware of the commercialisation of new technologies

32

and of consumer demands. It is also more likely to terminate a research programme if it is seen as not leading to results justifying continuation. In addition, competition in this area may lead to more efficient and low-cost technologies than centralised government research.

Market imperfections, such as price and regulatory distortions, in addition to the public good character of R&D, may result in a sub-optimal amount, or a sub-optimal composition of R&D. External effects, such as pollution or GHG emissions and the way in which they differ between alternative technologies are generally not embodied in relative prices. Market imperfections affecting energy efficiency and renewable energy may also reduce R&D expenditures by limiting the potential market for these technologies. The less serious these market imperfections are, the more powerful the argument that private industry will be willing to finance R&D on emission curtailment at the appropriate level.

Government's role should therefore primarily be directed at facilitating the efficient operation of energy markets by removing existing distortions. The introduction of a carbon tax can correct for the negative externality of carbon emissions, providing incentives to private industry for R&D on mitigation and the development of carbon-free or carbon-neutral energy sources. To the extent that such R&D has partly a public good character, governments may also provide fiscal stimuli to achieve an appropriate level of R&D. However, governments should be directly involved in energy R&D only if:

– the research is not likely to be performed by private industry;
– public funding is the cheapest and most efficient method.

Both criteria are more likely to be met by basic climate research, than by R&D in energy markets.

Although there is a growing tendency to leave more energy R&D to private industry, governments are still heavily involved in energy-related R&D. Securing long-term energy supply, environmental concerns and national security, are some of the reasons why governments feel a need to be involved in energy-related R&D. If the research has a long-term time horizon and is of general (non-applied) character, governments may indeed have to support the research because of differential public and private risk aversion and differences in public and private discount rates. However, little general guidance can be given on the appropriate extent of government involvement, and there is a definite risk of government capture by private interest and rent seeking behaviour induced by government financing of R&D.

The past composition of R&D may require reconsideration in the light of market imperfections. Over the period 1977-1990, IEA governments spent some $120 billion on energy-related R&D (IEA/OECD, 1991b). Of this sum almost 50 per cent was channelled into nuclear fission research, almost 12 per cent into nuclear fusion research, close to 15 per cent into fossil fuel related research and 9 per cent into electricity generation research in general. Finally, 5.8 per cent was spent on research on energy conservation and 9 per cent on renewable energy. This composition apparently suggests that renewable energy and energy efficiency, two options that have a considerable potential to mitigate the risk of global warming (see Part 3), have received relatively limited funding. While this composition may partly be the result of existing imperfections in the energy market, it is also likely to reflect the underdeveloped market for renewable energy and (possibly) the lack of suitable research projects.

Some reorientation of, and stimulation for, private R&D may be expected from the implementation of certain types of no-regrets measures (*e.g.* specification of energy efficiency standards) and from the introduction of carbon emission constraints or taxes, as these are likely to expand the market for technologies which mitigate carbon emissions and raise the pay-off to successful R&D in this area.

4.3. Policy making under uncertainty

4.3.1. *The insurance approach to global warming*

Even with an effective R&D programme, large uncertainties about climate change are likely to persist. It will, therefore, remain for policy makers to decide which policy actions are justified to avoid uncertain damages from uncertain climate change. Beyond the implementation of no-regrets options, further policy actions may be justified on the grounds that they provide insurance against possible climate change damage.

Little specific is known about the probability of climate change and the cost of its potential damage, as there is no past experience about the event. This makes it difficult to establish the correct "premium", *i.e.* the appropriate amount to spend on preventive action (mitigation and absorption). How much it is reasonable to "pay" depends on the potential damages from climate change, the probability of damages occurring and the preferences of the insurance taker, *i.e.* governments. A high degree of risk aversion, or use of a low discount rate, both imply high insurance premia, and therefore high acceptable costs of abatement measures.

Some alternative expenditure levels are depicted in Table A5.1 in Annex A, as a function of the various relevant variables which determine the size of "insurance premia", which were calculated for three different scenarios.[39] In each scenario, there is a 90 per cent probability that no damages of global warming occur, and a 10 per cent probability that there are damages, but with differing scales of damage assumed.[40]

Even though each scenario has a 90 per cent probability that no damage will occur, the 10 per cent probability that there could be major damages implies that it is rational to spend resources on preventing the (uncertain) damages, *i.e.* pay an "insurance premium". Annual insurance premia for different degrees of risk aversion, discount rates and probabilities of damages in terms of per cent of GDP are shown in Table A5.1. The value of insurance premia is fairly sensitive to the degree of risk aversion and the probability of damages, with the largest sensitivity being to the discount rate.[41]

Buying insurance against climate change has two aspects: *i)* reducing the risk of climate change occurring, *i.e.* investing in mitigation and sequestration; and *ii)* spreading the response cost, and thus risks of climate change, over the relevant parties. This second aspect concerns the question of who assumes the cost of response action. Both aspects are recognised in the FCCC, as the commitments undertaken by Annex 1 countries already aim at some mitigation efforts, whereas the FCCC also clearly recognises the need for joint policy action and burden sharing. This latter issue will require intensive international negotiations in the context of "joint implementation", dealt with in more detail in Part 6.

4.3.2. Uncertainty about policy effectiveness

The problem of uncertainty also affects the effectiveness of implemented policies. The effects of carbon taxation, efficiency measures or R&D programmes can only be predicted approximately. This implies that government policies may need to be tuned over time, to reach desired outcomes.

In principle, the implementation of policy measures (*e.g.* a carbon tax) should be gradual and predictable. If governments set and announce long-term targets, market expectations can adjust and investment decisions can take account of the future policy setting (*e.g.* the size of carbon tax rates). This would allow the capital stock to be adjusted gradually as fixed capital is replaced in the course of normal turn-over. Even if the announced policy lacked full credibility, it is likely that the threat of a future carbon constraint (for instance by implementation of a carbon tax) will lead to precautionary action by consumers and investors. Investors will choose less carbon-intensive technologies than they would have chosen without the presence of this possible carbon restraint.[42]

Periodic modification of instruments to reach desired outcomes would lead to considerable government-induced uncertainty, however, and could also be ineffective due to low short-term elasticities of substitution (Godard, 1993). Since capital stocks are slow to roll over, the short-term effect on emissions of – for example – a carbon tax may be relatively limited. Firms may at first choose to pay the tax, rather than abate emissions. As old capital is gradually replaced, they may start abating instead of paying the tax. At the same time final demand will gradually shift away from the energy-intensive output, due to its tax-induced relative price increase. Governments should be aware of these response lags, and not adjust instruments too often or too quickly to reach a required emission target. This slow response also implies that experimentation with tax rates may not be as simple and informative as sometimes suggested. However, a low initial carbon tax could provide some evidence of how the tax affects economic activity (Poterba, 1993).

Another element of policy uncertainty concerns the degree of natural adaptation to global warming that could take place (Pearce, 1991). Since several aspects of global warming may occur gradually, some adjustment of society to a changing environment may occur automatically. Although not costless, the degree of this process of natural adaptation can significantly affect the need for emission curtailment by government policy.

4.3.3. Building institutions

Implementation of a carbon tax or tradeable permit scheme will in practice require preparations, in particular if internationally co-ordinated action is envisaged. For the implementation of a national carbon tax, or an internationally harmonized tax, existing tax collection institutions would most likely be sufficient, although a harmonized tax could require the establishment of institutions to monitor and enforce the agreement. For an international tax fund or an international tradeable permit scheme international mechanisms would need to be established, supported by pertinent international institutions. It takes time to establish such institutions and to develop rules and procedures according to which they can function. Even more so, it could take some time before a credible global or multilateral coalition can be established to agree on the tasks and responsibilities of the newly created institution.

If a supra-national carbon tax fund would be considered a viable option, a global tax-collecting authority would need to be established, which would also be charged with distributing tax revenues among the different participants according to agreed criteria. This authority would also be responsible for monitoring carbon emissions and enforcing the tax regime.[43] The main problem with this option is that any tax which would have a credible effect on emissions, would generate large revenues which would make it unlikely that governments would allow the transfer of such power to an international organisation (Schelling, 1992).

An international tradeable emission quota (TEQ) scheme[44] would also require an international authority to monitor and enforce compliance, similar to those for an international tax system. Emissions trading within the countries involved could take place in national markets, but for the international trading an international market would be required.[45]

4.4. Optimal emission abatement over time

Although the objective of the FCCC is "..., stabilization of greenhouse gas **concentrations** in the atmosphere at a level that would prevent dangerous anthropogenic interference with the climate system", most climate change policy objectives are formulated in terms of stabilization or reduction of GHG **emissions**. However, stabilizing emissions at current levels would still lead to a steady rise in concentrations (Richels and Edmonds, 1993). A more relevant target for an international climate policy is therefore not the level of GHG emissions, but the level of GHG concentrations. Once such a concentration target has been defined for a future date, there is an infinite number of possible emission time-paths by which this target can be reached. An optimal time-path would minimise abatement cost over time, given the concentration target.

There are a number of considerations which call for delaying abatement to the later years of the time path, apart from the obvious reason that use of a positive discount rate implies that the present value of future expenditures is lower than that of identical current expenditures:

- abatement costs will probably fall over time, in particular if some investment is made now in pertinent R&D. In addition, existing capital stocks have a "sunk cost" character and will take time to be replaced by new capital stocks corresponding to less carbon-intensive technologies;
- awaiting confirmation of the greenhouse effect itself (its existence and extent) and reduction of uncertainties may justify postponing costly abatement measures to avoid the deadweight loss of premature and unnecessary action;
- a delayed abatement response may allow some adaptation to global warming, which can help to reduce abatement costs, in particular if the process of global warming is (very) gradual;
- finally, the gradual introduction of abatement policies may allow a learning process to take place (Kolstad, 1993), which could lower costs over time.

However, to take advantage of the reduced cost of equivalent future action will in many instances require the pre-announcement of future abatement requirements to allow anticipatory actions to take place. It is the elimination of the surprise element of abatement efforts which substantially lowers adjustment costs, rather than the postponement *per se*.

On the other hand, arguments can be made in favour of early abatement, beyond the obvious case of no-regrets measures: the earlier emissions are reduced, the greater the cumulative damages avoided. If damages are high and irreversible, early stabilisation of emissions below a plausible threshold level is required: the uncertain effects of global warming and, in particular, its potential catastrophic consequences may call for early action. Also, the cost function of emission curtailment is not linear, so that spreading emissions more evenly over a given period should *ceteris paribus* reduce overall curtailment costs.

The role of emission time paths is illustrated in Figure 4.1, which shows results of simulations by Richels and Edmonds (1993) with the Global 2100 and ERB models.[46] A maximum 500 ppmv[47] concentration level was defined for 2100, and three different emission paths were used to reach this concentration level. The least-cost scenario was that in which emissions were allowed to rise along the Bau trajectory up to 2010, were gradually reduced between 2010 and 2050, and were sharply reduced after 2050. The highest costs were calculated for the scenario which stabilised emissions at 1990 levels. The main factors leading to these results are the emergence of low-cost abatement measures over time, slow turn-over of fixed capital stocks and the 5 per cent discount rate used. The benefits of avoided damages were not integrated in this assessment, however, and are not necessarily identical for the alternative emission trajectories.

Unless there is a high preference to minimise climate change risks, an optimal time path of emission abatement, in terms of cost-optimization, is one that concentrates current policies on no-regrets policies, R&D,

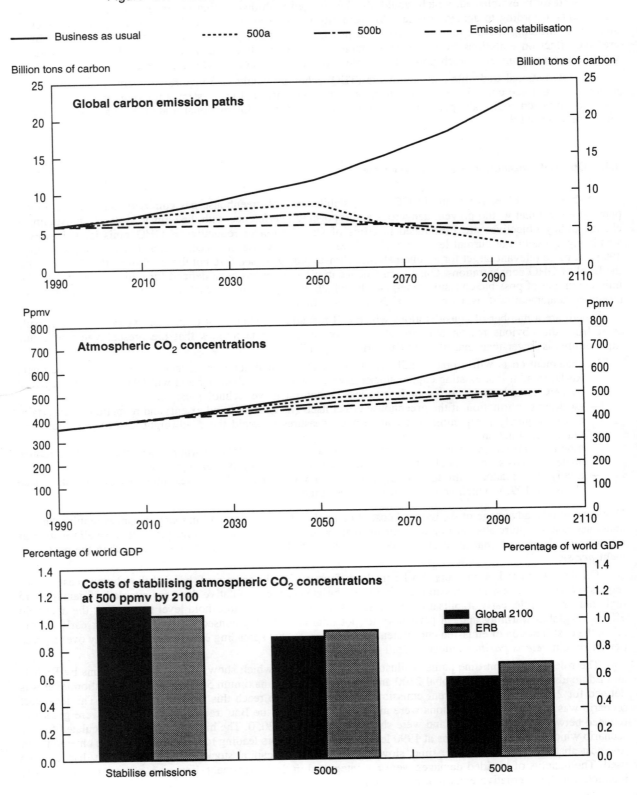

Figure 4.1. **Alternative emission time paths and associated costs**

——— Business as usual ······· 500a —··—··— 500b — — — Emission stabilisation

Billion tons of carbon

Global carbon emission paths

Ppmv

Atmospheric CO$_2$ concentrations

Percentage of world GDP

Costs of stabilising atmospheric CO$_2$ concentrations at 500 ppmv by 2100

Global 2100
ERB

Stabilise emissions   500b   500a

Source: Richels and Edmonds (1993).

36

institution building and the formation of effective international agreements. This optimal path would avoid costly abatement measures at the current stage, but would look very carefully at the design of such measures, to implement them if they were shown to be necessary at a later date. In this context it is interesting to note that both Cline – a proponent of the "don't wait" school – and Nordhaus – a proponent of the "wait and see" school – arrive at similar policy positions for the short term. It is only for the longer term that their respective views on policy needs diverge. The fact that these two camps are in basic agreement until at least the year 2010 about what should be done now points the way towards an acceptable initial strategy along the lines outlined here.[48]

4.5. Establishing a level playing field

An important element of an optimal policy design regarding climate change is the establishment of a framework in which the last dollar spent on each measure has an identical effect on reducing climate change risk. Climate change not only depends on CO_2 concentrations, but also on concentrations of other GHGs. As the goal is to stabilize concentrations of all GHGs, it is desirable to define a concentration target for all GHGs together (for example in terms of global warming potential, hereafter GWP), which allows trade-offs between the different gases. This would allow policy actions to concentrate on GHGs with relatively high damage potentials, long atmospheric lifetimes and low abatement costs.[49]

Given an abatement target, efficient policy requires the implementation of all available measures to a point where their marginal costs are equalised for a given contribution to achieving the target. For instance, implementation of a carbon tax would imply that an equivalent subsidy, per ton of carbon, would be required for permanent carbon sequestration (e.g. through afforestation), while biomass, as an essentially carbon-neutral fuel, would need neither taxation nor subsidisation. Tax rates, or equivalent measures, would also be needed for curtailment of emissions of other GHGs.[50]

One of the attractions of both a carbon tax and of tradeable emission quotas is their automatic tendency towards establishing a level playing field with respect to the large number of possible measures to reduce net carbon emissions (cf. Part 3). By leaving decision-making about the choice of measures (both type and scale) to individual market participants who have most information about marginal cost and effectiveness of alternative measures, chances to equalise marginal cost and benefits will be enhanced.[51] However, the presence of market imperfections may imply that some additional public policy measures, such as the provision of information or establishment of efficiency standards, may also be required to achieve cost-effectiveness.

5. The Fiscal Implications of a Carbon Tax

The objective of a carbon tax is to reduce carbon emissions through reductions in the use of fossil fuels. Ideally, a carbon tax would equate the marginal damage associated with climate change and the marginal cost of emission abatement. In practice, little is known about the marginal economic damage of climate change, so the objective of the carbon tax typically reverts to the "second best" goal of equating marginal costs of abatement among all emitters. To the extent that the carbon tax corrects for a negative externality[52] of carbon emissions (damages from climate change), it improves, rather than distorts, the functioning of the market, and the resulting revenues provide an opportunity to reduce the economic burden associated with other distortionary taxes.[53]

Motivated by the policy goals of reducing the risk of climate change and achieving a more efficient tax system, several Scandinavian countries have recently introduced carbon-type taxes as part of a revenue neutral tax reform package (OECD, 1993a). Similarly, original plans by the U.S. administration for a BTU tax were predicated on lowering other taxes, and the EC is currently studying revenue switching options, linking funds raised from a carbon/energy tax to lower taxes on labour income. Once the analysis of carbon taxes is expanded to encompass the efficiency of the revenue system, the comprehensive evaluation of carbon taxes must take account not only of their role as instruments of environmental management, but also their potential for reducing distortions from other taxes. In this sense a carbon tax could yield a "double dividend" – lower carbon emissions and a less distortionary tax system.[54]

5.1. Estimates of carbon tax revenues

Even moderate carbon tax rates could raise substantial amounts of revenue in both absolute and relative terms. A hypothetical $50 per ton OECD carbon tax[55] would raise approximately $150 billion based on 1990 carbon emissions, equivalent on average to about 2½ per cent of total OECD tax revenues (Table 5.1), ranging across countries from below 1 per cent to 6½ per cent. Countries like Sweden and Switzerland, which depend more on carbon-free fuels are at the lower end of the range. On the other hand, countries with lower tax burdens and a higher dependence on coal, such as Australia, the United States, Canada and Turkey are at the top end of the range. A carbon tax would induce greater energy efficiency (energy use per unit of GDP) and substitution towards less carbon intensive fossil fuels. As a consequence, despite a constant tax rate and rising CO_2 emissions, the growth in tax revenues would be slower than that of output, resulting in declining tax revenues as a percentage of GDP (Figure 5.1).[56] Furthermore, a carbon tax provides an incentive for research and development into less carbon-intensive production processes and fuels. If technological progress is rapid in the areas of renewable energy, energy-efficient appliances, carbon scrubbing technologies and so on, carbon emissions and therefore revenues will fall.

5.2. The use of carbon tax revenues

Compared with the existing structure of OECD tax revenues (Table 5.2), a $50 carbon tax[57] would yield revenues almost equal to those from property or payroll taxes in many OECD countries. These revenues from a carbon tax could be used in a variety of ways. Options include: reducing budget deficits, increasing general budget spending, "earmarking" for additional carbon abatement measures (including international side payments) and changing the tax structure by reducing taxes elsewhere, but keeping total revenues constant. Revenue-neutral tax reforms could target specific taxes or all taxes and could be implemented by narrowing the tax base or lowering the tax rate. It could also provide scope to reduce dependence on tax revenues from labour income. For each option, the fiscal and economic implications differ.

Table 5.1. **1990 OECD tax revenues implied by a hypothetical $50 per ton carbon tax**

	Total tax revenues		$50 per ton carbon tax[1]		
	Million US$	Per cent of GDP	Million US$	Per cent of GDP	Per cent of total tax revenue
United States	1 598 114	29.5	69 095	1.28	4.32
Japan	939 050	31.4	15 348	0.51	1.63
Germany[2]	539 953	37.6	9 959	0.69	1.84
France	522 800	43.8	6 188	0.52	1.18
Italy	428 459	39.1	6 962	0.64	1.62
United Kingdom	360 705	37.0	8 296	0.85	2.30
Canada	211 499	37.0	6 288	1.10	2.97
Australia	90 817	30.8	3 917	1.33	4.31
Austria	65 401	41.3	902	0.57	1.38
Belgium	86 220	44.8	1 819	0.95	2.11
Denmark	62 928	48.5	1 026	0.79	1.63
Finland	61 184	44.5	798	0.58	1.30
Greece	24 748	37.1	1 102	1.65	4.45
Iceland	1 962	32.3	32	0.53	1.64
Ireland	15 832	36.8	459	1.07	2.90
Luxembourg	4 391	48.8	149	1.65	3.39
Netherlands	126 468	44.6	2 723	0.96	2.15
Norway	16 325	37.3	517	1.18	3.17
New Zealand	48 881	46.2	381	0.36	0.78
Portugal	20 768	34.8	601	1.01	2.90
Spain	169 208	34.4	3 572	0.73	2.11
Sweden	129 699	56.9	815	0.36	0.63
Switzerland	71 193	31.5	692	0.31	0.97
Turkey	30 175	27.8	1 936	1.78	6.42
Total OECD[3]	5 626 782	34.6	147 308	0.91	2.62

1. Calculated as the tax rate ($50) multiplied by 1990 carbon emissions.
2. West Germany only.
3. Excluding Mexico.
Source: Revenue statistics of OECD Member countries, OECD (1992*d*); OECD Environmental Data (1993).

5.2.1. Earmarking revenues

How government revenues are raised and spent are usually treated as separate issues. However, earmarking revenues, especially those from a new tax, could generate broader public support for the introduction of the tax and make it more acceptable politically. Included in this category are side-payments to those agents who, for example, incur higher costs as a result of the policy change, including international transfers to encourage wider geographical participation in carbon-emission abatement schemes, an option discussed in more detail in Part 6. Earmarking could lead to inefficiencies as spending is not evaluated on the basis of its social benefits compared with alternative uses. Furthermore, the resulting levels of spending will be subject to the vagaries of receipts which may be too high or insufficient to finance appropriate outlays on environmental protection (climate change prevention).

5.2.2. Increase government spending

The main distinction between earmarking and increased government spending is that earmarked revenues do not necessarily imply a higher aggregate level of government spending. But, as with earmarking, arguments against linking new tax receipts to higher government spending are based on the separation of government financing and spending decisions. It makes little economic sense to increase public spending simply because tax revenues have increased (though in practice this causal link may be important for political reasons).

5.2.3. Reduce budget deficits

The use of carbon tax revenues to reduce the fiscal deficit can be seen as bringing forward a future tax increase. The policy issue from a public choice perspective then centres on whether carbon taxes are the

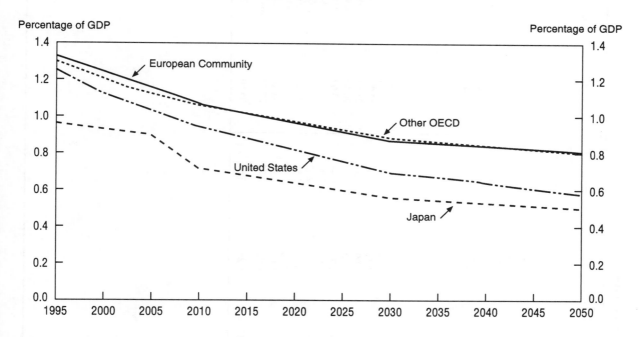

Figure 5.1. **Tax revenues implied by a hypothetical $50 per ton carbon tax in OECD countries**

Percentage of GDP

European Community

Other OECD

United States

Japan

Source: OECD GREEN model simulations.

appropriate new revenue source. Inter-generational equity questions are also involved, since tax *versus* debt financing impinges on the intertemporal distribution of the tax burden.

5.2.4. *Revenue switching*

Some studies have suggested that efficient (in the sense of compensating for a negative externality) carbon taxes combined with the reduction of other distortive taxes[58] can improve efficiency in the economy and hence contribute to raising economic welfare (Dower and Zimmerman, 1992). Empirical work on tax reform indicates that the highest efficiency gains occur when taxes on capital income are lowered. For example, Jorgenson and Wilcoxen (1994) find that GDP could actually increase if carbon tax revenues are used to lower taxes on capital income compared with the scenario where carbon tax revenues are redistributed as a lump sum. The gain in output is due to enhanced incentives to invest via an increase in the after-tax rate of return on investment, accelerating capital formation and potential output.[59] The same study also suggests that the impact of a carbon tax on GDP would be moderated if carbon tax revenues are used to lower taxes on labour income, but by a smaller amount. Comparable simulation experiments with other models find similar qualitative results as Jorgenson and Wilcoxen (Shackleton, *et al.*, 1992; Goulder, 1991). However, the majority of expert analyses suggest that the potential gains are difficult to determine and depend on specific conditions (including existing tax structures) which differ from country to country.

Potential labour market effects of tax switching have received increasing attention in many European countries, as unemployment rates have reached record post-war heights. However, determining the effect on employment levels of partly replacing taxes on labour income by a carbon tax is not straightforward. The necessary condition to raise employment is a shift in the burden of taxation away from labour to capital owners, resource owners or recipients of income transfers. In practice this is difficult to achieve, because even if a tax is nominally imposed on capital income, its economic burden ultimately falls on the least mobile factor of production, which is typically labour. Some analysts have cited the distortionary effects of a high and rising dependence on taxes on labour income as a possible explanation for weak employment growth (Standaert, 1992). A recent study by Bovenberg (1994) shows that the overall effect of carbon taxation (combined with tax reductions elsewhere) on employment is not clear and depends on the design of the tax and the existing tax

41

Table 5.2. **Structure of 1990 OECD tax revenues**

| | Total tax revenues | | Per cent of total tax revenue | | | | | |
	Millions US$	Per cent of GDP	Taxes on income, profits and capital gains	Social security contributions	Taxes on payroll and work force	Taxes on property	Taxes on goods and services	Other taxes
United States	1 598 114	29.5	43.16	29.53	0.00	10.84	16.47	0.00
Japan	939 050	31.4	48.31	29.22	0.00	9.04	13.19	0.24
Germany[1]	539 953	37.6	32.38	37.48	0.00	3.37	26.74	0.03
France	522 800	43.8	17.22	44.02	1.90	5.29	28.32	3.25
Italy	428 459	39.1	36.48	32.91	0.34	2.26	28.02	0.00
United Kingdom	360 705	37.0	39.47	17.06	0.00	8.69	30.51	4.27
Canada	211 499	37.0	47.93	14.23	0.00	9.21	27.42	1.21
Australia	90 817	30.8	57.20	0.00	6.10	8.96	27.74	0.00
Austria	65 401	41.3	25.53	32.87	6.03	2.73	31.50	1.34
Belgium	86 220	44.8	37.47	34.41	0.00	2.64	25.48	0.00
Denmark	62 928	48.5	58.27	3.07	0.64	4.21	33.62	0.20
Finland	61 184	44.5	43.11	21.74	0.00	2.38	32.64	0.13
Greece	24 748	37.1	19.83	30.46	0.69	4.62	44.38	0.02
Iceland	1 962	32.3	29.34	3.15	3.56	8.47	51.53	3.95
Ireland	15 832	36.8	36.90	14.84	1.31	4.68	42.27	0.00
Luxembourg	4 391	48.8	40.26	27.72	0.00	8.49	23.52	0.00
Netherlands	126 468	44.6	32.24	37.39	0.00	3.65	26.40	0.32
Norway	16 325	37.3	58.05	0.00	1.77	6.48	33.69	0.00
New Zealand	48 881	46.2	34.71	26.19	0.00	2.90	35.37	0.83
Portugal	20 768	34.8	25.70	27.46	0.00	2.42	43.81	0.61
Spain	169 208	34.4	30.64	35.42	0.00	5.52	28.39	0.03
Sweden	129 699	56.9	41.01	27.62	3.15	3.47	24.58	0.16
Switzerland	71 193	31.5	41.04	32.89	0.00	7.80	18.28	0.00
Turkey	30 175	27.8	33.47	19.65	0.00	2.28	27.92	16.69
Total OECD[2]	5 626 782	34.6	37.97	30.91	0.25	3.60	25.50	1.78

1. West Germany only.
2. Excluding Mexico.
Source: *Revenue Statistics of OECD Member Countries*, OECD environmental data 1993.

Table 5.3. **Macroeconomic impact of the EC tax switching proposal**

Study	Country/region	Model used	Model type	Tax	Offsetting revenue recycling	Time	Summary of results[1]	
							Employment	GDP
EC Commission (1992)	EC-12	Quest	Macroeconometric	EC tax[2]	Social security contributions	1993-1998	0	-0.7
EC Commission (1992)	EC-12	Quest	Macroeconometric	EC tax[2]	Value added tax		+0.1	-0.1
DRI (1993)	EC-11	DRI	Multi model systems	EC tax	Investment tax credit: 35% Corporate tax Social security contributions: 30%	1993-2005	Negative	-0.52
OECD (1992)	EC-12	GREEN	General equilibrium	EC tax	Lump sum	1995-2050	0[3]	-0.6
Manne and Richels (1992)	EC-12	Global 2100	General equilibrium	EC tax	Lump sum	1993-2030	0[3]	-0.4
Standaert (1992)	EC-4	Hermès	Macroeconometric	$10 per barrel of oil energy tax[2]	Social security contributions	1993-2005	+0.45	-0.12
Jorgenson and Wilcoxen (1994)	US	DW	General equilibrium	$15 per ton plus 5% increase per annum	Lump sum Labour rebate Capital rebate	1990-2020	–	-1.7 -0.7 1.1
EC Commission (1994)	EC-12	Quest	Macroeconometric	EC tax	Social security contributions	1993-2005	2.2	0.4

1. All results are given as per cent deviations from baseline at end-year of the period (except otherwise stated).
2. Fully introduced in 1993.
3. Model design excludes the analysis of employment effects resulting from tax switching.

Source: Based on Willems (1993).

43

structure. Others argue that the employment effects are small (Brechet, 1992). Still other studies examining the potential impacts of the EC carbon/energy tax proposal find a positive effect on employment (Majocchi, 1994). A summary of the key modelling results in this area is presented in Table 5.3.

Possibilities for impinging favourably on unemployment levels by changing the tax structure depend on pre-existing conditions in the labour market. If labour markets are free to balance labour supply and demand, the long-run effect of a tax on labour will affect employment, but not unemployment as the effects on labour supply and demand are symmetric. On the other hand, if labour markets do not clear because of policy regulations, for example minimum wages, more focused revenue switching, targeting taxes on low income labour affected by the minimum wage might increase employment and lead to a reduction in unemployment as well. Environment and taxation policies can be made mutually reinforcing, although achieving net-efficiency gains requires considerable detailed knowledge concerning the relevant demand and supply elasticities which are not known precisely and which will differ in the short and long run. Equity objectives may also constrain opportunities to reform the existing taxation structure using tax switching in the context of the introduction of a carbon tax.

5.3. Wider public finance implications

An important consideration when introducing any tax is the point of taxation. Implicitly, the discussion above assumed a carbon tax was imposed on the carbon content of end-user fossil fuel consumption, but this may not necessarily be the ideal choice. Where to tax the energy stream has implications for compliance, monitoring and enforcement costs, which affect efficiency; it is also likely to have distributional repercussions, both nationally and internationally.

Taxing fossil fuel producers or distributors has the advantage of administrative simplicity, since the number of players are limited and energy flows are already regularly monitored. In this case, at least the cost of monitoring overall compliance should not be excessive. Taxing at the producer level will also influence decisions along the entire energy stream. On the other hand, if the statutory point of tax incidence is at the consumer level, the effect on carbon emissions is smaller, since production and distribution losses in the energy system are not taxed, unless the tax is on gross carbon inputs to the items consumed. Taxing end-users could also be more complicated to administer due to the large number of carbon ''consumers'', although in countries with consumer energy taxes, existing tax systems could be readily adapted.

When levying the tax at the primary producer level, energy exporters, such as OPEC countries, would receive the tax revenue, provided there is international co-ordination and application of the tax, while energy-importing countries, such as Japan, would only raise small revenues despite large tax payments accruing to others. The statutory point of tax incidence also has distributional impacts within a country. If carbon taxes are levied at the producer level, the economic incidence of the tax will fall primarily on the least mobile production factor, which is typically labour – capital and energy can be more easily diverted to productive uses elsewhere, including abroad. On the other hand, consumer based taxes spread the tax burden more broadly, encompassing recipients of transfer incomes as well as labour incomes.

The choice of tax base is also important. In principle, it would be preferable to tax emissions directly, but in practice this is complicated since monitoring emissions is difficult to administer, in particular for household end-users and mobile sources. If there is a direct relationship between an intermediary product (fossil fuels) and emissions, it may be more efficient from a tax administration perspective to tax the product. For example, in the case of carbon emissions, the carbon content of fossil fuels is taxed. In this case, however, tax rebates (negative taxes) may be needed when use of the product does not entail emissions. For instance, some users of fossil fuels, like the petrochemical industry, do not burn the fuel and therefore generate lower carbon emissions than the carbon content of the fossil fuels they use. Some sources of carbon emission are ignored when the tax is levied on the carbon content of fossil fuels alone. For example, carbon emissions from cement production and land-use changes (deforestation) are not related to fossil fuel consumption, but account for about 20 per cent of global anthropogenic carbon emissions.

The implementation of carbon taxation becomes much more complicated in the international context. First, institutional arrangements for international taxation do not exist at present, and it is unlikely that most countries would allow the required transfer of sovereignty to take place. Secondly, enforcement mechanisms accepted at a national level, such as fines and sanctions are more difficult to enforce at an international level. An alternative, with less loss of sovereignty, is the possibility of harmonising individual country carbon taxes, taking into consideration overall economic and environmental objectives, though revenues are collected nationally. Assuming a harmonisation approach is accepted, the final form of the carbon tax will depend on the progress of negotiations concerning tax rates, exemptions, point of incidence, enforcement and monitoring procedures.

Although more difficult to implement, an effective international carbon tax will reduce the incentive to transfer energy intensive activities to non-taxed areas (carbon leakage). To the extent that carbon leakages are lower, the original purpose of the tax (reducing total CO_2 emissions) is upheld and a weakening of the revenue base is also avoided (see Annex B for a detailed discussion of carbon leakages).

In summary, carbon taxes offer the potential to raise substantial sums of revenues without incurring large compliance and enforcement costs if imposed on the carbon content of fossil fuels and tax rebates are given when needed (*i.e.* in the case of non-emission producing use), rather than on emissions directly. This approach has been adopted by all countries which have already imposed a carbon tax, and at the same time the carbon tax was introduced, tax rates on other bases were lowered. The emission reduction objective and the revenue raising objective for a specific carbon tax are in conflict: the more effective the tax is in curtailing emissions, the less effective it will be in raising revenue. Finally, scope to lower the excess burden of the tax system implies that abatement costs from carbon tax policies could be smaller than those estimated based on the standard assumption of lump sum revenue redistribution.

6. Joint Implementation

6.1. From cost efficiency to joint implementation

Effective and efficient GHG abatement is unlikely to be achieved without the participation and policy co-ordination of the major emitting countries (see Section 2.3 for a discussion of this point). A global agreement with uniform carbon taxes, or tradeable emission quotas, would tend to minimise aggregate abatement costs, but would also entail a very unequal distribution of these costs between countries. Therefore, international agreements for policy co-ordination could be elusive, despite aggregate benefits of co-operation. It will clearly be necessary to find a way of complementing the uneven distribution of abatement costs with compensatory side payments that satisfies all participating parties. Several such schemes are examined here.

The FCCC approach to the competing objectives of efficiency and equity is to separate the question of who pays from where emission abatement is implemented, by endorsing a provision known as joint implementation (Article 4 paragraph 2a). Joint implementation (hereafter, JI) is broadly defined as a class of policies which reduce the global costs of achieving given GHG abatement targets. JI could also be portrayed as a mechanism for compensating countries whose participation goes beyond their FCCC commitments for the costs incurred by their (voluntary) participation.

6.2. Joint implementation: negotiating side payments

A key part of JI schemes concerns the issues related to side-payments or compensation to specific parties. Using a GREEN scenario where Major emitters cut world CO_2 emissions by the equivalent necessary to stabilise ex-ante Annex 1 country CO_2 emissions at 1990 levels (already discussed in Part 2), and assuming Annex 1 countries compensate non-Annex 1 countries for participating, it is possible to quantify the benchmark levels of maximum and minimum compensation acceptable to each party in order to accomplish broader international co-operation.

For Annex 1 countries as a group the maximum amount of side payments to make it interesting to non-Annex 1 countries (China and India) to participate is the difference between the cost incurred under unilateral stabilisation and the cost incurred by Annex 1 countries under JI. In this case, the parties not belonging to the Annex 1 group, but jointly implementing the commitments of Annex 1 countries collect all the benefits from policy co-operation.[60] This is equivalent to Annex 1 countries being indifferent between unilaterally achieving the emission target (no co-operation) and jointly implementing the agreement with the Major emitters.

The minimum side-payment non-Annex 1 countries require for JI of the stabilisation agreement, is equivalent to the abatement costs non-Annex 1 countries incur (assuming they expect identical abatement benefits to accrue to them under either scheme).[61] The gap between the minimum and maximum compensation is illustrated in Figure 6.1. The lower line is the minimum compensation non-Annex 1 countries would require and the upper line is the maximum side-payment by Annex 1 countries.[62] The difference between the two amounts widens over the period and by 2050 the gap is approximately equivalent to 1.1 per cent of non-Annex 1 country GDP.

6.3. Joint implementation: partial schemes

Partial JI policies comprise bilateral co-operative agreements between parties (private firms, public or non-governmental organisations) in an industrialised country and a developing country. Such agreements are partly motivated by the anticipation of participants from industrialised countries that they will receive a "credit" against future emission curtailment obligations equal to the quantity of emissions prevented. Over the coming years international policy co-ordination might develop by programmes which closely resemble such offset

47

Figure 6.1. **Compensation bounds for Annex 1 JI agreement**[1]

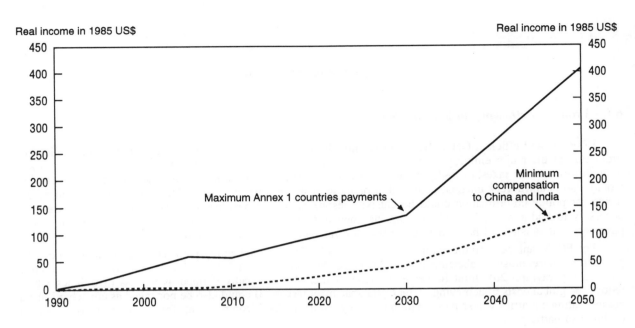

1. Major emitters stabilise Annex 1 CO_2 emissions at 1990 levels.
Source: OECD GREEN model simulations.

investments. Offsets are restrictive in numerous ways as a basis for conducting long term climate change policies, but they offer several advantages. Most importantly, offset projects facilitate immediate efforts to curtail GHG emissions without having to wait for the completion of a multilateral agreement. All that is needed is that the country investing in offset projects has an abatement obligation and, of course, agreement that abatement in a third country will be interpreted as fulfilling these abatement obligations.[63] Offsets offer an incentive for developing countries to participate in efforts to combat global warming as their abatement costs are financed by the sponsoring country and transfer of technology may also be enhanced. For these reasons offsets are of more immediate practical relevance than, for instance, tradeable quotas which presume a global emission target with an agreed allocation of emission quotas.

The experience to date with offset investments has been limited to small pilot projects. Mexico, in co-operation with Norway, has implemented a programme to introduce more energy efficient light bulbs, thereby lowering energy use and carbon emissions. A second pilot scheme is a co-operative agreement between the Netherlands, Poland and India. The objective here is to improve energy efficiency in electricity production, promoting a switch to lower carbon content fossil fuels by sponsoring the replacement of coal-burning power plants with units operating on natural gas.[64]

Co-ordination and funding of some of these pilot projects is currently organised by the Global Environment Facility – the interim FCCC financing mechanism. There are also other voluntarily organised offset schemes in place. Firms in OECD countries are interested in bilateral schemes because they anticipate some future abatement obligation and hope to accumulate eligible abatement credits by sponsoring abatement projects in LDCs under bilateral JI schemes. To avoid discouraging these initiatives, the U.S. Energy Act now includes a provision for agreeing and reporting emissions saved by companies undertaking voluntary abatement initiatives. Pilot projects help the development of monitoring, reporting and trading procedures, and provide data and knowledge about how a multilateral trading system might work. Experience with emission trading in the USA has shown that national offset schemes, characterised by bilateral trades, often precede and lead to more sophisticated market mechanisms.[65]

However, offsets pose implementation and other problems. They may, for example, discourage countries from participation at a later date (Bohm 1994). This is because the cheapest abatement options will be implemented first, leaving host countries at a higher level on their abatement cost curve than they would have been without the offset investments. Future abatement in developing countries will therefore be more expensive. Another difficulty with offsets is the information requirements needed for implementation. Because credits are only given for emission reductions below the baseline emission level, implementation of offset projects presupposes the amount of emissions avoided by a given investment can be measured. Since baseline emissions are subject to large uncertainty and influenced by a broad range of factors, computations of emissions saved are likely to be subject to dispute, raising the transactions costs involved with offsets. Even if countries genuinely attempt to calculate future emissions, considerable scope for contention remains. For example, a country seeking credit for a carbon sequestration project might attempt to exaggerate the benefits by claiming that the baseline scenario included extensive deforestation even if this was not its real intention. High transactions costs, as a result of complicated calculations of incremental costs and negotiations required for each offset project, could constrain the large scale use of offsets.[66]

An agreed set of guidelines and an estimation methodology on which basis a clearing house exchange could vet proposed offset investments might help the development of an organised offset market. A clearing house should also increase investor confidence in the system, lower transactions costs[67] and facilitate the sale of offset investment credits to third parties. Also, offsets and derivatives of offsets could provide the foundation for the evolution towards comprehensive JI schemes embracing efficient organised markets for GHG emission quotas or an international carbon tax combined with side payments.

6.4. Joint implementation: taxes or quotas?

Comprehensive global agreements are likely to be based either on a common carbon tax or on tradeable emission quotas (TEQs); the former operating on (relative) prices, the latter involving an explicit constraint on emissions. If the damage and cost functions were known and remained unchanged, both instruments would confront emitters with identical incentives.[68] However, great uncertainty exists in the assessment of both abatement costs and emission damages. Hence, making policy here involves balancing economic risks against environmental risks. In some cases knowing the cost of policy intervention may be essential (favouring the tax instrument), and in other situations guaranteeing a fixed environmental standard may be important (favouring the use of quotas).

Apart from judgements about uncertainty, there are other practical considerations governing any choice between carbon taxes and tradeable quotas as instruments to curtail emissions. With a national carbon tax, revenue collection and use remain under the discretion of governments, and tax administrations already exist. A carbon tax also gives flexibility to adjust other elements of the tax structure, maintaining the same aggregate tax revenue, which might bear on the overall abatement cost (see discussion in Part 5). On the other hand, quotas require a decision on their distribution and thus create a transparent link between efficiency and equity issues relating to climate change policies, which might help reduce resistance to implementing comprehensive climate change policies. Preferences with regard to each system vary across countries. In the United States, quotas have been experimented with whereas in Europe the tendency is to discuss policy options in terms of taxes and charges. It must be acknowledged that direct regulation remains the dominant approach to environmental policy in both regions.[69] Furthermore, the current version of the FCCC can be interpreted as advocating a regulatory approach, even though the wording of the Convention does contain a commitment (as yet unspecified) to the need for cost-effectiveness.

6.5. Distribution implications of comprehensive joint implementation schemes

6.5.1. Quota allocation principles

Numerous emission quota allocation rules have been proposed, reflecting a variety of international distributional considerations. They include basing the initial allocation of emission quotas on current levels of emissions (also known as grandfathering), emissions per capita, gross national product, population and cumulative emissions. Identifying general criteria which could form a basis for quota allocation or revenue redistribution is only part of the process of policy design. To be relevant, general criteria need to be translated into operational rules. For example, allocations could be made which pertain to conditions at a given point in time (a "static" reference base) or on the basis of past and future conditions (a "dynamic" reference base). In both cases, even if the same principle is employed, the implied allocation of quotas or tax financed side payments could be different. This would be the case, if for instance quotas are based on carbon emissions. Using a "static" reference base, such as

1990, would allocate 47 per cent of total quotas to OECD countries, but a "dynamic" reference base could gradually, as non-OECD emissions grow at a more rapid pace, lower the OECD share to 27 per cent by 2050. A potential problem, therefore, is that even if a rule exists which ensures the initial agreement among a group of countries, sustaining the agreement may become difficult as the incidence of costs as well as economic conditions determining quota allocation change over time.

6.5.2. Gains and losses from emission quota allocation rules[70]

GREEN simulations of abatement costs and emissions under different JI allocation rules do suggest that a carefully designed JI approach to climate change policy could help promote the effective achievement of FCCC objectives at minimum cost – although ultimately equity goals will depend on political judgement.

Three specific quota allocation rules are analysed in detail here; results obtained when simulating a variety of other rules are summarised in Annex A, Note 2. The emission target for all quota allocation rules is the reduction in CO_2 emissions from their baseline level by an amount equivalent to that resulting from the stabilisation of emissions in Annex 1 countries at their 1990 levels. Participating in the abatement effort are the countries pertaining to the group of Major emitters, *i.e.* all Annex 1 countries as well as China and India. This target corresponds to Scenario 4 in Part 2.

6.5.2.1. Quota allocation

The three allocation rules simulated here for illustrative purposes are:

i) "grandfathering" – quotas are allocated in proportion to 1990 emission shares,[71]
ii) "egalitarian" – quotas are allocated in proportion to 1990 population shares; and
iii) a "two-tiered" approach, which combines the first two rules with changing weights over time.[72]

The share of quotas allocated under each rule is presented in Table 6.1. The grandfathering rule is unlikely to attain the support of developing countries since China and India, having produced a small fraction of total emissions in 1990, receive only 15 per cent of the quota allocation. On the other hand, since more than 60 per cent of the Major emitters population reside in China and India, the egalitarian rule allocates quotas to this region well in excess of their current requirements.

OECD countries tend to receive a relatively large share of quota distribution (47 per cent) if emission quotas are distributed according to historic emissions, but a relatively small proportion (26 per cent) if based on 1990 population. The first quota allocation rule perpetuates the status quo, while the second jumps to a situation in which equal emission rights are accorded to each individual (on a static 1990 population base). The distinguish-

Table 6.1. **Quota allocation shares**

Percentage of total

| | Scenario 6.1 | Scenario 6.2 | Scenario 6.3 | | | | | |
| | Grandfathering permit allocation based on 1990 emission shares | Egalitarian permit allocation based on 1990 population shares | Two-tiered allocation rule[1] | | | | | |
	1995-2050	1995-2050	1995	2000	2005	2010	2030	2050
United States	27.1	7.9	25.2	23.3	21.4	19.4	13.6	7.9
Japan	6.8	3.9	6.5	6.2	6.0	5.7	4.8	3.9
European Community	16.6	10.2	16.0	15.3	14.7	14.0	12.1	10.2
Other OECD countries[2]	6.0	4.0	5.8	5.6	5.4	5.2	4.6	4.0
China	12.2	35.1	14.5	16.8	19.1	21.4	28.2	35.1
Former Soviet Union	20.9	9.1	19.7	18.5	17.3	16.1	12.6	9.1
India	3.0	26.1	5.3	7.6	10.0	12.3	19.2	26.1
Eastern Europe	7.3	3.8	6.9	6.6	6.2	5.9	4.8	3.8
Total volume[3]	..	..	5 074	5 192	5 287	5 469	6 448	8 260

1. The weights in per cent attached to each rule are shown in the main text, endnote 71.
2. Excluding Mexico.
3. Million tons of carbon.
Source: OECD GREEN Model simulations.

ing element of the two-tiered rule (Scenario 6.3) is to gradually shift the distribution of emission rights from the status quo to equal 1990 per capita quotas. With this allocation method China and India receive gradually increasing quotas in excess of their baseline scenario requirements, although fewer than the egalitarian criterion implies.

6.5.2.2.   *Quota trade*

Which countries/regions buy and sell quotas depends, both on a country's marginal abatement costs and the quota allocation rule chosen. The volume of trade in emission quotas for each of the three allocation rules is summarised in Figure 6.2. The egalitarian principle would strongly favour China and India, with India being the largest seller of emission quotas throughout the period, closely followed by China. By contrast, the small number of quotas Annex 1 countries receive under an egalitarian rule combined with their relatively high marginal abatement costs ensures that each Annex 1 country would require additional quotas throughout the simulation period. With the two-tiered rule each OECD country/region is a net buyer of quotas, but the volume of trade would be significantly smaller than under the egalitarian rule.

The grandfathering system would strongly favour the former Soviet Union, which becomes the major net seller of quotas by the turn of the century. It is able to sell a large proportion of its allocation because, since 1990 (the reference year), this region has experienced a large decline in energy consumption, resulting from both several years of negative output growth and gradual energy price liberalisation, inducing a rapid rise in energy efficiency. The grandfathering rule, however, is unlikely to attain support of developing countries since throughout the period these countries would have to purchase additional quotas. In particular, quota demand in China increases rapidly as the implicit carbon constraints tighten.

With the two tiered rule each OECD country/region is a net buyer of quotas; eastern Europe and the former Soviet Union are net sellers during the first 25 years, but then increasing energy demand in these regions necessitates the purchase of quotas. Most developing countries are net sellers of quotas over the simulation period.

6.5.2.3.   *Real income effects*

If a JI scheme among the Major emitters based on quotas results in lower income losses among Annex 1 countries than a unilateral scheme, and transfers received (quota sales) in India and China are higher than the minimum level of compensation (Section 6.2), both parties will be better off as a result of the JI scheme. In other words, co-operation between Annex 1 countries and China and India in jointly mitigating CO_2 emissions could benefit both groups of countries, as well as the global economy as a whole.[73] The net real income changes of each party under each of the quota allocation rules is shown in Figure 6.3.

Grandfathered TEQs save Annex 1 countries from considerable abatement costs, but clearly are of no interest to China and India (Figure 6.3, Panel 1). Similarly, the egalitarian rule (Panel 2) is unlikely to get the support of Annex 1 countries since, for the same level of global emission abatement, net income losses are greater than if the Annex 1 countries curtail emissions unilaterally for most of the period to 2050. India and China, on the other hand, are major beneficiaries from such a JI scheme. In the case where quotas are issued on the basis of a rule combining the grandfathering and egalitarian principle – a two tiered rule – Annex 1 countries, India and China experience favourable income changes compared with the scenario where Annex 1 countries curtail CO_2 emissions unilaterally (Panel 3, Figure 6.3). The two-tiered approach appears to ensure sufficient compensation and a more even distribution of net abatement costs among participating countries. Of course, the exact weights would be subject to negotiation, but the type of rule seems to offer some promise for a possible compromise.

6.6.   Global carbon tax fund

There is no unambiguously preferred method to implement climate change policies jointly. An international carbon tax fund is also compatible with the principle of joint implementation. This is similar to a uniform carbon tax, but revenues are not necessarily redistributed in proportion to amounts raised (as would be the case if the common carbon tax is implemented by national authorities in their own territories).

The effects of specific international carbon tax agreements can be simulated using GREEN with flexible assumptions about the use of revenues, since revenue reallocation is a specific element of policy design and not predetermined as in the case of quota allocation rules. In some key respects, however, the differences between an international carbon tax and tradeable quotas are minimal: if tradeable quotas are auctioned rather than allocated

Figure 6.2. **Volume of emission quota trading**[1]

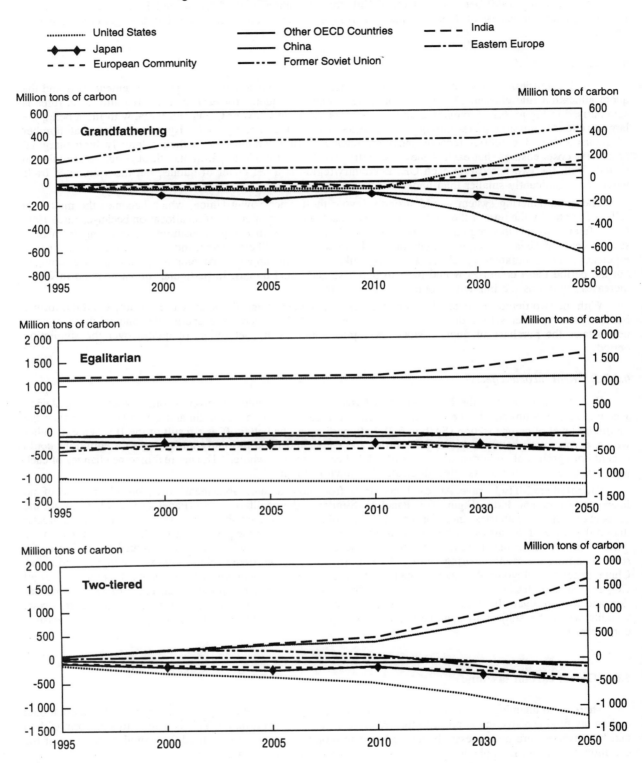

1. Major emitters stabilise Annex 1 CO_2 emissions at 1990 levels. A positive figure corresponds to a quota sale and a negative one to quota purchases.
Source: OECD GREEN model simulations.

Figure 6.3. **Mutual gains and losses from JI under alternative quota allocations**

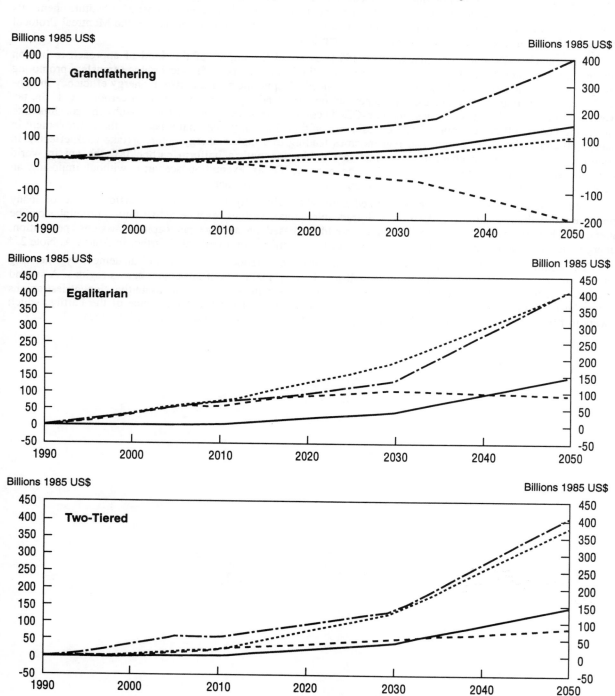

Source: OECD GREEN model simulations.

at no charge, the revenue raised in a competitive market would tend to be equivalent to the international carbon taxes collected to meet a given emission constraint. It is in principle also possible to design tax revenue reallocation so that the resulting redistributive implications are identical with those generated by a specific quota allocation rule.

A carbon tax fund offers greater flexibility to allocate the efficiency gains from JI, possibly facilitating agreement on burden sharing. The concept of a burden sharing arrangement incorporating the international recycling of tax revenues is not unprecedented. The Montreal Protocol includes a tax on ozone depleting substances, where part of the revenues is used to finance the incremental replacement cost of substitute chemicals which do not damage the ozone layer. The introduction of a compensation mechanism in the Montreal Protocol was a key factor in securing the participation of some large emitters.

A recent GREEN study (Burniaux, *et al.* 1993) explored the impact of this kind of approach to burden sharing. Several simulations linking revenues from an OECD carbon tax to fund technology transfers promoting energy efficiency in non-OECD countries were introduced. Despite the resulting rise in energy efficiency in non-OECD countries, policy effectiveness still depended on the broad regional coverage of a carbon tax. If the tax was imposed only in OECD countries, and non-OECD countries received transfers (financed by the tax) linked to enhancing energy efficiency, non-OECD emissions would decline only marginally because the improvement in energy efficiency increases output and real incomes leading to a higher energy demand (take-back effects). In contrast, if the transfer mechanism is applied in combination with a uniform carbon tax, the cut in world CO_2 emissions is three times larger than in the non-OECD tax exemption scenario, without imposing an excessive net burden on non-OECD regions participating in the agreement.

Redistributing carbon tax revenues linked somewhat arbitrarily to technology transfer is one of many possible redistribution options. Indeed, as with tradeable quotas, various revenue redistribution principles can be identified. For example, revenue redistribution could be based on average per capita emissions, population, energy intensity, carbon intensity and so on. Some of these options are investigated further in Annex A, Note 2.[74]

The common feature with all JI schemes is the objective to reduce global costs of abatement by extending the country coverage of the agreement and equalising the marginal costs of abatement across regions. A second characteristic is a mechanism to redistribute the total efficiency gains so as to compensate those countries/regions which bear the brunt of abatement costs. It is, however, the role of the first Conference of the Parties, which meets in March 1995, to determine the criteria governing the practical introduction of JI policies.

CONVERSION TABLES

A. Energy unit conversion table

	Joule	Calorie	Bfu	KWh	TCE	TOE	Barrel	B.cm
Joule	1.0	4 187	1 055.1	3.600E-06	2.931E+10	4.187E+10	5.736E+09	3.726E+16
Calorie	0.239	1.0	252.01	8.598E-05	7.000E+09	1.000E+10	1.370E+09	8.899E+15
Bfu	9.478E-04	3.968E-03	1.0	3412.0	2.778E+07	3.968E+07	5.437E+06	3.531E+13
KWh	2.778E-07	1.163E-06	2.931E-04	1.0	8 141.4	11 630.6	1.593E+03	1.035E+10
TCE[1]	3.412E-11	1.429E-10	3.600E-08	1.228E-04	1.0	1.430	0.196	1.271E-06
TOE[2]	2.388E-11	1.000E-10	2.520E-08	8.598E-05	0.699	1.0	0.137	8.899E-06
Barrel[3]	1.743E-10	7.299E-10	1.839E-07	6.276E-04	5.102	7.299	1.0	6.496E-06
B.cm[4]	2.684E-17	1.124E-16	2.832E-14	9.662E-11	7.868E-07	1.124E-06	1.539E-07	1.0

1. One ton of coal equivalent assumed to equal 7 million kilo calories.
2. One ton of oil equivalent assumed to equal 10 million kilo calories.
3. 7.3 barrels assumed to equal 1 ton of oil equivalent.
4. Billion cubic metres of natural gas.

B. Fossil fuel tax equivalents of carbon tax rates

Carbon tax (US$ per ton of C)			10	25	50	100	150	200
Corresponding CO$_2$ tax (US$ per ton of CO$_2$)			2.7	6.8	13.6	27.3	40.9	54.5
	Energy content (in GJ)	Carbon content (in ton/TJ)	Equivalent energy tax					
Ton of coal (US$/tce)	29.31	24.686	7.2	18.1	36.2	72.4	109	145
Barrel of oil (US$/barrel)	5.736	20.730	1.2	3.0	5.9	11.9	17.8	23.8
Ton of oil (US$/toe)	41.87	20.730	8.7	21.7	43.4	86.8	130	174
GBtu of gas (US$/GBtu)	1 055.1	13.473	142	355	711	1 422	2 132	2 843

C. Electricity tax equivalents of carbon tax rates (by energy source)

Carbon tax (US$ per ton of C)			10	25	50	100	150	200
	Heat rate (Bfu/kWh)	Carbon content (in ton/TJ)	Equivalent electricity tax					
Coal power plant (c/kWh)	9 000-10 000	24.686	0.23-0.26	0.58-0.65	1.15-1.30	2.30-2.60	3.45-3.90	4.60-5.20
Oil power plant (c/kWh)	9 800-13 600	20.730	0.21-0.30	0.53-0.75	1.05-1.50	2.10-3.00	3.15-4.50	4.20-6.00
Gas power plant (c/kWh)	9 000-10 400	13.473	0.12-0.15	0.30-0.38	0.60-0.75	1.20-1.50	1.80-2.25	2.40-3.00

Notes

1. This report was prepared under the supervision of Peter Sturm (Head of the Resource Allocation Division). Substantial contributions were provided by Jonathan Coppel, Hiro Lee, Joaquim Oliveira Martins and Dirk Pilat. Michael Feiner and Constantino Lluch are thanked for their suggestions on earlier drafts. Thanks also go to Jan Corfee-Morlot, Michael Daly, Andrew Dean, Jørgen Elmeskov, Tom Jones, Françoise Praderie, David Rubin and Ronald Steenblick for their helpful comments.

2. Annex A, Note 1 provides a fuller interpretation of the FCCC and outlines its main features.

3. A more detailed discussion of the uncertainties affecting the causal chain linking anthropogenic GHG emissions and their origins to climate change and the potential damage it may cause is presented in Annex D.

4. IPCC GHG emission projections reflect the combined efforts of numerous experts. Hence the reported range of estimates embodies the majority of professional findings. The assumptions underlying the IPCC scenarios are summarised in Panel B of Table 2.1. However, if all studies of GHG projections are surveyed (including outliers), the range of underlying assumptions as well as the band of possible emission paths would be even wider.

5. Even under harmonised assumptions with respect to economic growth and energy efficiency, the range of estimates may be large. For example, a "standardised" comparison exercise between GREEN and the 12RT model shows that baseline emissions can vary from 13.4 to 17 billion tons of carbon by 2050 (Manne and Oliveira Martins, 1994).

6. The basic assumptions underlying the scenarios referred to in this section are presented and discussed in Annex A, Notes 2 and 3.

7. Stabilising Annex 1 country CO_2 emissions at 1990 levels from the year 2000 onward, but assuming no major changes in trends in other countries, is estimated to delay a doubling of atmospheric CO_2 concentrations by only about 15 years, the rise continuing thereafter. This projection is based on the assumption of no major breakthrough in the supply of carbon-free or carbon-neutral energies, which would make the use of fossil fuels uncompetitive. Concentration levels are calculated from fossil fuel emissions using the methodology reported in Cohen and Collette (1991).

8. In fact the Intergovernmental Negotiating Committee for the FCCC has formally recognised that existing agreed commitments are inadequate for achieving the Convention's overall objective of maintaining concentrations below "dangerous" levels (INC 9).

9. Equalisation of marginal abatement costs is a necessary condition to achieve maximum welfare and thus efficiency, subject to an exogenous constraint on emissions, and thus for Pareto efficiency. Recently a number of studies have discussed the validity of this principle in the context of climate change policies (Chichilnisky, 1994); Chichilnisky and Heal, 1994; Chichilnisky, Heal and Starrett, 1993; Hourcade and Gilotte, 1994; and Bohm, 1993). The basic argument is that since carbon emission abatement is a global public good, equity and efficiency issues are not separable any more, and unless unlimited income transfers are feasible, Pareto efficiency requires a system with differentiated abatement prices, *i.e.* marginal abatement costs should not necessarily be equalised across countries. However, at this stage, joint optimisation of the levels of income and emissions is an exceedingly ambitious objective, given the uncertainties about the net benefits of stabilising climate and about income valuations.

10. Many of the relevant issues related to tradeable emission quotas are also discussed in OECD (1992*a*).

11. These simulations do not explore the potential for no-regrets policies; these are discussed below in Parts 3 and 4.

12. Real income is defined as the sum of household consumption, investment and government expenditure on goods and services.

13. Output and income gains and losses across regions are sensitive to whether output is valued at purchasing power parity (PPP) or official exchange rates. If PPP measures were used for the conversion of GDP, abatement cost disparities between OECD and non-OECD countries, and thus potential gains from policy co-ordination, would narrow.

14. For a discussion of the sensitivity of the carbon tax with respect to alternative specifications, see Annex A, Section 3.2.

15. A positive leakage rate implies the cut in emissions in a given region raises emissions in non-participating regions. The leakage rate is negative when an emission cut lowers emissions in non-participating countries.

16. See CEC (1992).

17. GREEN (as well as most other general equilibrium models) does not allow the analysis of problems of transitional unemployment caused by structural change.

18. Examples of such measures are orbiting mirrors to reflect incoming solar radiation, or "dusting" the atmosphere with particles, to achieve a similar effect. However, these measures are as yet far from practical application and therefore of limited immediate policy relevance.

19. Uncertainty about the extent and local manifestation of climate change makes *ex ante* adaptation virtually impossible.

20. Calculated as the ratio of world GDP (at 1985 prices and exchange rates) over world carbon emissions in 1990. Given the trend rise in energy efficiency, this implicit cost will rise steadily over time.

21. The case for population control to restrain GHG emissions is sometimes based on the argument that higher per capita income strengthens the preference for a cleaner environment. While this is indeed confirmed with respect to toxic emissions, there is no empirical evidence for such an inverse relationship between per capita income and the emission of non-toxic gases like CO_2.

22. The introduction of a carbon tax, accounting for the negative externalities of CO_2 emissions, will *ceteris paribus* lead to an increase in the price of fossil fuels and a shift in demand away from components using fossil fuels as an input. Such a price-induced change in consumption patterns is preferable to a **mandated** reduction in the use of fossil fuel intensive output.

23. Known conventional reserves of uranium were estimated at 3 million tons at 1 January 1993. 1992 production of uranium was only 36 246 tons. Besides these known reserves, additional resources of 3.9 million tons of uranium are probably available, whereas almost 10 million tons of uranium are speculative. At 1992 production volumes, this total resource base would suffice to supply some 470 years of current demand (NEA, 1994).

24. Geothermal energy is not renewable, but is included here since it has many properties comparable to the "real" renewable energy sources.

25. It is either only available in certain areas (hydro-power), or available for only limited periods (solar/wind energy). In addition, renewable energy is based on smaller power stations. Both problems make if difficult to integrate renewable energy in the existing system of energy supply.

26. A curtailment of CO_2 emissions can also reduce emissions of carbon monoxide considerably. Its direct impact on emissions of methane and N_2O, however, is relatively small.

27. Based on simulations with an updated version of GREEN, containing an (experimental) NO_x-SO_x module.

28. Emission factors are defined as the ratio of emissions to energy consumption. Based on past trends, NO_x/SO_x emission factors are assumed to decrease gradually over time in each region. See Complainville and Oliveira Martins (1994) for representative NO_x and SO_x emission factors and their data sources.

29. See, for instance, OTA (1991) for a discussion of this option.

30. However, an **optimal** carbon tax level would be difficult to determine, as it would require perfect knowledge of all the links in the causal chain from economic activity to climate change-induced damage discussed in Annex D, as well as of abatement costs.

31. The uncertainties concerning climate change policy are discussed in detail in Annex D.

32. The determination of the social discount rate is discussed in more detail in Annex A, Note 4.

33. See Annex A, Note 6 for more detail and some examples of no-regret measures.

34. Take-back effects refer to an increase in energy demand induced by real income gains and relative price changes due to gains in energy efficiency.

35. The U.S. National Action Plan contains a myriad of measures aiming at meeting FCCC emission targets for the United States, largely by encouraging economic agents to exploit potential no-regret measures, and by modifying existing regulations to make it possible and attractive for them to do so voluntarily.

36. DSM programmes refer to efforts to reduce energy demand (typically by raising energy efficiency in consumption). Such programmes are efficient if the marginal cost of energy supply exceeds the marginal cost of reducing energy demand.

37. The FCCC, in Article 4, recognises two aspects of the role of research and development (R&D). Firstly, in Section 1*g*, it mentions R&D aimed at improved understanding of the process of climate change, with the goal of reducing or eliminating the uncertainty concerning the causes, magnitudes and timing of climate change, the likely damages it entails, and the economic and social consequences of various response strategies. This type of R&D can help to provide guidance to mitigation, sequestration and adaptation policies. Secondly, under Section 1*c* it refers to the development of technologies that improve the ability to control, reduce or prevent anthropogenic emissions of GHGs.

38. Part 3 provides a brief overview of mitigation and sequestration measures.

39. The "rational insurance premium" is the annual payment (as a per cent of GDP) which equates the discounted present value of the annual premium payments with the present value certainty equivalent of the damages. The scenarios and the calculation of "insurance premia" are described in more detail in Annex A, Note 5.

40. In the first scenario, the damages rise by 0.05 per cent of GDP per year for the first 60 years from 1990 onwards and remain constant at 6 per cent of baseline GDP after 2050. In the second and third scenario there is a 10 per cent probability of catastrophic damages. In the second scenario, damages rise by 0.1 per cent of GDP annually for the first 30 years, but in 2020 a global catastrophe occurs and damages are 10 per cent of baseline GDP annually after 2020. In the third scenario, damages rise by 0.05 per cent of GDP annually for the first 60 years and in 2050 a global catastrophe

occurs and damages jump to 20 per cent of baseline GDP thereafter. The insurance premia are calculated for the 1990-2100 period, but it makes little difference to the results if infinite time horizons are used.

41. At an 8 per cent discount rate, even the probability of substantial damages (20 per cent of GDP from 2050 onwards), leads to a very low value of the present value certainty equivalent of the damage (0.03 per cent of GDP annually). For the first scenario, at a medium level of risk aversion, a 5 per cent discount rate and varying probabilities of damages occurring, society is willing to pay between 0.06 and 0.6 per cent of GDP annually to eliminate the risk of climate change. For the "catastrophic" scenarios insurance premia are substantially higher, unless the discount rate chosen is very large.

42. In fact there are definite indications that utility companies in the United States already discount the likelihood of future carbon constraints in their current choice of technologies and investment decisions (Manne and Richels, 1994).

43. Some experience with international institution building in this area is emerging. Under the FCCC countries are obliged to report both GHG emissions and the policies they have implemented to mitigate emissions.

44. Details of a global TEQ scheme are discussed in Chichilnisky and Heal (1995); a more cautious view is taken in OECD (1992b) and OECD (1993b), where the practical problems likely to be associated with global TEQ schemes are discussed.

45. Experience relevant to a future international market for tradeable emission quotas may be emerging as some utility companies in OECD countries have implemented carbon-offset projects in Mexico, Poland and Costa Rica, in the hope of being credited for emission reductions achieved against future abatement obligations.

46. For more details on these two models, see Manne and Richels (1992); and Barns, Edmonds and Reilly (1993).

47. The ppmv (parts per million by volume) indicator measures the concentration of CO_2 in the atmosphere. Current (1990) concentrations are 353 ppmv.

48. Details of Cline's suggested strategy are presented in OECD (1994), pp. 87-105.

49. In practice, a meaningful equivalence scale between different GHGs is difficult to establish. Atmospheric lifetimes of GHGs are uncertain, partly due to interactions between the various GHGs in the atmosphere. Due to this uncertainty, the GWP index, which used to serve as the basis for comparisons between GHGs (IPCC, 1990), has come under increasing criticism in recent years. Use of the GWP index in policy analysis also has limitations as it focuses on physical rather than economic effects (Schmalensee, 1993; Reilly and Richards, 1993). Annex D discusses these issues in more detail.

50. Curtailment of CO_2 emissions may have side-benefits in the form of reduced emissions of other GHGs, such as NO_x, SO_x and CO. In principle, these side benefits should be taken into account when setting equivalent GHG tax rates. However, in contrast to CO_2, emissions of these gases cannot in general be related to a typical fossil fuel, but mainly depend on combustion conditions.

51. Whether they are equalised at the "correct" level will, of course, depend on whether the tax rate chosen correctly reflects the negative externalities of carbon emissions, or whether the amount of quotas issued equalises marginal cost and benefits of emission reduction.

52. As long as carbon scrubbing is not economic, taxing the fuel input according to carbon content gives an incentive to curtail CO_2 emissions by reducing the use of fossil fuels, thereby reducing the risk of global warming. Note, however, that energy use *per se* does not induce negative externalities, although indirect side effects of energy consumption, depending on the source and use of energy, include traffic congestion, noxious emissions, the risk of misusing nuclear technology, acid rain and global warming.

53. Introduction of a tax to compensate for a negative externality will lead to an unambiguous increase in welfare only if no other distortions exist in the economy (a "first best" situation). In practice, it is usually assumed that such a welfare improvement occurs also under second best conditions, unless it can be shown that this is not the case.

54. Different meanings are sometimes attached to the notion of a "double dividend". Bovenberg and Mooij (1994) define three alternative concepts of "double dividends". The first is the gain from implementing a carbon tax compared with less efficient instruments to reduce emissions, the second is the gain from using carbon tax revenues to reduce other distortionary taxes, rather than returning these revenues in a lump sum manner, and the third is the gain from improving the tax system via tax reform, without counting any environmental benefits. The third case corresponds closely to the notion of a no-regrets policy, and, if these net benefits exist, should be adopted independent of any climate change policy considerations. This part of the paper focuses on the second type of double dividend where both environment and fiscal implications of a carbon tax are considered jointly.

55. In most OECD countries a $50 per ton of carbon tax is small relative to existing energy taxes. It is approximately equivalent to $6 per barrel of oil and would add about 3.8 cents to the gasoline price per litre.

56. Apart from carbon tax induced effects, the decline in the carbon tax/GDP ratio depicted in Figure 5.1 is partly due to the trend rise in energy efficiency and the penetration of carbon-free backstops.

57. A carbon tax could impact on company income tax receipts due to the deductibility of tax payments. Table 2 makes no adjustment for such an impact.

58. *Ceteris paribus* the size of the deadweight loss is greater, the higher the price elasticity of demand and supply of the good being taxed. The gain to the economy of reforming the tax system by substituting a carbon tax for some other tax will therefore depend on the size of the tax offset and on which taxes are reduced.

59. Whether the resulting increase in output leads to an increase in welfare as well depends on the relative size of the (social) rate of time preference and the rate of return on investment.

60. Real incomes in third countries (countries not forming part of the Major emitters group) will also be affected by a shift from uncoordinated policies to JI because of different behaviour of trade volumes and prices, especially for fossil fuels, under the two scenarios.

61. This abstracts from the gain from terms of trade improvements in India and China if Annex 1 countries implement the stabilisation agreement unilaterally, as well as from collateral benefits of local emission abatement (less air pollution) in non-Annex 1 countries if they participate.

62. In practice it is likely that the process of reaching agreement within the very heterogeneous Annex 1 group will also involve negotiations and require some form of side-payments, especially since some of the northern countries in this group (*e.g.* Canada and Russia) may actually reap net economic benefits from (moderate and gradual) global warming. Furthermore, and as shown in Part 2, Energy-exporting countries will gain from a JI scheme involving the Major emitters compared with unilateral implementation by Annex 1 countries. Energy-exporting countries could therefore be expected to be willing to contribute to the compensation of those non-Annex 1 countries where abatement costs increase under JI.

63. Even though neither definitive abatement obligations have been agreed on, nor a decision that firms in industrialised countries will indeed be credited for successful abatement abroad has been taken so far, a number of such projects are currently under way in anticipation of future agreements. Defining precise rules for such partial JI schemes and the applicability of abatement credits will be one of the initial tasks of the first Conference of the parties convening in 1995.

64. For a detailed description of these projects see Anderson (1993).

65. One example, established by the U.S. Clean Air Act, is the sulphur dioxide entitlement market. Rights to emit sulphur have been trading on the Chicago Board of Trade for over a year, and recently futures and swaps on these quotas have been introduced. See also OECD (1992a).

66. In addition to the technical problems referred to, there are political problems involving questions of national sovereignty (especially in the case of JI activities involving forestry) and issues concerning the effects of JI investments on both the rate and the type of technology transfers to LDCs. These issues are reviewed in more detail in Jones (1994).

67. The U.S. Clean Air Act expects to lower compliance costs using a form of offset system which is administered through a centralised clearing house. See Tietenberg, T.H. (1990) for details on how the system operates.

68. Other conditions include the absence of non-competitive market behaviour; for further details see Weitzman (1974).

69. Practical experience with emission quotas and carbon taxes has been limited, except for tradeable quotas in the United States and country specific carbon taxes in some Scandinavian countries. For an overview of experience to date see Tietenberg, T. (1992); see also Haugland (1994), where carbon taxes in selected OECD countries are compared.

70. For another detailed study of the economic implications of alternative emission quota allocations see Edmonds *et al.* (1993).

71. This rule is considered for analytical purposes and not because it is considered politically realistic.

72. The weights (expressed in percentages) attached to each rule are:

	1995	2000	2005	2010	2030	2050
1990 CO_2 emission share	90	80	70	60	30	0
1990 Population share	10	20	30	40	70	100

73. In addition both groups will, in principal, be interested in (benefit from) the reduced climate change risk, which is the overall objective of the policy.

74. See also Coppel (1994) for a discussion of alternative redistribution principles.

Bibliography

Alfsen, K.H., Birkelund, H. and Aaserud, M. (1994), "Secondary Benefits of the EU Carbon/Energy Tax", paper presented at the International Symposium on Economic Modelling, The World Bank, Washington DC, 22-24 June.

Anderson, R.J. (1993) "Joint implementation of climate change measures: an examination of some issues", *World Bank Working Paper*.

Atkinson, J. and Manning, N. (1994), "A survey of international energy elasticities" in Barker, T., Ekins, P. and Johnstone, N. (eds) *Global Warming and Energy Elasticities*.

Audus, H. (1994), "CO_2 removal and storage", in IEA/OECD, *Energy Technologies to Reduce CO_2 Emissions in Europe: Prospects, Competition, Synergy*, Paris, forthcoming.

Barns, D.W., Edmonds, J.A. and Reilly, J.M. (1992), "The Edmonds-Reilly-Barns Model", in *The Costs of Cutting Carbon Emissions: Results from Global Models*, OECD, Paris.

Bohm, P. (1993), "Should marginal carbon abatement costs be equalised across countries?", *Department of Economics, University of Stockholm Working Papers*, No. 1993:112 WE.

Bohm, P. (1994), "Making carbon-emission quota agreements more efficient: joint implementation versus quota tradeability" *Stockholm University Working Papers*, No. 10691.

Bovenberg, A.L. (1994), "Environmental taxation and employment" Working Paper, Tilburg University, The Netherlands.

Bovenberg, A.L. and de Mooij, R.A. (1994), "Environmental levies and distortionary taxation", *American Economic Review*, Vol. 84, No. 4, pp. 1085-1089.

Brechet, T. (1992), *Energy Tax in Europe: A VAT Variant with Hermes-Link*, Paris, Erasme.

Burniaux, J.M., Nicoletti, G. et Oliveira Martins, J. (1992), "GREEN: a global model for quantifying the costs of policies to curb CO_2 emissions", *OECD Economic Studies*, No. 19, Winter.

Burniaux, J.M. *et al.* (1993), "Carbon abatement, transfers and energy efficiency: evidence from GREEN", paper presented at the joint CEPR/OECD Development Centre Conference on "Sustainable Economic Development: Domestic and International Policy".

Chichilnisky, G, Heal, G. and Starrett, D. (1993), "International emission permits: equity and efficiency", mimeo.

Chichilnisky, G. (1994), Commentary on "Implementing a global abatement policy: the role of transfers", *The Economics of Climate Change*, OECD, Paris.

Chichilnisky, G. and Heal, G.M. (1994), "Who should abate carbon emissions? An international viewpoint", *Economic Letters*, Spring.

Chichilnisky, G. and Heal, G.M. (1995), "Markets for tradeable CO_2 emission quotas: principles and practice", *OECD Economics Department Working Papers*, No. 153.

Cohen, B.C. and Collette, J.M. (1991), "Fossil-fuel use and sustainable development", *International Journal of Global Energy Issues*, Vol. 3, No. 3, pp. 132-141.

Commission of the European Communities (CEC) (1992), "The climate challenge: economic aspects of the Community's strategy for limiting CO_2 emissions", *European Economy*, No. 51.

Commission of the European Communities (1994), "Taxation, employment and environment: fiscal reform for reducing unemployment", *European Economy*, No. 56.

Complainville, C. and Oliveira Martins, J. (1994), "NO_x/SO_xemissions and carbon abatement" *Economics Department Working Papers*, No. 151.

Coppel, J. (1994), "Implementing a global abatement policy: the role of transfers", in OECD (1994).

Dower, R. and Zimmerman, M. (1992), *The Right Climate for Carbon Taxes: Creating Economic Incentives to Protect the Atmosphere*. World Resources Institute, Washington DC, United States.

Edmonds, Jae, David W. Barns, Marshall Wise and My Ton (1993) *Carbon Coalitions (The Cost and Effectiveness of Energy Agreements to Alter Trajectories of Atmospheric Carbon Dioxide Emissions)*, Pacific Northwest Laboratories, Washington D.C.

Ekins P. (1994), "Rethinking the costs related to global warming", Birckbeck College, mimeo.

Godard, O. (1993), "Taxes", in: OECD, *International Economic Instruments and Climate Change*, Paris.

Goulder, L.H (1991), "Effects of carbon taxes in an economy with prior tax distortions: an intertemporal general equilibrium analysis for the US", Working Paper, Stanford University.

Grubb, M, Edmonds, J., ten Brink, P. and Morrison, M. (1993), "The costs of limiting fossil-fuel CO_2 emissions: a survey and analysis", *Annual Review of Energy and Environment*, Vol. 18, pp. 397-478.

Haugland (1994), "A comparison of carbon taxes in selected OECD countries", *OECD Environment Monograph No. 78*, Paris.

Hoeller, P and Coppel, J. (1992), "Energy taxation and price distortions in fossil fuel markets: some implications for climate change policy", *OECD Economics Department Working Papers*, No. 110.

Hourcade, J.C. and Gilotte, L. (1994), "Some paradoxical issues about an international carbon tax", presented at the Annual Conference of the European Association of Environment and Resource Economics, Dublin.

IEA/OECD (1989), *Electricity End-Use Efficiency*, Paris.

IEA/OECD (1991), *Greenhouse Gas Emissions – The Energy Dimension*, OECD Energy and Environment Series, Paris.

IEA/OECD (1991a), *Energy Efficiency and the Environment*, OECD Energy and Environment Series, Paris.

IEA/OECD (1991b), *Energy Policies of IEA Countries*, 1990 Review, Paris.

IEA/OECD (1993), *Electric Power Technologies: Environmental Challenges and Opportunities*, Paris.

IPCC (1990), *Climate Change – The IPCC Scientific Assessment*, Cambridge University Press, Cambridge.

IPCC (1992), *Climate Change 1992, The Supplementary Report to the IPCC Scientific Assessment*, Cambridge University Press.

Jaffe, A.B. and Stavins, R.N. (1993), "The energy paradox and the diffusion of conservation technology", *Center for Business and Government Working Paper, Energy 93-03*, John F. Kennedy School of Government, October.

Jones, T. (1994), "Joint implementation as a policy instrument for responding to climate change", paper presented to the IPCC Workshop in Tsukuba, Japan, January.

Jorgenson, D. and Wilcoxen, P. (1994), "The economic effects of a carbon tax", paper presented at IPCC Working Group Three Workshop in Tsukuba, Japan.

Joskow, P.L. and Marron, D.B. 1992), "What does a negawatt really cost? Evidence from utility conservation programs", *The Energy Journal*, Vol. 13, No. 4, pp. 41-74.

Kolstad, C.D. (1993), "Looking vs. leaping: the timing of CO_2 control in the face of uncertainty and learning", in Kaja, Y., Nakićenović, N. Nordhaus, W.D. and Toth, F.L. (eds.), *Costs, Impacts, and Benefits of CO_2 Mitigation*, IIASA, Laxenburg.

Krause, F., Koomey, J. and Olivier, D. (1994), *Energy Policy in the Greenhouse – Vol. 2, Least-Cost Insurance against Greenhouse Risks: The Cost of Cutting Carbon Emissions*, IPSEP, El Cerrito.

Liu, Leslie, A. (1994), "The Net Environmental Effects of Carbon Dioxide Reduction Policies", Master's thesis, Technology and Policy Program, Department of Electrical Engineering and Computer Science, Massachusetts Institute of Technology.

Majocchi, A. (1994), "The employment effects of Eco-taxes: a review of empirical models and results", paper prepared for OECD Environment Policy Committee and Committee on Fiscal Affairs Joint Sessions on Taxation and Environment.

Manne, A.S. and Richels, R.G. (1992), *Buying Greenhouse Insurance: The Economic Costs of CO_2 Emission Limits*, The MIT Press.

Manne, A.S. and Richels, R.G. (1994), "CO_2 hedging strategies – the impact of uncertainty upon emissions", in *The Economics of Climate Change*, OECD, Paris.

Manne, A.S. and Oliveira Martins, J. (1994), "Comparison of model structure and policy scenarios: GREEN and 12RT", *OECD Department of Economics Working Papers*, No. 146.

Nuclear Energy Agency (1994), *Uranium – 1993 Resources, Production and Demand*, Paris.

OECD (1991), *Responding to Climate Change: Selected Economic Issues*, Paris.

OECD (1992), "The economic costs of reducing CO_2 emissions", *OECD Economic Studies*, No. 19, Special Issue, Paris.

OECD (1992a), *Climate Change: Designing a Tradeable Permit System*, Paris.

OECD (1992b), *Climate Change: Designing a Practical Tax System*, Paris.

OECD (1992c), *Convention on Climate Change: Economic Aspects of Negotiations*.

OECD (1992d), *Revenue Statistics of OECD Member Countries: 1965-1991*, Paris.

OECD (1993), "The costs of cutting carbon emissions: results from global models", Paris.

OECD (1993a), *Taxation and the Environment Complementary Policies*, Paris.

OECD (1993b), *Economic Instruments and Climate Change*, Paris.

OECD (1994), *The Economics of Climate Change*, Proceedings of an OECD/IEA Conference, Paris.

OECD (1994a), *Global Change of Planet Earth, Megascience: The OECD Forum*, Paris.

Office of Technology Assessment (OTA), Congress of the United States (1991), *Changing by Degrees – Steps to Reduce Greenhouse Gases*, Washington DC.

Pearce, D. (1991), "Evaluating the socio-economic impacts of climate change: an introduction", in OECD, *Climate Change – Evaluating the Socio-Economic Impacts*, Paris.

Poterba, J.M. (1993), "Global warming policy: a public finance perspective", *Journal of Economic Perspectives*, Vol. 7, No. 4, Fall, pp. 47-64.

Reilly, J.M. and Richards, K.R. (1993), "Climate change damage and the trace gas index issue", *Environmental and Resource Economics*, Vol. 3, February, pp. 41-61.

Richels, R. and Edmonds, J. (1993), "The economics of stabilizing atmospheric concentrations", EPRI, Palo Alto, mimeo.

San Martin, R.L. (1989), "Environmental emissions from energy technology systems: the total fuel cycle", in IEA/OECD, *Energy Technologies for Reducing Emissions of Greenhouse Gases*, Paris

Sanstad, A.H., Koomey, J.G. and Levine, M.D. (1993), "On the economic analysis of problems in energy efficiency: market barriers, market failures, and policy implications", Lawrence Berkely Laboratory, January.

Schelling, T.C. (1992), "Some economics of global warming", *American Economic Review*, Vol. 82, No. 1, pp. 1-14.

Schmalensee, R. (1993), "Comparing greenhouse gases for policy purposes", *The Energy Journal*, Vol. 14, No. 1, pp. 245-255.

Shackleton, *et al.* (1992), "The efficiency value of carbon tax revenues", US. Environmental Protection Service, Washington DC.

Shah, A. and Larsen, B. (1992), "Carbon taxes, the greenhouse effect, and developing countries", *World Bank Working Papers*, WPS 957, Washington DC.

Spencer, D.F. (1994), "Open ocean macroalgal farms for CO_2 mitigation and energy production", in IEA/OECD, *Technology Responses to Global Environmental Challenges*, Conference Proceedings, Paris.

Standaert, S. (1992), "The macro-sectoral effects of an EC-wide energy tax: simulation experiments for 1993-2005", *European Economy*, Special Edition No. 1.

Tietenberg, T. (1990), "Economic Instruments for Environmental Regulation", *Oxford Review of Economic Policy*, Vol. 6, No. 1, pp. 17-33.

Tietenberg, T. (1992), "Relevant experience with tradeable entitlements" in UNCTAD, *Combating Global Warming: Study on a Global System of Tradeable Carbon Emission Entitlements*, New York.

UNCTAD (1992), *Combating Global Warming: Study on a Global System of Tradeable Carbon Emission Entitlements*, New York.

Waide P, and Boyle, S. (1993), "Towards a fossil free energy future", Technical Annex for Greenpeace International, Greenpeace, Amsterdam.

Weitzman, M.L. (1974), "Prices vs. quantities", *Review of Economic Studies*, Vol. 41, No. 128.

Willems, S. (1993), "Environment/employment opportunities arising from fiscal shift away from distortionary taxes and in favour of environmental taxes", European Commission, internal DGXI document, Brussels.

World Energy Council (1992), *1992 Survey of Energy Resources*, London.

Appendix

Glossary of Terms/Abbreviations

AEEI coefficient: Autonomous energy efficiency improvement. Harrod-neutral energy-augmenting technical progress.

Aerosols: Particles, other than water or ice, suspended in the atmosphere. Help to scatter incoming radiation from the sun and work as condensation nuclei for cloud formation. Sulphate aerosols form the major type of anthropogenic aerosols.

Afforestation: The establishment of forests on land not previously forested.

Annex 1 countries: Annex 1 signatories of the FCCC agreement; the group includes OECD, the Former Soviet Union (FSU) and most countries in eastern Europe.

Anthropogenic: Made by people or resulting from human activities.

Atmospheric concentration: Measure of the amount of greenhouse gases present in the world's atmosphere.

Atmospheric lifetime: For every greenhouse gas except CO_2, this is defined as the ratio of the atmospheric content to the total rate of removal. For CO_2, it corresponds to the time it takes for the atmospheric CO_2 level to adjust to a new equilibrium if sources or sinks change.

Backstop technology: Technology for producing a non-conventional energy source assumed to become commercially available in the future.

Baseline scenario: Scenario which describes the path of carbon emissions and other relevant variables in the absence of policies designed to curtail emission growth, except for the removal of existing energy subsidies.

Bau: Business-as-usual scenario. See baseline scenario, except that in this scenario no removal of existing energy subsidies is foreseen.

Biomass: Organic matter from which fuels can be extracted, *e.g.* wood, plants, animal waste.

Bottom-up models: Disaggregated modelling of the systems that provide and use energy services; generally includes both energy supply and end-use.

BTU: British thermal unit.

Carbon content: Amount of carbon emitted per unit of energy consumed.

Carbon-free backstop fuel: Fuel based on carbon-free energy source.

Carbon-free electricity: Electricity produced from carbon-free energy, *e.g.* solar, wind. Excludes hydro-energy and nuclear fission.

Carbon leakage: Increase in CO_2 emissions resulting from a displacement of emitting activities towards countries not participating in a regional agreement to curb emissions.

Carbon tax: Excise tax on fossil fuels, in proportion to the carbon content of each fuel.

CFCs: Chlorofluorocarbons. An important type of greenhouse gas, being phased out under the Montreal Protocol.

CFC-11: $CFCl_3$ (trichlorofluoromethane), a type of CFC.

CFC-12: CF_2Cl_2 (dichloro-difluoromethane), a type of CFC.

CH_4:   Methane. A major greenhouse gas.

CO: Carbon monoxide. A gas which works as an ozone precursor (see below).

CO_2:   Carbon dioxide. The main greenhouse gas.

CO_2 fertilization: Feedback mechanism in which increased CO_2 concentrations increase photosynthesis of plants and therefore plant growth.

Co-generation: Recycling of heat generated during manufacturing or industrial power production.

CoP: Conference of the Parties. Body responsible for co-ordinating and reviewing the obligations of the signatory nations of the FCCC, and for promoting the exchange of information.

DAEs: Dynamic Asian Economies. Hong Kong, Philippines, Singapore, South Korea, Taiwan and Thailand.

DSM: Demand-side management. Policies of utility companies designed to encourage costumers to use electricity more efficiently.

Eastern Europe: Bulgaria, Czech Republic, Hungary, Poland, Romania, Slovakia and the former Republic of Yugoslavia.

Egalitarian principle: Allocation of tradeable emission permits based on population shares.

EIS: Energy-Intensive Sectors.

EJ: Exajoule, or 10^{18} Joule.

EMF-12:   Energy Modelling Forum, exercise number 12. A comparison of carbon emission abatement cost estimates by different models. Based at Stanford University.

Energy Exporting Countries: OPEC and other energy-exporting countries. See Table 4 in Burniaux, *et al.* (1992) for a full list of countries.

Energy intensity: The amount of energy required per unit of output.

Energy tax: Excise tax on energy use.

Equivalent variation: The change in real income necessary to ensure that a consumer's utility prior to a policy change is the same as after the policy change. Or, equivalently, the maximum a consumer would be willing to pay to prevent the policy change.

FCCC: Framework Convention on Climate Change.

Flue gases: Exhaust gases from electrical power plants.

Free-riding: Situation where one country or individual benefits from actions taken by other countries or individuals, without incurring the costs or taking its own policy actions.

GEF: Global Environmental Facility. Fund managed by UNDP, UNEP and IBRD.

Geo-engineering: Measures that intervene in the earth's atmosphere and biosphere to limit global warming, for instance measures to screen the earth from incoming radiation.

Geothermal energy: Energy (heat) extracted from an underground, natural heat source.

Gigaton: 10^9 (billion) ton.

Global Warming Potential (GWP):   The time integrated contribution to radiative forcing from the release of 1 kg of trace gas relative to the release of 1 kg of CO_2 (The GWP index for CO_2 is therefore by definition equal to one).

Grandfathering: Initial allocation of tradeable emission rights based on current emissions.

Greenhouse gas (GHG):   Any gas in the atmosphere that absorbs infrared radiation in the atmosphere.

GREEN: The OECD's General Equilibrium Environmental Model.

Halocarbons: Compounds containing carbon and at least one halogen (bromine, chlorine, fluorine, iodine or astatine). Includes CFCs, HFCs and HCFCs.

Horizontal equity: Principle of equal treatment of all countries in a similar position, under a joint implementation (JI: see below) agreement.

IEA: International Energy Agency.

IGCC: Integrated Gasification Combined Cycle. Relatively efficient and clean power plant technology in which coal is converted into a synthetic gas before combustion.

INC: Intergovernmental Negotiating Committee on the Framework Convention for Climate Change.

IPCC: Intergovernmental Panel on Climate Change.

Joint implementation (JI):   Policies which attempt to reduce the costs of achieving and implementing GHG abatement by international cooperation and coordination of measures.

London Amendments: Amendments to the Montreal Protocol on ozone-depleting compounds.

Major emitters: Annex 1 countries, plus China and India.

Montreal Protocol: International agreement on the regulation of ozone-depleting compounds.

Mtoe: Million tons of oil equivalent.

NMHCs: Non-methane hydrocarbons. A group of gases which work as ozone precursors.

NMVOCs: Non-methane volatile organic compounds. A group of gases which work as ozone precursors.

N_2O: Nitrous oxide. A greenhouse gas.

No-regrets measures: Measures which can be implemented at a net economic benefit or at zero net economic cost.

NO_x: Nitrogen oxides. An ozone precursor.

O_3: Ozone. An important greenhouse gas which results from complex interactions in the atmosphere, involving NO_x, CO, NMHCs and CH_4 (the ozone precursors).

Offset agreement: Joint implementation scheme in which a country, with an initial emission target, invests in curtailment measures in another country and receives a corresponding credit against its own target equal to the quantity of emissions avoided.

OH: Hydroxyl radical. Short-lived compound that influences the atmospheric lifetime of methane and the ozone chemistry of the atmosphere.

Ozone precursors: Gases which help to create ozone in the atmosphere. Includes CO, NO_x, CH_4 and NMHCs.

Photosynthesis: The process in which plants produce carbohydrates and oxygen from carbon dioxide and water, by using energy from sunlight and in the presence of chlorophyll.

Photovoltaic power: Technology which converts the radiant energy of the sun directly into electricity.

Phytoplankton: Tiny floating plants in the oceans (for instance algae).

ppmv: parts per million by volume (measure of atmospheric concentration).

Radiative forcing: The way in which radiation of the sun is absorbed and scattered by the earth's atmosphere.

Reserves: Those occurrences of minerals that are identified, measured and economically and technically recoverable with current technologies and prices.

Resources (or yet-to-find reserves): Occurrences of minerals with less certain geological and economic characteristics.

Resource base: The sum of reserves and resources.

RoW: Rest of the World. All countries not included in one of the other 11 groupings in the GREEN model.

Ruminants: Group of animals which generate methane during digestion. Includes cattle and sheep.

Sequestration: Processes which remove carbon dioxide from the atmosphere and retain it (for some time) in a carbon sink, for instance trees.

Sink: Vehicle for removal of a gas from the earth's atmosphere, in which the gas is absorbed permanently or semi-permanently. Major carbon sinks are oceans, soils and forests.

SO_x: Sulphur oxides. Gases which help to create sulphate aerosols.

Synfuels: Fuels produced by a chemical synthesis process, such as those produced from the gasification or liquefaction of coal.

Take-back: Increased energy use resulting from energy efficiency enhancing measures, due to changes in relative prices and income.

Terajoule: 10^{12} (trillion) Joule, equals $2.78 * 10^5$ kilowatt/hours.

Teragram: 10^{12} (trillion) grammes, or 1 million tonnes.

Top-down models: Macro-economic modelling of interactions between economic activity and energy use.

Toronto-type agreement: International agreement with differentiated abatement targets between OECD and non-OECD countries.

Tradeable emission quotas: Rights to GHG emissions which are tradeable across countries.

Uniform carbon tax: Carbon tax rate common to all parties participating in the (regional, global) carbon abatement coalition.

Vertical equity: Principle of favourable treatment under a JI agreement of countries at lower capital incomes relative to those at higher scales.

Annex A

TECHNICAL BACKGROUND INFORMATION

This Annex provides technical background information to various sections of the main text. See the table of contents for a list of the subjects covered.

Annex A

TECHNICAL BACKGROUND INFORMATION

This Annex provides technical background information to various sections of the main text. See the table of contents for a list of the subjects covered.

TABLE OF CONTENTS

Note 1. An Interpretation of the UN Framework Convention on Climate Change 71
    A1.1. FCCC objectives 71
    A1.2. Cost efficiency and equity 72
    A1.3. Policy instruments 72

Note 2. Model Simulations: Assumptions and Results 74
    A2.1. The baseline scenario 74
    A2.2. Gains from international co-operation 76
        A2.2.1. Carbon taxes 77
        A2.2.2. Real income gains and losses 78
    A2.3. Joint Implementation and the burden sharing issue 79
        A2.3.1. Tradeable emission quota allocation 80
        A2.3.2. International carbon tax fund 81

Note 3. Sensitivity Analysis on Baseline Emissions and Marginal Abatement Cost 85
    A3.1. CO_2 emissions in the baseline 85
    A3.2. Cost of stabilising emissions in Annex 1 countries 87

Note 4. The Discount Rate and Climate Change Policy 89
    A4.1. Sensitivity analysis over the 1990-2100 period 89
    A4.2. Sensitivity analysis over a 300-year time horizon 91
    A4.3. What is the appropriate rate of discount? 93
    A4.4. Intergenerational comparison 93
    A4.5. Shadow price of capital approach to discounting 93

Note 5. Risk Aversion and Insurance Premia 95

Note 6. Raising Energy Efficiency 99

Notes 101

Bibliography 103

Note 1. **An Interpretation of the UN Framework Convention on Climate Change**[1]

by

Jonathan Coppel

The United Nation's Framework Convention on Climate Change (FCCC) signed at the Earth Summit in Rio de Janeiro in the summer of 1992 defines a comprehensive framework within which greenhouse gas (GHG) abatement, absorption and adaptation policies towards reducing the threat of global warming can develop. Over 150 countries signed the FCCC, and the minimum number of countries required to ratify the agreement (50) has by now been greatly exceeded. In keeping with the notion of a framework convention, the FCCC lays out the main considerations that should govern future policy and specifies – although not very precisely – the obligations of signatory nations. Details on choice of policy instruments, implementation strategies, monitoring, enforcement and adequacy of the commitments are left to be determined in future protocols to the convention.

A1.1. FCCC objectives

Recognition that unilateral responses to the threat of climate change would prove ineffective, but that mutual co-operation could generate significant potential gains, provided a strong incentive to reach an international agreement. The result of intense negotiation is the FCCC, a document explicitly focused on the necessity for implementing global solutions. The first sentence of the FCCC states that, "change in the earth's climate and it's adverse effects are a common concern of humankind". It then declares, in the preamble, that "the global nature of climate change calls for the widest possible co-operation by all countries and their participation in an effective and appropriate response, in accordance with their common but differentiated responsibilities and respective capabilities and their social conditions".

Two fundamental concerns expressed in the FCCC are equity and economic efficiency. These principles are not, however, the primary objectives of the FCCC, but are intended to guide the process to achieve effective co-operation. The primary objective of the FCCC is stated explicitly in environmental terms to achieve a "... stabilisation of greenhouse gas concentrations in the atmosphere at a level that would prevent dangerous anthropogenic interference with the climate system" (Article 2 FCCC). Currently, any operational interpretation of this goal will inevitably be controversial, given pervasive uncertainty in this area.

As many uncertainties attach to the prediction of climate change, specifying and enforcing rigid climate-change response initiatives without reliable information on the policies' costs and benefits would have involved a major risk. A target could imply expensive, unnecessary responses; or it may be insufficient, entailing large damages. By avoiding hasty implementation of rigid action plans, the FCCC gives parties time to assemble more information on the various and large uncertainties pertaining to the likelihood and possible impacts of climate change and the costs of responding to this risk. Nonetheless, despite massive uncertainty the FCCC contains immediate, but modest commitments which can – if and when necessary – evolve into more ambitious actions in response to new scientific and economic information.

The FCCC obligations, in effect, can be interpreted as a precautionary ("insurance") response to the risk of adverse impacts from climate change. At the same time initial commitments might also serve to set precedents and establish institutions better prepared, through experience, to implement stronger policy measures at a later date – if deemed necessary. In support of these capacity and institution-building activities, and more broadly the effective implementation of the convention, Article 7 of the FCCC formally establishes the Conference of the Parties (COP), a body explicitly responsible for co-ordinating and reviewing the obligations of the Parties (*i.e.* signatory nations of the FCCC) and promoting the exchange of information. Several other subsidiary institutions are also created whose purpose is to assess available scientific information and promote activities that clarify and reduce climate science uncertainties.

A1.2. Cost efficiency and equity

Achieving policy co-operation among a large number of heterogeneous countries is more likely if the policy process and policy outcomes are perceived to be fair by a maximum of them. Intermediate objectives of economic efficiency and equity are integral parts of this process and, as noted earlier, are two principles which pervade the FCCC. The equity objective is elaborated in Principles 1 and 2 (Article 3) where ideas of inter-generational fairness, differentiated burdens, depending on individual countries' capabilities, and the responsibility for developed country parties to take the lead in combating climate change are introduced. Principle 3 expresses a wish for parties to consider policies and measures which deal with climate change effectively and efficiently, so as to attain given targets at the lowest possible cost. Typically, however, cost effectiveness is not necessarily compatible with equitable outcomes as perceived by the parties.

The FCCC was able to attract broad support, and establish at least the necessary condition for cost effective and equitable GHG abatement and absorption, by separating the issue of where these activities are sourced from the question of who pays. The FCCC identifies three distinct country groups, each with different responsibilities. These are the OECD economies (Annex 2 countries),[2] countries in transition (eastern Europe and the former Soviet Union) and developing countries. The first two groups of parties represent the Annex 1 countries. Annex 1 countries have accepted several broad commitments: to limit greenhouse gas emissions, enhance removals by sinks and play a leading role assisting developing countries to implement the FCCC objective. Specifically, Annex 1 countries engage themselves to take immediate action towards reducing the risk of harmful climate change. No precise definition of immediate action is stipulated, but some clarifying guidelines are outlined in Article 4 paragraph 2a. In particular, Annex 1 countries pledge to enact measures which "will demonstrate that developed countries are taking the lead in modifying longer term trends in anthropogenic emissions consistent with the objective of the Convention, recognising that the return by the end of the present decade to earlier levels of anthropogenic emissions ... would contribute to such modification...''. The base year implied by "earlier levels'' is suggested in paragraph 2b of the FCCC as 1990, but countries in transition are allowed "a certain degree of flexibility'' notably with respect to the base year chosen, in order to enhance the ability of these countries to address climate change (Article 4, paragraph 2g). All other parties pledge to provide comprehensive information on anthropogenic GHG emissions in their territories.

Consistent with the precautionary approach, although not necessarily motivated by it, the FCCC gives no indication whether the commitment to introduce policies/measures which aim to stabilise Annex 1 emissions continues beyond year 2000. It is the responsibility of the COP, as supreme body of the FCCC, to review the adequacy of the commitments, given the latest available assessment of the risks and impacts of climate change.

A1.3. Policy instruments

The FCCC demonstrates no preference for a specific kind of instrument; it only stipulates that adopted policies must be communicated to the COP. Hence the FCCC does not ensure cost-effective policy responses. Cost-effectiveness will depend on the choice of policy instrument, which is left for each party to decide. The objective, however, of achieving commitments cost efficiently and equitably narrows the possible choice of instruments. Again, without being specific, the FCCC provides scope potentially to abide by these two principles simultaneously via a provision which has become known as joint implementation (JI). Specifically, Article 4, paragraph 2a states: "developed country Parties and other Parties included in Annex 1 may implement ... policies and measures jointly with other Parties and may assist other Parties in contributing to the achievement of the objective of the Convention''.

One of the attractions of JI is that it facilitates climate change policies among a wider coalition of countries, providing an incentive to put into place abatement policies in countries with low costs. At the same time, the economic costs of climate change policies can be redistributed. JI could also be portrayed as a mechanism for compensating countries whose participation goes beyond their FCCC commitments for the costs incurred by their (voluntary) participation. Although the principle of JI is embodied within the FCCC, it is not yet known what JI will actually mean when it is applied in practice. The COP will consider operational matters at its first meeting in March 1995.

Provisions for compensation relating to signatory commitments are also embodied in the FCCC. Article 4, paragraph 3 broadly outlines the responsibility of developed country parties to: "provide new and additional financial resources to meet the agreed full costs incurred by developing countries in complying with their obligations". In addition, financial resources, including for the transfer of technology, are available if a developing country implements initiatives (consistent with Article 4, paragraph 1) which mitigate the threat of climate change. These resources are meant to cover the agreed full incremental costs of adopted measures. Currently, no universally accepted definition of the incremental costs of climate change measures exist. This issue, as well as how funds provided by developed country parties, are redistributed, the types of measures and policies, programme priorities and their eligibility criteria, are currently being actively considered by the Conference of the Parties.

Note 2. **Model Simulations: Assumptions and Results**

by

Jonathan Coppel and Hiro Lee

This note provides supplementary detail on the GREEN simulations discussed in Parts 2 and 6 of the main paper. It also reports the findings from additional, but closely related simulation experiments not discussed in the main paper. The next section outlines the key assumptions and relevant features of the GREEN model baseline scenario.[3] The following section elaborates on the gains from international co-operation. This is followed by an analysis centring on the issue of burden sharing in joint implementation agreements under different tradeable emission quota allocation rules. The final section also focuses on joint implementation and the burden sharing question, but in the context of an international carbon tax fund.

A2.1. The baseline scenario

The baseline scenario describes the path of carbon emissions expected in the absence of policies designed to curtail their growth. The baseline assumptions are broadly similar to those underpinning the IPCC reference case scenario IS92A,[4] summarised in Table 2.1 of the main paper. The underlying GDP and population growth assumptions over the period 1990-2050 are summarised in Table A2.1. These are largely based on the guidelines used for the OECD Model Comparisons Project[5] and the Energy Modelling Forum Number 12 (EMF 12)[6] exercise updated for recent trends.

Two important policy assumptions are explicitly built into the baseline scenario. First, it is assumed that any existing subsidies on oil will be gradually eliminated by the year 2000 and those on coal and natural gas by 2010 to reflect major price reforms that have been instigated or planned in several countries currently subsidising the production of fossil fuels. Table A2.2 shows the 1985 level of fossil fuel subsidies in each GREEN country/ region. The existing level of energy taxes in the benchmark year (1985) is assumed to remain unchanged over time. Secondly, the baseline does not assume any discretionary policy action to curtail carbon emissions. Consequently, policy commitments by FCCC signatories to reduce CO_2 emissions, such as those contained in the U.S. government "Climate Change Action Plan" are not included.

The average global baseline emissions growth rate is 1.8 per cent per annum – 0.3 percentage points higher than annual energy demand growth – reaching, 17 billion tons of carbon annually by 2050. The OECD share of global emissions gradually declines from 47 per cent in 1990 to 35 per cent in 2050 (Table A2.3). After an initial period of negative emission growth in the former Soviet Union and Eastern Europe, linked to the current output decline, this region's share of global emissions declines further, by 7 percentage points, to 17 per cent in 2050. As a result, the relative importance of emissions among Annex 1 countries falls from 71 per cent in 1990 to 51 per cent in 2050. Reflecting above average output growth, China becomes the largest single carbon emitter: its 10 per cent share of global emissions in 1990 almost doubles by 2050. Baseline emissions are sensitive to assumptions on output growth (which itself is a result of assumptions concerning labour force and labour efficiency growth), fossil fuel supply elasticities, technical progress and energy back-stop prices. Note 3 in this Annex provides more information on the sensitivity of baseline emissions with respect to economic and technical assumptions.

Table A2.1. Real GDP and population projections underlying the baseline scenario in GREEN

| | 1990 level[1] | | Per annum percentage changes | | | | | | | | | |
| | | | 1990-2000 | | 2000-2010 | | 2010-2030 | | 2030-2050 | | 1990-2050 | |
	RGDP	POP	RGDP	POP	RGDP	POP	RGDP	POP	RGDP	POP	RGDP	POP
United States	4 177 802	249.9	2.6	0.7	2.1	0.6	1.9	0.3	1.6	-0.1	2.0	0.3
Japan	1 514 575	123.5	3.7	0.3	2.7	0.1	2.5	-0.2	2.2	-0.3	2.6	-0.1
European Community	2 477 665	324.0	2.2	0.1	1.7	0.0	1.5	-0.2	1.3	-0.3	1.6	-0.1
Other OECD countries[2]	875 779	126.8	2.2	1.2	1.7	0.9	1.5	0.6	1.3	0.2	1.6	0.6
Former Soviet Union	721 603	288.8	0.0	0.6	2.3	0.5	3.0	0.4	2.2	0.2	2.1	0.4
Eastern Europe	268 322	120.7	0.0	0.4	2.3	0.3	3.0	0.2	2.3	0.1	2.1	0.2
China	549 483	1 117.4	6.0	1.3	5.0	0.9	4.3	0.6	3.5	0.2	4.4	0.6
India	227 206	831.9	4.6	1.8	4.4	1.4	3.9	1.0	3.4	0.6	4.0	1.1
Dynamic Asian economies	322 481	189.7	4.4	1.4	4.2	1.1	3.7	0.7	3.2	0.3	3.7	0.8
Brazil	229 257	150.2	4.4	1.7	4.2	1.2	3.7	0.9	3.2	0.5	3.7	1.0
Energy-exporting countries	1 248 431	743.7	3.6	2.3	3.4	2.0	3.1	1.5	2.7	0.9	3.1	1.5
Rest of the World	728 803	993.8	3.5	2.6	3.1	2.3	2.7	1.9	2.4	1.2	2.8	1.8
OECD[2]	9 045 821	824	2.6	0.5	2.1	0.3	1.8	0.1	1.6	-0.2	1.9	0.1
Annex 1 countries[3]	10 035 747	1 234	2.4	0.5	2.1	0.3	1.9	0.2	1.7	-0.1	1.9	0.2
Major emitters[4]	10 812 436	3 183	2.6	1.1	2.3	0.8	2.1	0.5	1.8	0.2	2.1	0.6
World	13 341 407	5 260	2.8	1.6	2.5	1.3	2.3	0.9	2.0	0.5	2.3	1.0

1. Real GDP (RGDP) in millions of 1985 US dollars, population (POP) in million persons.
2. Excluding Mexico.
3. Annex 1 is defined as OECD countries, Eastern Europe and the former Soviet Union.
4. Major emitters are defined as Annex 1 countries, India and China.
Source: OECD GREEN Model database.

Table A2.2. **1985 Energy subsidy rates in GREEN**

Per cent of producer price

	Coal	Oil	Gas
United States	–	4	–
Japan	–	–	–
European Community	–	–	–
Other OECD [1]	–	–	–
Former Soviet Union	56	88	88
Eastern Europe	52	39	17
Energy-exporting countries	3	36	21
China	55	2	11
India	42	42	50
Dynamic Asian economies	–	17	–
Brazil	–	24	42
Rest of the World	–	18	–

1. Excluding Mexico.
Source: OECD GREEN model database.

Table A2.3. **CO₂ emissions growth in the baseline scenario**

	Per cent, average annual rate					Million tons	Per cent	
	1990-2000	2000-2010	2010-2030	2030-2050	1990-2050	1990	1990	2050
United States	1.5	1.2	1.0	1.1	1.2	1 350.3	22.9	16.0
Japan	3.9	0.5	1.4	1.9	1.8	333.1	5.6	5.8
European Community	1.6	0.7	0.8	1.2	1.0	823.5	13.9	9.0
Other OECD countries [1]	1.8	1.3	1.2	1.1	1.3	295.4	5.0	3.7
Energy-exporting countries	2.2	2.0	2.4	2.5	2.3	423.6	7.2	10.0
China	2.6	2.5	2.8	2.9	2.8	600.6	10.2	18.0
Former Soviet Union	-1.7	1.0	2.1	2.0	1.2	1 055.3	17.9	12.9
India	3.0	3.1	3.2	3.2	3.2	151.2	2.6	5.8
Eastern Europe	-1.9	0.7	1.9	1.9	1.1	359.4	6.1	4.0
Dynamic Asian economies	3.7	3.0	2.8	3.0	3.0	108.2	1.8	3.8
Brazil	2.9	2.2	2.5	3.3	2.8	96.2	1.6	2.9
Rest of the world	2.9	2.8	2.4	2.2	2.5	310.3	5.3	8.0
OECD [1]	1.9	1.0	1.0	1.2	1.2	2 802.4	47.4	34.5
Annex 1 countries [2]	0.8	1.0	1.3	1.5	1.2	4 217.1	71.4	51.5
Major Emitters [3]	1.1	1.3	1.7	1.9	1.6	4 968.9	84.1	75.3
non-OECD	0.9	2.8	2.5	2.6	2.2	3 104.9	52.6	65.5
non-Annex 1 countries	2.7	2.5	2.7	2.8	2.7	938.4	15.9	24.7
World	1.4	1.5	1.9	2.1	1.8	5 907.2	100.0	100.0

1. Excluding Mexico.
2. OECD countries, the former Soviet Union and Eastern Europe.
3. Annex 1 countries, China and India.
Note: Carbon emissions in million tons of carbon, share and growth rates in percentages.
Source: OECD GREEN Model simulations.

A2.2. Gains from international co-operation

Marginal abatement costs tend to increase more than proportionately with abatement and differ across countries/regions. This suggests that expanding participation and equalising marginal costs of abatement among a wider coalition of countries could lower the total cost of attaining a given emission target, but could also result in an uneven regional distribution of abatement costs. These points are explored by simulating a suite of agreements, with a common emission target, starting with OECD participation and country specific carbon taxes and then successively incorporating larger country coalitions eventually encompassing global participation and a uniform carbon tax.

The emission curtailment target chosen for the analysis is the stabilisation of Annex 1 country CO_2 emissions at their 1990 level, or the reduction of world CO_2 emissions from baseline equivalent to Annex 1 stabilisation. This target reduces growth in Annex 1 baseline emissions by almost 1 percentage point per annum and represents a 26 per cent cut from global baseline emissions in 2050. The results suggest that the average global costs of emissions cuts could be reduced by 0.9 per cent of real world income under a global co-ordinated abatement agreement, compared with an uncoordinated abatement effort among OECD countries. This is approximately equivalent to $120 billion per annum (at 1985 prices and exchange rates; Table A2.4, scenarios S.1 and S.5).

Table A2.4. Summary of average real income losses when different country coalitions reduce emissions by a fixed amount [1]

Per cent deviation from baseline

	Four OECD regions cut emissions in equal proportions to stabilise Annex 1 emissions at 1990 levels (S.1)	A uniform carbon tax to achieve the emission target is imposed on:			
		The OECD (S.2)	Annex 1 countries (S.3)	Major emitters (S.4)	The global coalition (S.5)
Average real income over the period 1990-2050 [2] (% relative to baseline)					
United States	−0.53	−0.55	−0.51	−0.24	−0.16
Japan	−1.67	−1.17	−0.80	−0.34	−0.19
European Community	−0.85	−0.87	−0.58	−0.24	−0.14
Other OECD countries [3]	−0.52	−0.56	−0.23	−0.08	−0.07
Energy-exporting countries	−3.62	−3.32	−0.31	0.07	−0.18
China	−0.52	−0.47	0.21	−1.19	−0.79
Former Soviet Union	−1.35	−1.32	−0.70	0.41	0.52
India	−0.07	−0.07	0.09	−0.74	−0.52
Eastern Europe	0.10	0.08	−0.37	0.26	0.36
Dynamic Asian economies	−0.35	−0.29	0.09	0.12	−0.30
Brazil	0.14	0.12	0.52	0.43	−0.22
Rest of the world	−0.65	−0.62	0.04	0.10	−0.55
OECD [3]	−0.85	−0.76	−0.56	−0.25	−0.15
Annex-1 countries	−0.86	−0.77	−0.57	−0.20	−0.10
Major emitters	−0.79	−0.71	−0.46	−0.33	−0.19
World	−1.07	−0.97	−0.36	−0.22	−0.22

1. The emission reduction from baseline is equivalent to that resulting from stabilising Annex 1 countries' emissions at their 1990 levels. Since the target is always an *ex ante* reduction of emissions among participating countries the *ex post* level of world emissions varies slightly between scenarios mainly due to different leakage rates.
2. Real income is defined as the sum of domestic household consumption, investment and government expenditure.
3. Excluding Mexico.
Source: OECD GREEN Model simulations.

A2.2.1. Carbon taxes

Carbon taxes in 2050 required to meet the emission target range between $426 per ton of carbon in Other OECD countries, if country/region specific taxes are imposed in OECD countries (Scenario S.1) and $25 if participation is global and taxes are uniform (Scenario S.5). The profile of carbon taxes over the simulation period are also very different, especially from 2010 onwards when the growth in carbon taxes needed to achieve the emission target under each scenario diverges (Figure A2.1). Compared with the case where only OECD countries curtail emissions (Scenarios S.1 and S.2), required carbon taxes in all other cases are considerably lower. Simply extending the country base of the tax to include Eastern Europe and the former Soviet Union (Scenario S.3) reduces the average tax compared with an agreement among OECD countries alone by about 70 per cent. The "Major emitters" case where China and India are also included in the carbon tax scheme (S.4), results in carbon taxes very similar to those implied by a global co-operation agreement (S.5). Initial taxes (1995) among Major emitters start at $6 per ton of carbon and rise gradually, reaching $37 in 2050. The reason why tax

Figure A2.1. **Uniform carbon tax under alternative participation scenarios[1]**

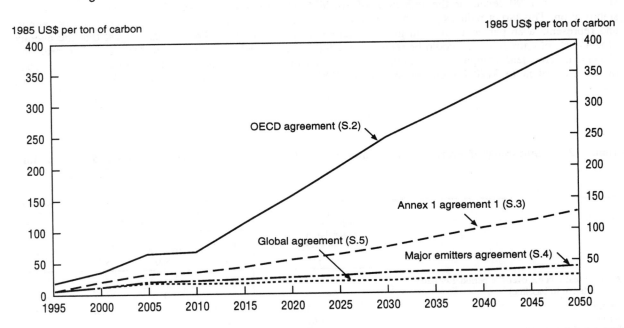

1985 US$ per ton of carbon

1985 US$ per ton of carbon

1. The global *(ex ante)* CO_2 emission reduction from baseline is identical for all scenarios, corresponding to the stabilisation of emissions in Annex 1 countries at their 1990 levels.
Source: OECD GREEN model simulations.

rates are similar in these two cases is linked to the fact that Major emitters account for about 84 per cent of global baseline emissions in 1990, and this share is relatively constant over the simulation period.

Once non-OECD countries are involved in a stabilisation agreement, the distribution of emission cuts shifts sharply away from OECD countries with relatively high marginal abatement costs to countries with low costs (Figure A2.2). Under global participation (S.5) curtailed emissions in OECD countries would account for 27 per cent of the total in 2050. In the case where country participation is limited to Annex 1 countries (S.3), OECD nations still have to implement sharp cuts. However, relative abatement in 2050 is largest in the former Soviet Union (67 per cent below baseline). In general, when non-OECD countries also participate, (Scenarios S.3 to S.5) the coal intensive countries like the former Soviet Union, China and India make the largest proportional emission cuts.

If country participation in a carbon abatement agreement is less than global, "carbon leakages" or "off-shore" effects, could modify the global abatement level achieved. Under each of the scenarios presented in Part 2 of the main paper, leakage rates are consistently small. Annex B provides more detail on the channels of carbon leakage and their sensitivity to model assumptions.

A2.2.2. *Real income gains and losses*

Imposing a uniform carbon tax within a global coalition achieves the emission stabilisation target at lowest cost (Figure A2.3). The potential benefits in terms of cost savings are considerable. When OECD countries stabilise the equivalent of Annex 1 emissions at 1990 levels (S.2), average global incomes are 1.0 per cent below baseline. If the same target is achieved under global participation, average incomes are 0.2 per cent below baseline. Even if the agreement is confined to the Major emitters (S.4) – representing about 35 countries – the average real income loss in the OECD region is reduced by almost 70 per cent compared with unilateral OECD abatement (from 0.85 per cent to 0.25 per cent).

It is not, however, only OECD countries which would benefit from expanded co-operation. Energy Exporting countries are the single largest gainer. Most notably, the average real income change in Energy Exporting countries improves from –3.6 to 0.1 percentage points when co-operation widens from OECD countries (S.1) to

Figure A2.2. **Emission reductions in 2050 under alternative participation scenarios**[1]

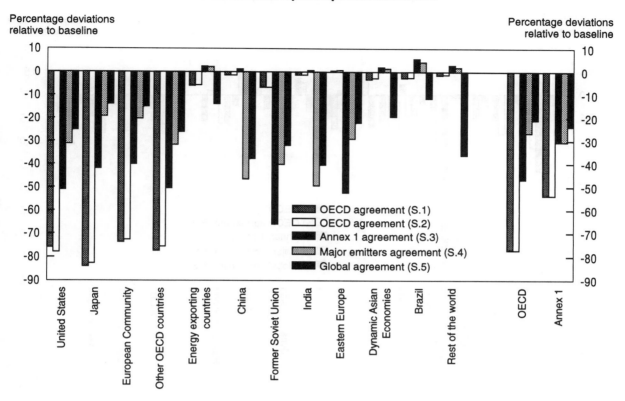

1. The global *(ex ante)* CO_2 emission reduction from baseline is identical for all scenarios, corresponding to the stabilisation of emissions in Annex 1 countries at their 1990 levels.
Source: OECD GREEN model simulations.

involve the Major emitters (S.4). The gains are smaller if Energy Exporters also participate (S.5), but still impose lower losses compared with an agreement among only OECD countries. The reason these countries would prefer an agreement which secures broad coverage is linked to the greater efficiency of achieving emission cuts by curbing coal rather than oil demand and hence limiting the adverse impact of a carbon tax on Energy Exporters terms of trade (Table A2.5).

Not all countries reduce their real income losses when more cost-effective agreements are implemented. Such agreements achieve lower costs of abatement by shifting the burden of stabilising emissions to countries with low marginal abatement costs. Typically, these tend to be the coal-based developing economies of India and China whose real incomes, relative to no climate agreement, fall by more than in any other country/region. Average real incomes in China switch from a small gain relative to baseline (0.2 per cent) if Annex 1 countries stabilise emissions to losses of up to 1.2 per cent. In India welfare losses are smaller, but triple the global average.

A2.3. Joint Implementation and the burden sharing issue

As the distribution of abatement costs under the efficiency scenario is unlikely to be politically acceptable, it may require substantial income redistribution to enlist global or broad participation. The burden sharing issue is explored further in this section using the GREEN model to simulate the distributive implications of explicit quota

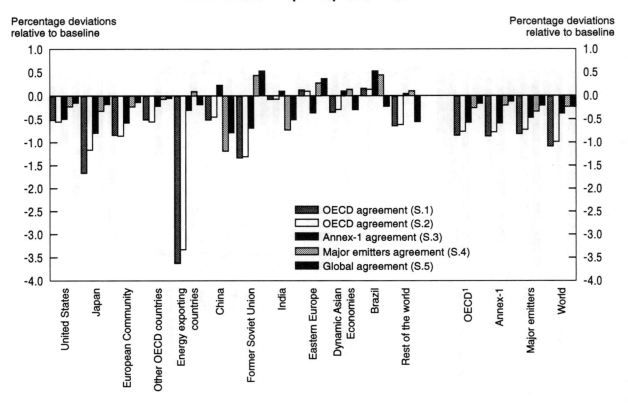

Figure A2.3. **Average real income changes over the period 1990-2050 under alternative participation scenarios[1]**

Percentage deviations relative to baseline

Percentage deviations relative to baseline

- OECD agreement (S.1)
- OECD agreement (S.2)
- Annex-1 agreement (S.3)
- Major emitters agreement (S.4)
- Global agreement (S.5)

United States / Japan / European Community / Other OECD countries / Energy exporting countries / China / Former Soviet Union / India / Eastern Europe / Dynamic Asian Economies / Brazil / Rest of the world / OECD[1] / Annex-1 / Major emitters / World

1. The global *(ex ante)* CO_2 emission reduction from baseline is identical for all scenarios, corresponding to the stabilisation of emissions in Annex 1 countries at their 1990 levels.
Source: OECD GREEN model simulations.

allocation principles. As before, the emission target assumed for the analysis is a cut in world baseline CO_2 emissions by Annex 1 countries with the co-operation of India and China (the Major emitters group) equivalent to stabilising Annex 1 country emissions at 1990 levels. This target corresponds to Scenario 4 in Part 2 of the main paper.

A2.3.1. *Tradeable emission quota allocation*

Numerous emission quota allocation rules have been proposed based on diverse rationale (see Table A2.6). A country/region's initial quota allocation obviously depends critically on the rule adopted. Table A2.7 shows the initial quota shares implied by different allocation rules. All rules, apart from the "two-tiered" and grandfathering rules, described in Part 6 of the main paper, result in allocations very different from current emission shares.

The value of trade in emission quotas for each of the allocation rules is summarised in Table A2.8. Non-OECD countries tend to sell a large number of quotas when initial distributions are based on measures linked to population (*e.g.* egalitarian, redistributive and equity). By contrast, OECD countries are net sellers of quotas if quota distribution is related to either current emissions (grandfathering) or efficiency (carbon emissions per unit of GDP).

The distribution of net abatement costs varies widely between countries. Table A2.9 summarises the average net real income losses for each allocation rule. Net real income changes within a country/region also span a wide range depending on how quotas are allocated. For example, average real income in India and China could be

Table A2.5. **Summary of terms of trade changes under different country participation scenarios**

Per cent deviation relative to baseline in a given year

	2000	2010	2030	2050
Scenario 1				
Energy exporters	-3.31	-5.20	-7.43	-3.77
OECD[1]	1.08	1.96	3.12	2.70
Annex 1 countries	0.85	1.58	2.56	2.43
Major emitters	0.79	1.46	2.21	1.60
Scenario 2				
Energy exporters	-2.40	-4.67	-7.62	-4.21
OECD[1]	0.82	1.65	3.02	2.81
Annex 1 countries	0.34	0.65	1.35	1.62
Major emitters	0.36	-2.30	1.14	0.92
Scenario 3				
Energy exporters	-1.26	-2.60	-0.54	7.07
OECD[1]	0.44	0.92	0.39	-2.68
Annex 1 countries	0.11	0.34	-0.06	-2.36
Major emitters	0.12	-2.61	-0.11	-1.68
Scenario 4				
Energy exporters	-0.84	-1.72	0.67	4.84
OECD[1]	0.30	0.61	0.00	-1.11
Annex 1 countries	0.10	0.21	-0.10	-0.87
Major emitters	0.06	-2.75	-0.28	-1.22
Scenario 5				
Energy exporters	-1.08	-2.08	1.01	2.51
OECD[1]	0.32	0.61	-0.04	-0.23
Annex 1 countries	0.10	0.15	-0.03	-0.03
Major emitters	0.06	-2.79	-0.23	-0.29

1. Excluding Mexico.
Source: OECD GREEN Model simulations.

1.7 per cent below baseline under the grandfathering rule, but 4.1 per cent above baseline if quotas are distributed according to the redistributive rule. Real income losses among OECD country/regions tend to lie within a comparatively narrower range (-1.0 per cent to -0.3 per cent).

A2.3.2. *International carbon tax fund*

One advantage of an international carbon tax fund approach is the greater flexibility in redistribution arrangements to reach a joint implementation agreement.[7] If it transpires that the distribution of costs in a climate agreement is not as anticipated, it could be, in some cases, easier to adjust the tax fund allocation rules. As with tradeable quotas, there are numerous conceivable kinds of international carbon tax fund agreements. Two such agreements are explored in more detail here. Inevitably, numerous overly simplistic and arbitrary assumptions are required on issues which in practice would presumably be decided on the basis of political and economic considerations.

The scenarios and assumptions underlying the analysis in this section are a uniform carbon tax applied among the Major emitters such that baseline emissions are reduced by an amount equivalent to emission stabilisation at 1990 levels in Annex 1 countries, with 75 per cent of Annex 1 carbon tax revenues diverted to an international carbon tax fund. Donor regions are assumed to contribute in proportion to their 1990 emission shares. All countries/regions participating in the agreement are assumed to receive payments from the fund in proportion to their population. The revenue redistribution rule is therefore similar to the egalitarian quota distribution principle. The second scenario is an identical emission target achieved through a uniform carbon tax, but only OECD countries contribute to the international fund. Eastern Europe and the former Soviet Union (countries belonging to the Annex 1 group) are subject to the carbon tax, but retain carbon tax revenues within the region. The smaller amount of fund revenues available ($134 billion in 2050) are redistributed to China and India in proportion to population in these two countries.

Table A2.6. Quota allocation rules

Rule	Rationale
1. Grandfathering. Quotas allocated on the basis of country/region emission shares in a given year.	Relatively easy to define and measure.
2. Egalitarian. Quotas allocated in proportion to country/region population shares in a given year.	Easy to measure and appeals to the principle that every person has an equal right to use the atmosphere.
3. Efficiency oriented. Quotas allocated in proportion to the inverse of relative country/region carbon intensity measured by the ratio of CO_2 emissions to GDP, scaled by population size.	Favours countries which use lower carbon emitting and more efficient energy sources.
4. Redistributive. Quotas are allocated in inverse proportion to a country/region's GDP per capita, scaled by population size.	Favours poor countries giving a positive flow of funds to developing countries.
5. Equity plus efficiency oriented. Quotas are allocated in inverse proportion to a country/region's fossil fuel consumption per capita.	Tends to favour poor developing countries and countries which promote carbon free energy sources and energy efficiency.
6. Hybrid schemes. Numerous possibilities exist. Principle is combining the preceding rules by attaching predetermined weights (which may change over time) to two or more allocation criteria.	Depends on the combination of rules. Practical implication may be greater political acceptability via a gradual transition from the status quo towards a rule implying a more egalitarian distribution of quotas.

Table A2.7. Initial quota shares under different allocation rules

	Redistributive	Efficiency	Equity	Grandfathering	Egalitarian
	Per cent of total				
United States	0.2	15.4	1.9	27.1	7.9
Japan	0.2	11.0	4.0	6.8	3.9
European Community	0.7	19.8	4.1	16.6	10.2
Other OECD countries [1]	0.3	7.7	4.5	6.0	4.0
China	42.0	18.2	20.6	12.2	35.1
Former Soviet Union	2.8	2.7	2.3	20.9	9.1
India	52.7	23.8	59.2	3.0	26.1
Eastern Europe	1.1	1.5	3.5	7.3	3.8

1. Excluding Mexico.
Note: The different quota allocation rules are explained in detail in Table A2.6.

Table A2.8. Value of net trade in emission quotas by 2050 [1]
$US billion

Quota allocation rule	Region		
	OECD [2]	FSU and Eastern Europe	China and India
Redistributive	−176	−58	234
Efficiency	5	−57	52
Equity	−130	−52	182
Grandfathering	14	22	−36
Egalitarian	−90	−29	119
Two-tiered [3]	−90	−29	119

1. A positive figure corresponds to a quota sale and a negative figure to a quota purchase.
2. Mexico excluded.
3. Although the distribution of quotas under the two-tiered rate in 2050 is identical with the egalitarian rule, the value of quota trade in 2050 may not be identical because the initial quota distribution differs, which leads to a different dynamic path of income.
Source: OECD GREEN Model simulations.

Carbon taxes in both cases rise gradually, reaching around $43 per ton in 2050. The international tax fund will then receive just over $200 billion in 2050 (Scenario 1, Table A2.10) – 0.6 per cent of Annex 1 country GDP. In both simulations the United States would be the major contributor. In relative terms, India would be the main recipient country, receiving $69 billion – equivalent to 2.8 per cent of its GDP – under the first scenario. Average real income losses in both tax fund scenarios are approximately the same, except in the former Soviet Union and Eastern Europe (Figure A2.4). These regions switch from an average real income loss of 2.1 per cent

Table A2.9. **Summary of average real income losses under different quota allocation rules**[1]

Per cent deviation relative to baseline

Quota allocation rule	Region			
	OECD[2]	Annex 1	China and India	World
Redistributive	−1.0	−1.1	4.1	−0.2
Efficiency	−0.3	−0.5	0.3	−0.2
Equity	−0.8	−1.0	2.5	−0.2
Grandfathering	−0.3	−0.1	−1.7	−0.2
Egalitarian	−0.7	−0.7	2.0	−0.2
Two-tiered	−0.5	−0.5	1.0	−0.2

1. Average real income over the period 1990-2050. Real income is defined as the sum of domestic household consumption, investment and government net expenditure.
2. Excluding Mexico.
Source: OECD GREEN Model simulations.

Table A2.10. **Carbon fund flow in 2050**

Billions of 1985 US dollars

Panel A, Scenario 1[1]

Contributing regions	Recipient regions								
	United States	Japan	EC	Other OECD[3]	FSU	Eastern Europe	China	India	Sub-total
United States	4.2	1.7	4.2	2.6	5.0	1.9	23.0	22.2	64.7
Japan	1.0	0.4	1.0	0.6	1.2	0.5	5.7	5.5	16.0
European Community	2.6	1.0	2.6	1.6	3.1	1.2	14.0	13.5	39.5
Other OECD[3]	0.9	0.4	0.9	0.6	1.1	0.4	5.0	4.9	14.1
Former Soviet Union	3.3	1.3	3.3	2.0	3.9	1.5	17.9	17.3	50.6
Eastern Europe	1.1	0.4	1.1	0.7	1.3	0.5	6.1	5.9	17.2
Sub-total	13.1	5.2	13.1	8.0	15.7	6.1	71.7	69.3	**202.0**

Panel B, Scenario 2[2]

Contributing regions	China	India	Sub-total
United States	32.9	31.8	64.7
Japan	8.1	7.9	16.0
European Community	20.1	19.4	39.5
Other OECD[3]	7.2	7.0	14.2
Sub-total	68.3	66.0	**134.3**

1. Annex 1 countries contribute 75 per cent of carbon tax revenues to the carbon fund and all participants receive revenues in proportion to their respective populations in 2050.
2. Only OECD countries contribute to the carbon fund and revenues are redistributed in proportion to the respective populations of China and India in 2050.
3. Excluding Mexico.
Source: OECD GREEN Model simulations.

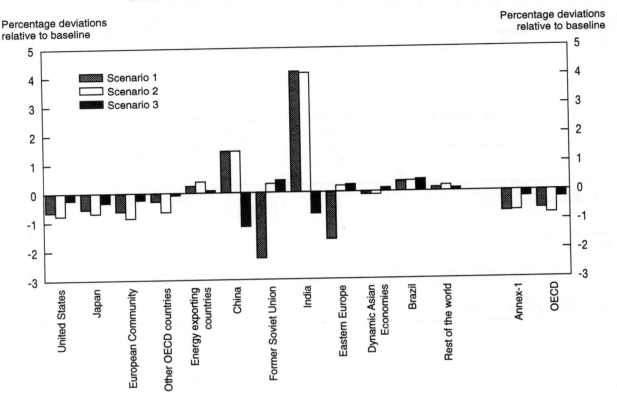

Figure A2.4. **Average real income changes over the period 1990-2050 under alternative international carbon fund agreements**

Note: See text for definition of scenarios 1 to 3.
Source: OECD GREEN model simulations.

relative to baseline if contributions are paid into the fund (Scenario 1), to a gain of 0.3 per cent if carbon tax payments are recycled within the region (Scenario 2). As would be expected under a tax fund with revenue redistribution based on population shares, the regional distribution of economic gains and losses are similar to those implied under the egalitarian quota allocation rule.

Comparing real income changes from these two tax fund agreements with an agreement achieving the same target, but without international recycling of tax revenues (Scenario 3), illustrates how the redistribution of tax funds could modify the regional distribution of net abatement costs: without international revenue recycling, China and India would incur the largest relative income losses compared with gains under each of the tax fund scenarios (Figure A2.4).

Note 3. **Sensitivity Analysis on Baseline Emissions and Abatement Cost**

by

Hiro Lee

This note reports the results of various sensitivity tests under different assumptions and parameter values on: *i)* the baseline carbon emissions scenario; and *ii)* the marginal abatement cost of stabilising Annex 1 CO_2 emissions (as measured by a uniform carbon tax).

A3.1. CO_2 emissions in the baseline

The sensitivity of the baseline CO_2 emissions to GDP growth, the rate of "autonomous energy efficiency improvement" (AEEI), the price and date of introduction of backstop technologies, inter-fuel elasticities of substitution, and supply elasticities of fossil fuels are summarised in Table A3.1. The following twelve sensitivity tests were conducted.

(A1)   High GDP growth: the baseline GDP growth rates are increased by 1 percentage point per annum in all regions.

(A2)   Low GDP growth: the baseline GDP growth rates are reduced by 1 percentage point per annum in all regions.

(A3)   Low AEEI: this parameter is reduced from 1.0 to 0.5 per cent per annum throughout the 1990-2050 period in all regions.

(A4)   Low carbon-based backstop (CBS) price: the price of carbon-based synthetic fuel is reduced by 50 per cent (from \$50/barrel to \$25/barrel).

(A5)   High CBS price: the price of carbon-based synthetic fuel is increased by 50 per cent (from \$50/barrel to \$75/barrel).

(A6)   Low carbon-free backstop (CFBS) prices: the prices of carbon-free liquid fuel and electric backstops are reduced by 50 per cent (from \$100/barrel and 75 mills/kwh to \$50/barrel and 37.5 mills/kwh, respectively).[8]

(A7)   High CFBS prices: the prices of carbon-free liquid fuel and electric backstops are increased by 50 per cent (from \$100/barrel and 75 mills/kwh to \$150/barrel and 112.5 mills/kwh, respectively).

(A8)   A delay in the introduction of carbon-free backstops from 2010 to 2030.

(A9)   High inter-fuel elasticities of substitution: the inter-fuel elasticities of substitution are doubled in all regions (in the base specification, they are set at 0.25 for old capital and 2 for new capital).

(A10)   Low inter-fuel elasticities of substitution: the values of these elasticities are halved in all regions.

(A11)   Low supply elasticity of coal: this parameter value is reduced to 1.0 in all regions (in the base specification, the elasticity ranges between 4 and 5).

(A12)   Low supply elasticity of crude oil in Energy-exporting countries: the supply elasticity of crude oil is set at 0.1 throughout the period (in the base specification, the supply elasticity is gradually reduced from 3 to 1 over the period 1990-2050).

The results of sensitivity tests (A1) and (A2) indicate that the levels of carbon emissions are extremely sensitive to GDP growth rate assumptions.[9] The AEEI is also found to be a key parameter that can influence the emission levels significantly (A3).

While each alternative assumption on GDP growth and AEEI affects the emission levels almost uniformly in all regions, a different specification on backstop prices, inter-fuel elasticities of substitution, and supply elasticities of fossil fuels each leads to substantially different impacts across regions. The results of experiment A4 indicate that when a 50 per cent lower price of carbon-based backstop energy is assumed, it can drastically

Table A3.1. Sensitivity of carbon emissions to changes in key assumptions

Per cent deviations from baseline in 2050 (unless otherwise indicated)

	Baseline CO$_2$ emission in 2050 (million tons)	(A1) High GDP growth	(A2) Low GDP growth	(A3) Low AEEI	(A4) Low CBS price	(A5) High CBS price	(A6) Low CFBS price
OECD countries	5 886	77.7	−44.6	15.5	87.0	−12.7	−40.0
FSU and Eastern Europe	2 884	79.9	−45.8	16.1	12.7	−1.7	−8.2
China and India	4 063	73.3	−44.2	13.4	20.0	5.7	−11.2
Annex 1 countries	8 769	78.4	−45.0	15.7	62.6	−9.1	−29.6
Major emitters	12 832	76.8	−44.7	15.0	49.1	−4.4	−23.8
World	17 040	77.2	−45.0	15.2	60.1	−7.3	−26.4

	(A7) High CFBS price	(A8) Introduction of CFBS in 2030	(A9) High inter-fuel elasticity of substitution	(A10) Low inter-fuel elasticity of substitution	(A11) Low supply elasticity of coal	(A12) Low supply elasticity of oil
OECD countries	10.4	4.8	11.3	−5.5	−5.0	−3.6
FSU and Eastern Europe	0.3	0.2	13.0	−20.1	−15.7	1.0
China and India	0.6	0.4	−6.5	4.5	−32.5	5.2
Annex 1 countries	7.1	3.6	11.8	−10.3	−8.5	−2.4
Major emitters	5.0	3.0	6.0	−5.6	−16.1	−0.9
World	4.7	2.9	6.9	−5.3	−12.9	−0.6

1. (A1)-(A12): see the text for more detailed descriptions of alternative specifications.
2. Figures for (A8) and (A12) indicate deviations from the baseline in 2010.
Source: OECD GREEN Model simulations.

increase emissions relative to the standard specification case because of the very high carbon content of this backstop.[10] The differences across regions in per cent deviations from the baseline in 2050 can be attributed to differences in the consumption shares of carbon-based backstop. In OECD countries the share of synthetic fuel increases from 10.6 per cent (baseline) to 43.9 per cent of total primary energy consumption (by 33.3 percentage points) by 2050, whereas in the former Soviet Union and Eastern Europe it increases from 2.2 to 9.7 per cent (by 7.5 percentage points).

A surprising result is that a higher price of carbon-based backstop energy does not lead to a reduction in carbon emissions (relative to the baseline) in China and India as in the other regions (experiment A5). An extremely large consumption share of coal in China and India, combined with a very high elasticity of substitution between coal and the backstop substitute, can to large extent explain this result.[11] A sharp increase in the relative price of oil after 2030 also contributes to this result. While the share of synthetic fuel declines from 6.8 to 2.1 per cent of the total primary energy consumption in these countries in 2050, the share of coal increases from 77.0 to 83.4 per cent.[12] In other words, the combined consumption share of coal and carbon-based synthetic fuel increases from 83.8 to 85.5 per cent, inducing higher emission levels in China and India relative to the base specification. In OECD countries, by contrast, an increase in the synthetic fuel price reduces the combined share of coal and carbon-based synthetic fuel from 39.3 to 35.7 per cent and increases consumption shares of natural gas, conventional electricity, and the carbon-free electric option in 2050, inducing lower emission levels.

Alternative assumptions for the prices of the carbon-free liquid fuel and the electric backstop lead to expected results (experiments A6 and A7). Lower prices will significantly reduce emission levels in all regions, but the impact is particularly large in OECD countries where the share of carbon-free electric backstops in 2050 increases from 15.6 to 68.7 per cent. Higher prices will have an opposite effect, but the effect on emission levels in the former Soviet Union, Eastern Europe, China and India is negligible because the market shares of carbon-free backstops remain extremely small for these countries. A 20-year delay in the introduction of carbon-free backstop energy has a significant impact on CO$_2$ emissions in 2010 only in the OECD countries (experiment A8).[13]

Different values of inter-fuel elasticities of substitution will also have varying impacts on emission levels across regions (experiments A9 and A10). In OECD countries, a higher degree of substitutability between fossil fuels will speed up the replacement of oil by coal in response to increases in the relative price of oil during the

2020-2050 period, raising CO_2 emissions. In non-OECD countries, both the magnitudes of energy subsidies and their differences across fossil fuels in the base year (1990) play an important role. In the former Soviet Union, for example, crude oil and natural gas have been much more heavily subsidised than coal, and the gradual phase-out of energy subsidies over the 1990-2010 period will sharply increase the domestic prices of oil and gas relative to coal. The higher inter-fuel substitutability will thus intensify the replacement of oil and gas by coal in the former Soviet Union, leading to a higher emission level compared with the baseline. In China, by contrast, coal has been most heavily subsidised while the subsidy rates on oil and gas have been relatively low. As a result, during the period of energy subsidy phase-out the relative price of coal will increase sharply, lowering the market share of coal. In the baseline, the coal share in China and India combined declines from 71.9 per cent in 1990 to 64.5 per cent in 2010. A doubling of inter-fuel substitution elasticities will reduce this share to 54.3 per cent in 2010. Although the consumption share of coal increases more rapidly after 2010 under this assumption, reaching 74.1 per cent by 2050, this value is still 3 percentage points below the baseline share in 2050, resulting in a lower emission level in China and India. A reduction in inter-fuel substitution elasticities has an opposite impact from the increase in these parameter values in each region.[14]

Low supply elasticities of coal and oil will limit the extent of increase in consumption of these fossil fuels resulting from an increase in overall demand for primary energy over time. When low supply elasticity of coal is assumed, it reduces the market share of coal over time compared with the baseline (experiment A11). The larger the baseline market share of coal, the larger the reduction in CO_2 emissions. When low supply elasticity is assumed for oil, however, the impact on CO_2 emissions is ambiguous (experiment A12). It depends upon the relative magnitudes of changes in demand for fuels with different carbon intensities. In OECD countries demand for natural gas (less carbon intensive than oil) increases more than that for coal (more carbon intensive than oil) compared with the baseline, whereas the opposite occurs in the former Soviet Union, Eastern Europe, and particularly China and India. Low supply elasticities of fossil fuels also accelerate the penetration of carbon-free backstop energy in OECD countries, but this effect is insignificant in non-OECD countries.

A3.2. Cost of stabilising emissions in Annex 1 countries

The sensitivity of the cost of stabilising CO_2 emissions by Annex 1 countries at their 1990 levels to different assumptions on key exogenous variables and parameter values is examined here. The following eight sets of sensitivity tests are conducted:

(B1) High GDP growth (the same growth rate assumption as A1).
(B2) Low GDP growth (the same growth rate assumption as A2).
(B3) Low AEEI (the same AEEI parameter assumption as A3).
(B4) Low CBS price (the same carbon-based backstop price assumption as A4).
(B5) Low CFBS prices (the same carbon-free backstop price assumption as A6).
(B6) High inter-fuel elasticities of substitution (the same elasticity specification as A9).
(B7) Low supply elasticity of coal (the same elasticity specification as A11).
(B8) Low supply elasticity of crude oil in Energy-exporting countries (the same elasticity specification as A12).

For each experiment, the uniform carbon tax rate needed to stabilise Annex 1 CO_2 emissions at 1990 levels is plotted in Figure A3.1. The diagram displays a striking contrast between the high sensitivity of carbon tax rates to assumptions on GDP growth, AEEI and backstop prices (B1-B5) and the low sensitivity of tax rates to variations in key parameter values (B6-B8). The former is not surprising since the baseline emissions are highly sensitive to different assumptions on growth rates, AEEI and backstop prices, as shown in the previous section. What is extremely important, however, is understanding the degree of uncertainty on the carbon abatement cost that can result from different GDP growth rates, AEEI and backstop energy prices. Research and development on carbon-free backstop technology appears to be a particularly attractive option if they lead to a reduction in prices of carbon-free backstop fuels.

The reason why the tax rate is insensitive to variations in, for example, inter-fuel elasticities of substitution is the existence of two opposing forces. On the one hand, the larger the values of inter-fuel elasticities, the higher the emission levels (A9 and A10), requiring higher carbon taxes to stabilise Annex 1 emissions. On the other hand, larger elasticity values implies that a given carbon tax rate will ceteris paribus lead to a greater reduction in emissions. The net effect on marginal abatement cost of stabilising Annex 1 emissions depends on the relative magnitudes of these two opposing effects. The result of sensitivity test B6 indicates that the former effect is barely larger than the latter in all years except 2005. Although not plotted in Figure A3.1, variations in inter-

Figure A3.1. Uniform tax rate required to stabilise carbon emissions in Annex 1[1] countries

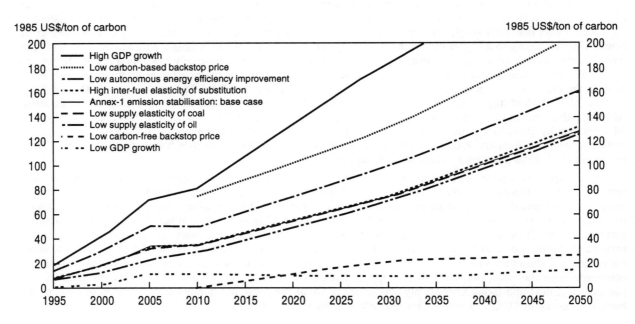

1985 US$/ton of carbon

Legend:
- High GDP growth
- Low carbon-based backstop price
- Low autonomous energy efficiency improvement
- High inter-fuel elasticity of substitution
- Annex-1 emission stabilisation: base case
- Low supply elasticity of coal
- Low supply elasticity of oil
- Low carbon-free backstop price
- Low GDP growth

1. See the text for a more detailed identification of the different scenarios.
Source: OECD GREEN model simulations.

factor elasticities of substitution and Armington trade substitution elasticities are also found to affect the carbon tax rates only marginally.

Lower supply elasticities of fossil fuels will reduce the growth rate of carbon emissions, thereby lowering the tax rate necessary to stabilise Annex 1 emissions (experiments B7 and B8). There is also an opposite secondary effect here; *i.e.*, when the supply elasticity is lower, a higher tax rate is required to reduce a given amount of emissions. An interesting result is that, for the parameter values chosen, the carbon abatement cost is more sensitive to the reduction in the supply elasticity of oil than that of coal. This is explained by two factors. First, the supply elasticity of oil is reduced to 0.1 while that of coal is reduced to only 1.[15] The relative price increase for oil is therefore larger than that for coal. Second, oil is the most important source of energy in Annex 1 countries (OECD countries in particular), at least until 2010 in the baseline scenario. The sharply higher oil price will necessitate a lower carbon tax rate than in the base specification case. After the potential oil supply constraint becomes binding around 2030, the difference in the cost of abatement between the Annex 1 stabilisation scenario with base oil supply elasticity and that with low oil supply elasticity becomes much smaller than in earlier periods.

Note 4.   **The Discount Rate and Climate Change Policy**

by

Hiro Lee

The choice of the discount rate plays a critical role in evaluating the effects of public projects. This choice is particularly important in the cost-benefit analysis of climate change policies due to the extremely long time horizon of global warming and to the desynchronisation between costs of policy action and the resulting benefits (damages avoided). Since CO_2 has a long atmospheric lifetime in the range of 50-200 years, actions (or non-actions) today can affect economic welfare in a distant future. Given the large time horizons of climate change issues, many of the benefits of current policy action will accrue to future generations, while much of the cost of action will be born by the current generation in the form of foregone consumption.

The results obtained in this Annex suggest that unless the appropriate discount rate for climate change policies is low (*e.g.* 3 per cent or less) or the time lag between incurred costs and realized benefits is relatively short, delaying costly abatement policy is justified. Under most circumstances, a gradual abatement policy appears to be preferable to an aggressive abatement policy, but the discount rate plays a critical role in both abatement scenarios.

A4.1.   Sensitivity analysis over the 1990-2100 period

There is considerable disagreement on the appropriate rate of discount for climate change policy. (A brief review of this discussion is provided in Sections A4.3 to A4.5.) Thus, a sensitivity analysis is conducted to examine to what extent the choice of a particular discount rate makes a difference for the comparison of costs and benefits of carbon abatement under a time horizon from 1990 to 2100. In the subsequent section (A4.2), a 300-year time horizon is used, where costs and benefits are significantly more desynchronised. Both cases assume a constant average annual real GDP growth rate of 2 per cent over the entire period.

Two alternative assumptions on the time path of the abatement cost are considered:

1. Early abatement (C1). The cost/GDP ratio increases with time, peaks in year t^*, and gradually declines until a certain abatement target is achieved. Thereafter, the cost of stabilising global atmospheric carbon concentrations will become a constant fraction of world GDP.
2. Gradual abatement (C2). The cost/GDP ratio increases much more gradually than the early abatement scenario. After it reaches a certain ratio, it will remain constant.

In both cases, the abatement cost schedule can be approximated by a logistic function. Specifically, the cost of stabilising the global carbon emissions in year t (C_t) is defined as:

$$C_t = \frac{a_1}{1 + 100 \cdot e^{-b_1 t}} \quad \textit{for } 0 < t \leq t^*$$

$$C_{t^*} = \frac{a_2}{1 + 100 \cdot e^{-b_2(t - t^*)}} \quad \textit{for } t > t^* \qquad \text{(A4.1)}$$

where a_1, a_2, b_1 and b_2 are parameters, and C_t is expressed as a percentage of world GDP. Parameter a_1 determines the maximum level of C_t, a_2 the maximum level of cost reduction from C_{t^*}, and the b parameters determine the shape of the function. Two cost curves, labelled C1 and C2, are drawn in Figure A4.1. They correspond to the two cost scenarios outlined above ($a_2 = 0$ for C2).

Figure A4.1. Benefit and cost curves under alternative specifications over the 1990-2100 period

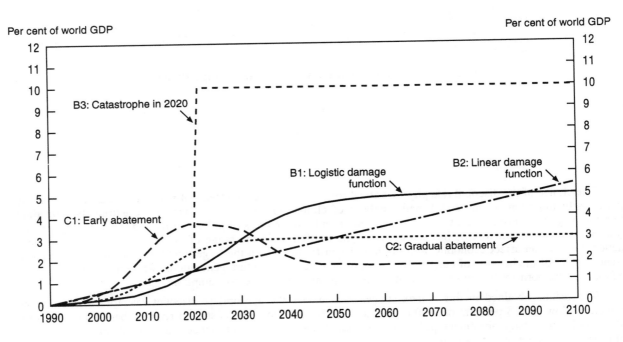

Source: OECD.

The benefit of emission curtailment in year (B_t) is assumed to be the damage that is prevented by stabilisation of global atmospheric carbon concentrations. Three alternative forms of damage functions (damage is also expressed in percentages of world GDP) are considered:

a) Logistic damage function (B1). The damage/GDP ratio in the absence of carbon abatement policy will increase gradually, then reaches a maximum level at some point in the future. It is given by:

$$B_t = \frac{a}{1 + 100 \cdot e^{-bt}} \qquad (A4.2)$$

where it is assumed that benefits of avoided damage will be realised with a lag after costs are born, but the benefit/GDP ratio will become larger than the cost/GDP ratio during the time horizon. This implies that $a > a_1$ and $b < b_1$.

b) Linear/exponential damage function (B2). Damage increases monotonically with a rise in temperature and can be expressed as

$$B_t = |\overline{D}| \left[\frac{(\Delta T)^t}{2.5} \right]^k \qquad (A4.3)$$

where $\overline{D}$ is the damage (in percentage of world GDP) that will result from a rise in the temperature of 2.5°C, ΔT is the difference in the expected change in temperature per annum relative to the base year between no policy action and the global emission stabilisation (t = 0 corresponds to 1990), and k is the exponent in the relationship of damage to warming ($k = 1$ implies a linear function).

c) Catastrophe scenario (B3). Under this hypothesis, a catastrophe occurs at a future date $\tilde{t}$ if no policy action is taken, causing a drastic reduction in GDP equal to $\tilde{D}$: for $t < \tilde{t}$, damage increases at a constant rate β. That is,

$$B_t = \beta t \text{ for } t < \tilde{t}$$

$$B_t = \tilde{D} \text{ for } t \geq \tilde{t} \qquad (A4.4)$$

90

Damage/benefit curves associated with each of the three scenarios are plotted and labelled B1-B3 in Figure A4.1 ($\tilde{t}$ = 2020 in B3).

Four different discount rates (3, 4, 5 and 8 per cent) are applied to compute present values (PVs) of benefits and costs over the 1990-2100 period associated with the corresponding benefit and cost curves.[16] Table A4.1 summarises the ratios of the PV of benefits to the PV of costs for different combinations of benefit and cost curves; the following results are worth noting:

Table A4.1.   **Sensitivity of cost-benefit ratios to the discount rates over the 1990-2100 period**

Benefit curve	Discount rate (%)	Cost-benefit ratio when cost curve is:	
		C1	C2
B1	3.0	1.42	1.31
B1	4.0	1.18	1.22
B1	5.0	0.98	1.13
B1	8.0	0.62	0.91
B2	3.0	1.17	1.08
B2	4.0	0.98	1.02
B2	5.0	0.85	0.97
B2	8.0	0.66	0.95
B3	3.0	3.38	3.13
B3	4.0	2.95	3.06
B3	5.0	2.58	2.97
B3	8.0	1.84	2.67

Source: See the main text for a description of cost and benefit curves.

- The lower the discount rate, the larger the benefit-cost ratio would be. When the discount rate is 3 per cent, all combinations of benefit and cost curves hypothesized for the analysis yield a ratio greater than one. When the discount rate is 8 per cent, the ratio exceeds one only in the catastrophe scenario (B3).
- If the discount rate is 4 per cent or greater, the PV of costs is higher for early abatement (C1) than for more gradual abatement (C2), resulting in higher benefit-cost ratios for the latter abatement scenario; the benefit-cost ratios are much less sensitive to the discount rates when the cost curve is C2.
- If a catastrophe occurs early (2020), then benefits exceed costs for a wide range of discount rates. However, this result depends critically upon the date of occurrence (see next section).

A4.2.   Sensitivity analysis over a 300-year time horizon

The literature on climate change suggests that there is large desynchronisation between costs of carbon abatement and benefits of prevented damage (see *e.g.* Cline, 1992; d'Arge, *et al.*, 1982; Nordhaus, 1991; Peck and Teisburg, 1992). A second set of experiments is thus conducted extending the time horizon to 300 years and using a much longer lag between abatement costs incurred and damages avoided.[17] Two cost and three benefit curves are plotted in Figure A4.2; the results of the sensitivity of the benefit-cost ratios to the discount rates are summarised in Table A4.2.

Three important results emerge. First, when costs and benefits are more desynchronised, the benefit-cost ratios become substantially smaller. For benefit curves B1' and B2', the PV of benefits exceeds that of costs only when the discount rate is 3 per cent (or lower) and a gradual abatement policy (represented by cost curve C2') is implemented. Second, the benefit-cost ratios also become more sensitive to the discount rates, particularly when early abatement (represented by cost curve C1') is pursued. Third, even in the (late) catastrophe scenario, it does not pay to implement an aggressive abatement policy unless the discount rate is low. For gradual abatement, the PV of costs exceeds that of damages avoided for a wide range of discount rates, but it barely exceeds one when the discount rate is relatively high.

Figure A4.2. **Benefit and cost curves under alternative specifications over the 1990-2100 period**

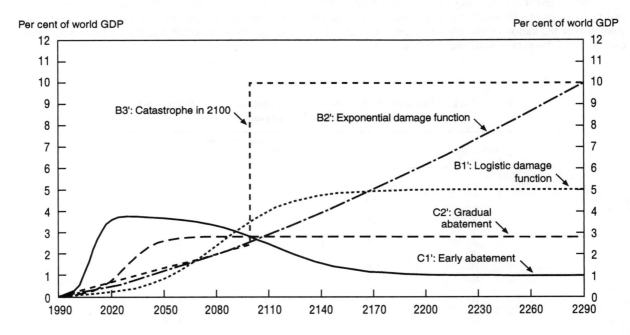

Per cent of world GDP

Source: OECD.

Table A4.2. **Sensitivity of cost-benefit ratios to the discount rates over the 1990-2290 period**

Benefit curve	Discount rate (%)	Cost-benefit ratio when cost curve is:	
		C1'	C2'
B1'	3.0	0.84	1.05
B1'	4.0	0.43	0.75
B1'	5.0	0.27	0.57
B1'	8.0	0.13	0.42
B2'	3.0	0.89	1.11
B2'	4.0	0.45	0.78
B2'	5.0	0.30	0.64
B2'	8.0	0.18	0.59
B3'	3.0	1.63	2.03
B3'	4.0	0.83	1.42
B3'	5.0	0.52	1.11
B3'	8.0	0.33	1.08

Source: See the main text for a description of cost and benefit curves.

A4.3. What is the appropriate rate of discount?

Given the high sensitivity of benefit-cost ratios of carbon abatement projects to the discount rate, the debate on what discount rate should be used for climate change policy is reviewed. Some analysts, Cline (1992) in particular, advocate a low discount rate of about 2 per cent. Others, including the World Bank (*e.g.* Birdsall and Steer, 1993) and Nordhaus (1991), argue that in principle the same discount rate should be used for all projects because investible resources should be channelled to projects with the highest environmental, social, and economic rates of return.[18]

In a first-best world with optimal resource allocation, and if policies do not involve comparisons between generations, the "correct" discount rate can be defined unambiguously: it should equal the social rate of time preference (SRTP), which in turn will equal both the private producer rate of interest and consumer rate of interest (Arrow, 1966; Stiglitz, 1982).[19] In a second-best world, an appropriate rate of discount depends upon several factors, including the types of market imperfections prevailing (*e.g.* an imperfectly competitive capital market and imperfect information) and distortions causing misallocation of resources (*e.g.* various taxes and their distortionary effects). Lind (1982) and Stiglitz (1982) argue that under such circumstances the appropriate rate of discount depends upon the nature of the project under study, and suggest in principle that there should be a different discount rate for each project.

A4.4. Intergenerational comparison

Decisions regarding as to what extent CO_2 emissions are mitigated in the next few decades will affect the welfare of future generations. Mishan (1975) argues that there is no satisfactory way of determining social worth at different points of time. Thus, the extent to which future generations should be entitled to share the resources that are available today is an important policy question. Weiss (1989) contends that future generations are entitled to inherit environmental resources that are at least as good as those the preceding generations.[20] Schelling (1983) argues that the notion of time preference only makes sense for an individual or a group of individuals during their life times, so that there cannot be time preference between generations. Using discounting between generations has little to do with time preference, but rather expresses the degree of concern today's generation has for other generations.

Cline (1992) shares the views of Mishan, Weiss and Schelling and asserts that the "pure" rate of time preference should be set equal to zero. Birdsall and Steer (1993), however, note that a zero pure rate of time preference implies that the welfare of people living two or three centuries from now is valued exactly the same as that of people living today, even if there are many poor people around different parts of the world today. They also cite the evidence that many consumers in developing countries are willing to borrow at high interest rates, indicating that they value current consumption highly relative to future consumption. This would imply a relatively high pure rate of time preference, at least for consumers in developing countries.

Cline's SRTP is a summation of the pure rate of time preference PRTP (which is set at zero) and a discount factor for future income growth representing declining marginal utility of income as per capita income rises. For the second component of the SRTP, he uses a rate of 1.5 per cent, assuming a long-term annual per capita income growth g of 1 per cent and the degree of risk aversion θ (the absolute value of the elasticity of marginal utility with respect to consumption) of 1.5 (Cline, 1992, 249-55). More precisely:

$$SRTP = PRTP + g.\theta = 0 + (1.0)\ (1.5) = 1.5$$

A4.5. Shadow price of capital approach to discounting

Public investment draws resources from both consumption and private investment. The social rate of discount should therefore be a weighted average of the SRTP and the (higher) rate of return on private investment.[21] Arrow (1966), Feldstein (1970), and Lind (1982) suggest that the appropriate procedure is to convert all effects of a project to consumption-equivalents as follows: first, compute a shadow price of capital. Second, multiply the project costs that represent a displacement of private capital by the shadow price. Third, add the resulting amount to the costs that represent a displacement of consumption. The adjusted stream of consumption units should then be discounted at the SRTP.

The shadow price of capital is defined as the present value of the future stream of consumption benefits associated with a dollar of private investment discounted at the SRTP. Different formulations have been suggested by various authors for the computation of the shadow price (*e.g.* Bradford, 1975; Lind, 1982, 1986; Cline, 1992). Within relatively reasonable bounds on the rate of return on private capital and the SRTP, the shadow price of capital typically ranges between 1.0 and 5.0.[22]

Cline (1992) argues that policy actions to reduce the risk of global warming draw resources primarily out of consumption, and this is one of the reasons why he advocates a relatively low rate of discount for greenhouse analysis. Specifically, Cline uses 0.8 for the share of displaced consumption and 0.2 for the share of displaced private investment. Thus, he calculates the discount rate to be:

$$d = \beta_c i + \beta_I \lambda_k i = (0.8)\,(1.5) + (0.2)\,(2)\,(1.5) = 1.8$$

where β_C and β_I are the shares of displaced consumption and private investment, i is the SRTP, and λ_K is the shadow price of capital.

While Birdsall and Steer (1993) have no problem with Cline's formula for computing the discount rate, they question the appropriateness of his choice of parameters β. Following their line of reasoning, what matters for purposes of allocating scarce investment resources is the capital share displaced and those projects with the highest returns should be undertaken. Nordhaus (1991) making a similar argument, notes that a low discount rate for evaluating climate change policy and a considerably higher return on capital are inconsistent. He contends that in this case efficient policy would require investing in high-return capital today and then use the return of those investments to slow climate change in the future.[23]

The World Bank recommends that the appropriate discount rate should be based on the assumption that all of a project's resources can potentially be used for other investments. In addition, if one assumes per capita income growth of 2 per cent and a pure rate of time preference of 1 per cent, then the SRTP would be equal to 4 per cent and the discount rate would be about 8 per cent.[24] The controversy on the appropriate rate of discount, however, is likely to continue because there is a considerable disagreement on the shares of displaced capital investment and consumption, the appropriate pure rate of time preference, and the shadow price of capital.

Note 5. **Risk Aversion and Insurance Premia**

by

Hiro Lee

This note provides several numerical examples of the income a society is willing to forgo ("insurance premia") in order to avoid the risk of climate change. Three alternative scenarios of the damage function under no policy action over the 1990-2100 period are considered and summarised in Figure A5.1. As defined below, there are two possible states in each scenario: one state where catastrophe (or high damage) occurs within the policy relevant time horizon and the other where no damage will ever be incurred.

Scenario 1: With probability p_1 climate change will cause damage equivalent to 0.1t per cent of GDP during the first 60 years (1990-2049), where t = 0 corresponds to year 1990. From 2050-2100, damage will be equivalent to 6 per cent of GDP. The alternative (with probability $1 - p_1$) is that no damage will occur during the 1990-2100 period.

Scenario 2: There is a probability p_2 that damage will be equivalent to 0.1t per cent of GDP during the first 30 years (1990-2019), then it jumps to 10 per cent of GDP from 2020-2100, against the alternative of no damage with probability $(1 - p_2)$.

Figure A5.1. **Uncertainty in damage from climate change**

Scenario 1

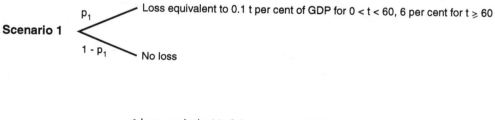

p_1 — Loss equivalent to 0.1 t per cent of GDP for 0 < t < 60, 6 per cent for t ≥ 60

$1 - p_1$ — No loss

Scenario 2

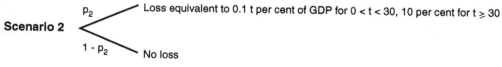

p_2 — Loss equivalent to 0.1 t per cent of GDP for 0 < t < 30, 10 per cent for t ≥ 30

$1 - p_2$ — No loss

Scenario 3

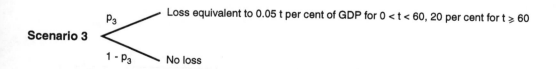

p_3 — Loss equivalent to 0.05 t per cent of GDP for 0 < t < 60, 20 per cent for t ≥ 60

$1 - p_3$ — No loss

Note: The time horizon is from 1990 (t = 0) to 2100 (t = 110).
Source: OECD.

Figure A5.2. **Risk aversion and certainty equivalents**

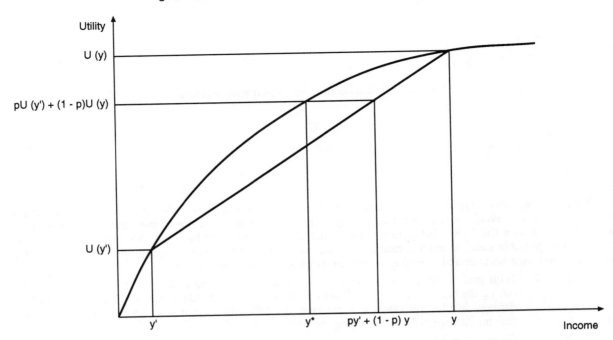

Source: OECD.

Figure A5.3. **Utility functions with constant risk aversion**

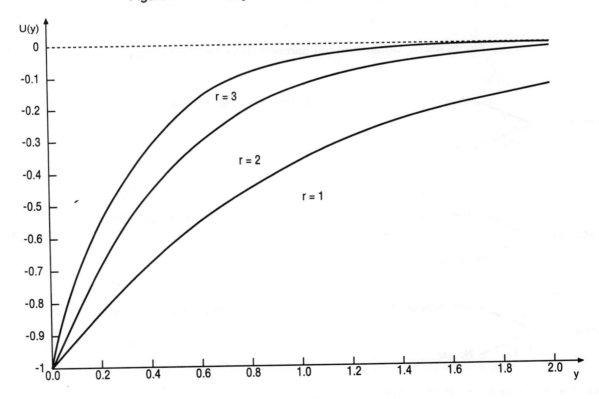

Source: OECD.

Scenario 3: There is a probability p_3 that damage will be equivalent to 0.05t per cent of GDP during the first 60 years (1990-2049), then it jumps to 20 per cent of GDP from 2050-2100, against the alternative of no damage with probability $(1 - p_3)$.

If an individual or the society as a whole is risk averse, then its utility function is concave. Suppose that its income will equal y' with probability p and y with probability $(1 - p)$. If $U(y)$ is continuous and strictly increasing with y, then there exists a certainty equivalent income $y*$ such that:

$$U(y*) = pU(y') + (1 - p)\ U(y) \qquad (A5.1)$$

where $y* < py' + (1 - p)y$. In other words, the society is willing to pay an "insurance premium", Z, equal to:

$$Z = [py' + (1 - p)y] - y* \qquad (A5.2)$$

in order to protect against the risk of income variation (Figure A5.2).

A conventional measure of (absolute) risk aversion (known as the Arrow-Pratt measure of risk aversion) is given by:

$$r(y) = -U''(y)/U'(y) \qquad (A5.3)$$

Solving the differential equation $-U''(y)/U'(y) = r$ *gives the utility function with a constant risk aversion, r.*

$$U(y) = -e^{-ry} \qquad (A5.4)$$

Figure A5.3 plots several utility functions of this functional form for alternative values of r.

Table A5.1. **Output society is willing to forgo to eliminate the risk of climate change**

Scenario [1]	Degree of risk aversion (r)	Discount rate (d), per cent	Probability of disaster (p)	Insurance premium, per cent of GDP [2]
1	**0.5**	5.0	0.10	0.07
1	**1.0**	5.0	0.10	0.16
1	**2.0**	5.0	0.10	0.40
1	**3.0**	5.0	0.10	0.70
1	**4.0**	5.0	0.10	1.00
1	2.0	**3.0**	0.10	3.07
1	2.0	**4.0**	0.10	1.16
1	2.0	**5.0**	0.10	0.40
1	2.0	**8.0**	0.10	0.05
1	2.0	5.0	**0.01**	0.06
1	2.0	5.0	**0.05**	0.24
1	2.0	5.0	**0.20**	0.58
1	2.0	5.0	**0.50**	0.60
2	2.0	**3.0**	0.10	6.15
2	2.0	**4.0**	0.10	3.39
2	2.0	**5.0**	0.10	1.50
2	2.0	**8.0**	0.10	0.15
3	2.0	**3.0**	0.10	9.81
3	2.0	**4.0**	0.10	4.20
3	2.0	**5.0**	0.10	1.16
3	2.0	**8.0**	0.10	0.03

1. See the text for a description of the scenarios.
2. Per cent of annual GDP society is willing to forgo every year during the 1990-2100 period to avoid the risk of climate change.
Note: A 2 per cent per annum growth rate of output is assumed in all cases.
Source: OECD Secretariat calculations.

Assuming that the social welfare function can be represented by equation (A5.4), the per cent of annual income the society is willing to forgo to avoid the risk of climate change is computed under alternative assumptions on *a)* the degree of risk aversion, *b)* the social rate of discount, and *c)* the probability of catastrophe (p_1, p_2 and p_3 in scenarios 1, 2 and 3, respectively). The results, summarised in Table A5.1, are calculated as follows:

   i) In each scenario, the present value (PV) of income in each state is computed, assuming the GDP growth rate (g) of 2 per cent.[25]
   ii) The value of y^* that satisfies equation (A5.1) is computed.[26]
   iii) The PV of aggregate income or GDP society is willing to forgo in order to eliminate the risk (equation A5.2) is calculated.
   iv) The PV is converted to per cent of annual GDP from period 0 forever.

The rational yearly insurance premium (the percentage of GDP the society is willing to sacrifice), is given in the last column of Table A5.1. In the first scenario, it ranges from 0.07 to 1.00 per cent of GDP when the degree of risk aversion (r) is varied from 0.5 to 4.0 while the discount rate (d) and the probability of disaster (p) are fixed at 0.05 and 0.10, respectively. This indicates that the premium is quite sensitive to the degree of risk aversion and is highly sensitive to the discount rate. This is because a small variation in d causes a significant change in the PV of income. When a relatively high d (*e.g.* 8 per cent) is used, the difference in the PVs between the two states becomes extremely small. Finally, a variation in p also changes the premium but by a lesser magnitude than the variation in d or r, especially when it is increased from 0.10. Figure A5.2 suggests that the difference $[py' + (1 - p)y] - y^*$ is relatively insensitive to p for a wide intermediate range of p values.

When the probability of a catastrophic climate change is positive in later years (scenarios 2 and 3), the premium becomes even more sensitive to the discount rate. In the third scenario, the society is willing to sacrifice almost 10 per cent of its income to avoid such a possibility when d is 3 per cent, r is 2.0 and p is 0.1. When d is 8 per cent, however, its willingness to sacrifice any amount of income largely disappears for a wide range of r and p values. This is because even when there is a 10 per cent probability that GDP is reduced by half, if that risk is not present for the next 100 years, it makes very little difference for the PV of income at a 8 per cent discount rate.

In the real world, there are more than two possible states. On the one hand, research to date suggests that the probability of catastrophic climate change which reduces the world GDP by more than 10 per cent is likely to be very low. On the other hand, the probability that no damage will occur for the next 100 years under no policy action is also likely to be very low. Between these two extremes, there exists a number of possibilities for different magnitudes of expected damages, each with an unknown probability. Two possible, polar, states were assumed because the existence of three or more possible states would vastly complicate the analysis and make it less transparent.

Note 6. **Raising Energy Efficiency**

by

Dirk Pilat

In Part 3 of the main paper it was suggested that substantial energy savings might be possible in many energy end-use categories and in primary energy supply. The potential for energy efficiency improvements is shown in Table A6.1. This table shows the present average energy efficiency of various end-use categories and the best, currently available, technology, implying the possibility that substantial energy savings are now available for most end-use categories discussed here.[27]

The main energy uses in the residential sector are space heating and cooling, lighting, water heating and appliances. For all these areas significant technical potential for energy efficiency improvements exists. For the largest source of energy use in this sector, space heating, heat losses can be reduced through improved building designs, improved insulation, and double- or triple-glazing of windows. For domestic appliances, the largest potential for gains in energy efficiency exist in refrigeration. A gap of 30-50 per cent exists between the energy requirements of currently-used installations and commercially available, and cost effective, best practice in this area (IEA/OECD, 1991*b*). Smaller energy-saving potential exists for cooking, washing machines and dish washers. Lighting makes up a small proportion of residential energy use, but offers a considerable energy-saving potential. Incandescent light bulbs can be replaced by energy-efficient compact fluorescent light bulbs.

The main energy uses in the commercial sector are space heating and cooling, lighting and office equipment. Energy costs are often only a small proportion of total cost in this sector, which implies that it is usually not a priority area for management attention. Technical potential for efficiency improvements in space heating and cooling are similar to those of the residential sector. Fluorescent light bulbs are already more widely used in the commercial sector than in the residential sector, but improvements in lighting control systems can provide further substantial savings (IEA/OECD, 1991*b*). In office equipment, some gains are possible as well.

Transport is an end-use sector characterised by rapid growth of energy demand. Most of the expected energy savings in transport are based on improved fuel efficiency of vehicles. The long-term technical potential here is large, but there is often a trade-off between fuel efficiency and other vehicle characteristics, such as performance, costs and safety. Improved fuel efficiency can be achieved by reduced vehicle weight, transmission improve-

Table A6.1.   **Examples of potential energy efficiency improvements by end-use category**

Average potential for all IEA countries

End-use category (unit of energy use in parentheses)	Present average technology	Present best available technology	Presently available savings (%)	Potential best technology[1]	Potential savings (%)
Domestic lighting (Kwh/household/year)	320	120	62.5	100	68.8
Refrigerators (Kwh/litre/year)	2	1.5	25.0	0.45	77.5
Washing machines (Kwh/kg)	0.62	0.45	27.5	0.30	51.7
Passenger cars (litres/100 km)	10	8	20.0	6.3	37.0
Aluminium production (Kwh/kg)	16.45	13.5	18.0	12.0	27.1
Paper pulp production (toe/metric ton)	0.43	0.27	37.3	0.24	44.2

1.   Energy-efficiency improvements obtained by integrating demonstrated state-of-the-art technology (as of 1990) into current practice between 1990 and 2005.
Source: IEA/OECD (1991), *Energy Efficiency and the Environment*, Paris.

ments, aerodynamic designs, engine design and various other technical aspects which reduce energy loss (IEA/OECD, 1991b). The use of electric vehicles, the introduction of speed limits, increased use of public transport and telecommuting may also provide considerable energy savings, but there is a trade-off with performance, mobility and other transport characteristics relevant to consumers. This implies that such measures are far from being perfect substitutes of present technology and are therefore difficult to evaluate in a cost-benefit analysis.

The industrial sector accounts for approximately one-third of energy use in OECD countries. There is much variation in energy-intensity between industries. The more energy-intensive industries are paper and paperboard, aluminium, iron and steel, cement and gypsum. In these industries, energy inputs constitute more than 20 per cent of total production costs (IEA/OECD, 1991b), making energy efficiency a priority area for management attention. However, many opportunities for energy saving in the industrial sector remain: there is scope for improved process design, more efficient drives and motors and the recycling of process heat. IEA/OECD (1991b) suggests possible energy savings between 10 and 40 per cent in energy-intensive industries such as aluminium, steel, pulp and cement, mostly based on a move from average practice to available best practice.

The production of electricity also offers significant opportunities for reduced distribution and generation losses, for co-generation and for retrofitting of existing power plants with more energy-efficient and cost-effective technologies (IEA/OECD, 1993). An illustration of efficiency characteristics and carbon emissions from existing and emerging fossil-fuel power plants is provided in Table A6.2. Compared with current average coal-based power plants, CO_2 emission reductions of 15 to 20 per cent appear to be currently feasible, and additional reductions of 20 to 25 per cent may be available in the medium term as technology in this area improves further (IEA/OECD, 1991a, 1993). These modern power plants typically also emit much less sulphur and nitrous oxides per unit of usable energy than current technologies.

Co-generation is a more efficient method of energy use, although it can also be seen as a more efficient method to produce electricity. It has various applications, primarily in factories needing process heat, but also in district heating systems. Combined generation of heat and power (CHP) can lead to overall efficiency of energy conversion up to 80 per cent (compared to less than 40 per cent in currently used technologies; see IEA/OECD, 1993), in particular, if new power plants can be located close to industrial areas in need of process heat, or to residential areas to provide district heating.

Efficiency measures may be capable of achieving a significant reduction of carbon emissions. However, although such measures lead to a one-time fall in emissions, they do not help in reducing the growth in energy demand permanently. In this respect, efficiency measures alone are likely to be insufficient to solve the problem of global warming. They also may have a take-back effect attached, *i.e.* the initial savings of increased energy efficiency may be partly offset by income and substitution effects entailed by the induced fall in relative prices of energy.

Table A6.2. **Efficiency and CO_2 emissions from fossil-fuelled power plants**[1]

Technology	Power Plant efficiency (%)	CO_2 emissions (kg/Mwh)	CO_2 emission reduction compared with conventional technology (%)
Coal power plants:			
Conventional technology	33	1 000	0
Improved conventional technology	38	850	15
Emerging technologies[2]	42-48	650-750	25-35
Emerging technologies combined with fuel cells	55-60	550-600	40-45
Gas power plants:			
Conventional technology	45-50	400-450	0
Gas-fired power plant combined with fuel cells	65-70	300	25-34

1. Figures are indicative, precise emission levels depend upon plant design.
2. For instance, PFBC (Pressured Fluidised Bed Combustion) and IGCC (Integrated Gasification Combined Cycle) power plants. These are technologies which are currently being installed.
Source: Based on IEA/OECD, *Electric Power Technologies: Environmental Challenges and Opportunities*, Paris, 1993

Notes

1. The risk with any interpretation of the FCCC is that the particular interpretation may not be accepted by all signatory parties: critics may feel that specific targets or types of policy instrument are being advocated. The interpretation of the FCCC presented here is not intended this way, but aims to provide a structure upon which possible international agreements can be evaluated in order to inform negotiators; the objective is **not** to recommend a particular negotiating stance for any of the Parties.

2. Mexico is not included among Annex 2 countries.

3. For a detailed description of the model see Burniaux, Nicoletti and Oliveira Martins (1992).

4. IPCC (1992).

5. See OECD (1993), p. 145.

6. See Weyant (1993).

7. In particular the amount and criteria according to which tax revenues are redistributed could be easily tailored to policy priorities: to support technology transfer to developing countries, or any other relevant criterion, including those not related to carbon emissions.

8. Mills are one-thousandth (0.001) of a U.S. dollar.

9. A 1 percentage point increase and 1 percentage point reduction in the GDP growth rate will have substantially different magnitudes of impact on energy demand when cumulated over 60 years. A simple comparison between $(1 + 0.01)^{60} = 1.82$ (82 per cent increase) and $(1 - 0.01)^{60} = 0.55$ (45 per cent reduction) illustrates this point.

10. The carbon emission coefficient for carbon-based backstop energy used in GREEN is 39.0 tons of carbon per terajoule, based on Energy Modelling Forum No. 12 assumptions. As a comparison, the coefficient on coal (the most carbon-intensive ''natural'' fossil fuel) is 24.7.

11. A Constant Elasticity of Substitution (CES) of 10 is assumed in GREEN.

12. The ratio of demand for coal to that for synthetic fuel depends upon the price of coal relative to synthetic fuel, the substitution elasticity and the share parameters. See Van der Mensbrugghe (1994, p. 29) for a detailed exposition of how aggregate energy demand is decomposed into demand for conventional fuels and their associated backstop substitutes.

13. By 2050, the impact of a late introduction of carbon-free backstop energy on CO_2 emissions becomes negligible even in OECD countries as the market share of backstops will mainly be determined by the relative prices of backstops. However, atmospheric CO_2 concentrations would still be affected because annual emissions between 2010 and 2050 would have been higher.

14. It is worth noting that, as shown in columns (A9) and (A10) of Table A3.1, the impact of doubling or halving the elasticities of substitution is not symmetric.

15. The coal supply elasticity of 1.0 is quite low considering that the degree of competition in the coal market is relatively high in most countries and that coal reserves are assumed to be infinite over the period to 2050.

16. The 3 per cent discount rate used here approximately corresponds to Cline's (1992) 2 per cent discount rate because our assumption on the real growth of output (2 per cent) is 1 percentage point higher than Cline's assumption.

17. Extending the time horizon from 300 years to infinity makes very little difference to the present values of costs and benefits, unless the discount rate is zero.

18. It may also be argued that because uncertainty is particularly large in the context of climate change analysis, this should *ceteris paribus* drive up the discount rate.

19. The SRTP is the rate at which society is willing to exchange consumption today for consumption in the future. While most theoretical models assume an identical rate of time preference for all individuals (the representative consumer assumption), in practice this rate should be computed as a weighted average of individual rates of time preference.

20. She cites international law in areas such as fishery rights and marine pollution to support her argument.

21. The private rate of return on investment is greater than the SRTP because of taxation of capital income, uncertainty of investment returns, and capital market imperfections.

22. Lind (1986) suggests that the best point estimate of the shadow price is about 2.5, whereas Cline (1992, Annex 6A) estimates that the shadow price values are typically in the range of 1.5 to 2.

23. An immediate policy action is of course justified if it gives a net benefit at a relatively high discount rate (*e.g.* 8 per cent).

24. Since the opportunity cost of capital is generally lower in industrialised countries than in developing countries, Birdsall and Steer (1993) advocate a lower rate (*e.g.* 5 per cent) for the former.

25. For example, the present value of income in the ''no damage'' scenario, and for an infinite time horizon will be:

$$PV(y) = \sum_{t=0}^{\infty} \left[\frac{1+g}{1+d} \right]^{t} y_0 = \frac{1+d}{d-g} \ y_0 \ , \ d > g$$

Changing the time horizon from infinity to 110 years will affect $PV(y)$ marginally to:

$$PV(y) = \frac{1+d}{d-g} \left[1 - \left(\frac{1+g}{1+d} \right)^{111} \right] y_{0'} \ , \ d > g$$

Since an increase in the growth rate will have an almost identical effect as the same percentage point reduction in the discount rate (not identical because d is both in the numerator and denominator of the first term), the sensitivity of insurance premia to the growth rate assumption is not experimented with.

26. This implies that:

$$y^* = - \ \frac{\log \{ - [pU(y') + (1-p)U(y)] \}}{r}$$

where all income terms are expressed in present values.

27. More extensive discussion is available in specialised studies (for instance, IEA/OECD, 1989; IEA/OECD, 1991).

Bibliography

Arrow, K.J. (1966), "Discounting and public investment criteria", in Kneese, A.V. and Smith, S.C. eds., *Water Research*, Johns Hopkins University Press for Resources for the Future, Baltimore.

Arrow, K.J. (1982), "The rate of discount on public investments with imperfect capital markets", in Lind, R.C. *et al.*, eds., *Discounting for Time and Risk in Energy Policy*, Resources for the Future, Washington DC.

Baumol, William J. (1978), "On the social rate of discount", *American Economic Review*, Vol. 68 (September), pp. 788-802.

Birdsall, Nancy and Andrew Steer (1993), "Act now on global warming – but don't cook the books", *Finance and Development*, Vol. 30 (March), pp. 6-8.

Bradford, David F. (1975), "Constraints on government investment opportunities and the choice of discount rate", *American Economic Review*, Vol. 65 (December), pp. 887-99.

Burniaux, J.M., Nicoletti, G. and Oliveira Martins, J. (1992), "GREEN: A global model for quantifying the costs of policies to curb CO_2 emissions", *OECD Economic Studies*, No. 19, Winter.

Chichilnisky, Graciela and Geoffrey Heal (1993), "Global environmental risks", *Journal of Economic Perspectives*, Vol. 7 (Fall), pp. 65-86.

Cline, William R. (1992), *The Economics of Global Warming*, Institute of International Economics, Washington DC.

Cline, William R. (1993), "Give greenhouse abatement a fair chance", *Finance and Development*, Vol. 30 (March), pp. 3-5.

d'Arge, Ralph, William, C., Schulze, D. and David, S. Brookshire (1982), "Carbon dioxide and intergenerational choice", *American Economic Review*, Vol. 72 (May), pp. 251-56.

Feldstein, Martin S. (1970), "Financing in the evaluation of public expenditure", Discussion Papers 132, Harvard Institute of Economic Research, Cambridge, MA.

Gramlich, Edward M. (1990), *A Guide to Benefit-Cost Analysis*, 2nd edition, Prentice Hall, Englewood Cliffs, NJ.

IEA/OECD (1989), *Electricity End-Use Efficiency*, Paris.

IEA/OECD (1991*a*), *Greenhouse Gas Emissions – The Energy Dimension*, Paris.

IEA/OECD (1991*b*), *Energy Efficiency and the Environment*, Paris.

IEA/OECD (1993), *Electric Power Technologies: Environmental Challenges and Opportunities*, Paris.

IPCC (1992), *Climate Change 1992, The Supplementary Report to the IPCC Scientific Assessment*, Cambridge University Press.

Kolb, Jeffrey A. and Joel D. Scherage (1990), "Discounting the benefits and costs of environmental regulations", *Journal of Policy Analysis and Management*, Vol. 9, pp. 381-90.

Kreps, David M. (1990), *A Course in Microeconomic Theory*, Harvester Wheatsheaf, New York.

Lind, Robert C. (1982), "A primer on the major issues relating to the discount rate for evaluating national energy options", in Lind, R.C. *et al.*, eds., *Discounting for Time and Risk in Energy Policy*, Resources for the Future, Washington DC.

Lind, Robert C. (1986), "The shadow price of capital: implications for the opportunity cost of public programs, the burden of debt, and tax reform", in Heller, W.P. *et al.*, eds., *Social Choice and Public Decision Making: Essays in Honor of Kenneth Arrow*, Vol. 1, Cambridge University Press, Cambridge.

Manne, Alan, Robert Mendelsohn, and Richard Richels (1993), "MERGE – a model for evaluating regional and global effects of GHG reduction policies", manuscript, Stanford University, November.

Mishan, E.J. (1975), *Cost Benefit Analysis: An Informal Introduction*, Allen and Unwin, London.

Nordhaus, William D. (1991), "Economic approaches to greenhouse warming", in Dornbusch, R. and Poterba, J.M. eds., *Global Warming: Economic Policy Responses*, MIT Press, Cambridge, MA.

OECD (1993), "The costs of cutting carbon emissions: results from global models", *OECD Documents*, Paris.

Peck, Stephen C. and Thomas J. Teisberg (1992), "CETA: a model for carbon emissions trajectory assessment", *Energy Journal*, Vol. 13, pp. 55-77.

Schelling, Thomas C. (1983), "Climate change: implications for welfare and policy", in National Research Council, *Changing Climate*, National Academy Press, Washington DC.

Stiglitz, Joseph E. (1982), "The rate of discount for benefit-cost analysis and the theory of the second best", in Lind, R.C. *et al.*, eds., *Discounting for Time and Risk in Energy Policy*, Resources for the Future, Washington DC.

Van der Mensbrugghe, Dominique (1994), "GREEN: the reference manual", *OECD Economics Department Working Papers*, No. 143, OECD, Paris.

Weiss, Edith B. (1989), *In Fairness to Future Generations: International Law, Common Patrimony, and Intergenerational Equity*, The United Nations University and Transnational, Tokyo and Dobbs Ferry, NY.

Weyant, J. (1993), "Costs of reducing global carbon emissions", *Journal of Economic Perspectives*, Vol. 7, Autumn.

Annex B

UNILATERAL EMISSION CONTROL, ENERGY-INTENSIVE INDUSTRIES AND CARBON LEAKAGES

by

Joaquim Oliveira Martins

TABLE OF CONTENTS

B1. Introduction 109

B2. Emission abatement and competitiveness in energy-intensive sectors 109
     B2.1. Energy-intensive industries and carbon emissions 109
     B2.2. Competitiveness and comparative advantage 111

B3. Unilateral abatement policy and carbon leakages 112
     B3.1. Leakage mechanisms: an illustrative case study with GREEN 112
            B3.1.1. Changes in trade flows 113
            B3.1.2. Changes in world energy markets 113
     B3.2. How sensitive are carbon leakages to alternative model specifications? 115
     B3.3. Other possible leakage mechanisms 118

B4. Carbon leakages in the context of an agreement involving FCCC – Annex 1 countries 119

Notes 122

Bibliography 124

B1. Introduction

This annex analyses two policy issues related to an agreement that has only partial geographical coverage, *e.g.* a scenario in which the stabilisation of emissions is achieved unilaterally within FCCC-Annex 1 countries.[1] The first issue, concerns the view that unilateral emission curtailment will be particularly damaging for the competitiveness of energy-intensive industries and, for this reason, these industries should be exempted from carbon taxation.

The second issue concerns the possibility that emission reduction in one region could be to some extent offset by increased emissions elsewhere due to "carbon leakages". These leakages would entail a loss of effectiveness and weaken the rationale for taking unilateral actions in the first place.

This annex shows how energy-intensive industries relate to the level of carbon emissions and discusses the notion of competitiveness. The effects of carbon leakages will be analysed, and, in particular, sensitivity analysis is carried out in order to identify on which key parameters the size of leakages depends. Even in the case where the leakage rate is small, the results show that there could be large impacts of Annex 1 unilateral of emissions on trade flows, especially for energy and energy-intensive products.

B2. Emission abatement and competitiveness in energy-intensive sectors

Proposals to tax fossil-fuels in order to control carbon emissions have raised concerns about adverse effects for the competitiveness of energy-intensive sectors (EIS)[2, 3] and hence have led to suggestions that those sectors be exempt from taxation for environmental purposes.[4] Two problems with this suggestion are discussed here: the role of EIS sectors in total carbon emissions and the appropriate interpretation of the notion of competitiveness.

B2.1. Energy-intensive industries and carbon emissions

Using International Energy Agency (IEA) statistics it is possible to identify the consumption of fossil-fuels in the energy-intensive sectors. The share of emissions from industrial sectors in overall emissions is given in Table B1. In 1991, emissions from the aggregate manufacturing industry represented between 17 to 25 per cent, and those from Energy-intensive industries 11 to 21 per cent of total carbon emissions in OECD countries. From Table B1 it can also be seen that in a majority of countries carbon emissions from EIS grew faster than those in other industrial sectors over the period 1960-91. As an indication of the economic weight of these sectors and potential adjustment problems, Table B2 shows the share of manufacturing employment in the energy-intensive sectors in some OECD countries. Depending on the country, the share in total manufacturing employment of the energy-intensive sectors ranges from 10 to 18 per cent by the end of 1980s.

A cross-sectional analysis allows for a quantification of the link between EIS specialisation and emissions. Data used are from the GREEN model database, which contains input/output tables and data on fossil-fuel consumption for 70 countries in 1985. An equation was estimated, relating emissions per capita to income per capita, average primary energy prices and a variable reflecting country-specialisation in energy-intensive sectors, the share of gross output of energy-intensive sectors (*EISGO*) in total gross output (*GO*). Results are as follows:[5]

$$Log\left(\frac{Em}{N}\right) = \underset{(-5.2)}{-3.76} + \underset{(18.2)}{0.94}\ Log\left(\frac{GDP}{N}\right) \underset{(-4.2)}{-0.35}\ Log\ (P_E) + \underset{(4.8)}{0.37}\ Log\left(\frac{EISGO}{GO}\right)$$

$$Nobs = 70 \qquad R^2 = 0.85$$

Table B1. Shares of energy-intensive and total industries in carbon emissions[1]

	Total economy — Carbon emissions (in million tons)			Total economy — Emission average p.a. growth rate (in %)	Total industry — Carbon emissions (in % of total economy)			Total industry — Emission average p.a. growth rate (in %)	Energy-intensive industries — Carbon emissions (in % of total economy)			Energy-intensive industries — Emission average p.a. growth rate (in %)
	1960	1973	1991	1960-91	1960	1973	1991	1960-91	1960	1973	1991	1960-91
OECD												
United States	824.8	1 354.4	1 469.3	1.7	27.2	23.1	17.4	0.1	..	..	..	..
Japan	74.7	281.9	326.2	4.0	38.5	40.6	29.3	2.7	15.5	32.8	21.1	4.3
Germany	140.5	303.5	269.0	2.3	31.1	25.6	19.3	1.1	15.2	17.2	15.0	2.3
France	72.5	147.8	121.6	1.2	35.7	27.1	24.8	0.1	17.9	17.5	18.9	2.0
Italy	32.6	105.1	119.5	3.4	37.1	31.1	20.7	1.3	18.7	24.7	17.0	3.0
United Kingdom	158.4	190.2	166.6	-0.2	25.7	26.3	16.2	-2.2	14.1	17.1	10.5	-1.6
Canada	55.2	107.2	130.8	2.8	24.9	25.2	25.4	3.3	8.5	12.5	18.9	6.7
Australia	30.4	52.5	77.1	2.9	39.2	23.9	17.3	0.0	8.8	11.4	11.2	3.6
Mexico	..	34.8	94.6	5.9	..	22.1	22.7	6.5	..	8.6	17.5	10.6
Spain	14.3	43.2	67.0	4.9	34.2	36.1	22.3	3.4	18.4	27.9	18.8	6.1
Non-OECD[2]												
Indonesia	..	9.6	41.1	8.1	..	19.6	22.6	9.2	..	4.0	16.2	15.2
Venezuela	..	17.6	29.4	2.9	..	17.4	27.3	5.6	..	3.5	1.5	10.7
Iran	..	18.5	55.1	6.1	..	35.8	11.9[3]	2.9	..	2.0	0.6	-4.9
Iraq	..	4.3	12.5	8.0	..	14.0	3.7[4]	-1.5	..	..	..	..
South Africa	..	47.2	95.5	4.3	..	30.5	20.0	1.5	..	16.9	11.7	2.0
Algeria	..	3.6	17.5	9.7	..	17.1	8.3	7.6	..	..	..	..
Egypt	..	6.1	24.4	8.0	..	33.6	35.7	7.7	..	3.4	5.7	9.8
China	..	258.0	649.0	5.2	..	..	30.5[3]	5.1	..	..	30.5[3]	6.5
Former Soviet Union	..	719.8	947.0	1.9	..	29.4	24.2[3]	0.6	..	20.4	19.6	5.2
India	..	62.1	177.4	5.6	..	37.6	33.2	5.2	..	4.8	5.7	2.1
Bulgaria	..	18.7	16.1	0.7	..	13.2	13.2	5.0	..	14.1	10.1	-1.2
CSR	..	56.9	51.8	0.2	..	35.0	18.2	-3.5	..	9.0	8.2	2.3
Hungary	..	18.7	18.1	0.5	..	20.3	11.1	-1.7	..	14.2	7.5	-1.5
Poland	..	88.4	93.7	1.2	..	17.7	10.3	-1.3	..	8.1	15.0	7.0
Romania	..	33.4	34.6	1.9	..	29.1	27.8	1.6	..	12.2	0.0	4.4
Yugoslavia	..	19.6	29.0	3.6	..	32.6	0.0	-0.2	..	..	..	..
Hong Kong	..	3.2	10.8	6.9	..	18.6	14.5	4.6	..	..	..	..
Philippines	..	8.4	11.6	1.5	..	20.5	18.8	1.0	..	2.8	11.1	8.7
South Korea	..	20.0	78.5	7.4	..	29.7	36.1	8.1	..	7.6	23.5[5]	21.9
Taiwan	..	11.2	36.2	6.5	..	36.4	37.0	6.9	..	22.7	30.1	8.6
Thailand	..	7.2	26.2	6.7	..	18.8	14.5	4.6	..	10.6	7.6	4.0
Brazil	..	37.0	69.8	3.7	..	27.5	29.7	4.3	..	18.5	25.1	5.7
Argentina	..	26.6	28.9	0.7	..	16.7	15.7	0.2	..	2.3	4.3	3.6

1. Total fossil-fuel related carbon emissions. ".." indicates that data are not available.
2. Growth rate from 1971 to 1991 (or last available year).
3. Corresponds to 1990 data.
4. Corresponds to 1988 data.
5. Corresponds to 1983 data.

Source: IEA, Energy Balances for Member and non-Member countries and Secretariat's calculations.

Table B2. Employment in energy-intensive industries (EIS)

In thousands

| | | ISIC Codes | | | | | | Share of EIS/total manufacturing |
		341	351	352	371	372	300	
Australia	1988	27.1	18.0	33.9	46.9	33.2	1 219.0	13%
Canada	1988	116.3	87.6	0.0	59.0	43.9	1 859.4	16%
Finland	1990	41.4	13.8	10.5	12.6	4.5	462.7	18%
France	1990	103.3	118.8	172.5	185.0	49.5	4 425.9	14%
Germany (West)	1989	204.1	342.7	313.6	466.0	183.8	8 696.0	17%
Italy	1988	146.5	159.4	135.4	135.4	30.7	5 085.1	12%
Japan	1989	357.0	260.3	317.4	470.8	168.2	15 118.0	10%
Netherlands	1988	21.9	57.8	33.0	19.9	14.1	921.0	16%
Norway	1989	11.8	9.3	5.6	8.4	11.8	288.8	16%
Sweden	1989	56.2	20.4	23.7	33.4	12.0	979.8	15%
United Kingdom	1989	110.9	160.5	185.1	153.4	60.6	5 512.0	12%
United States	1989	713.4	430.9	536.2	478.8	286.2	19 418.0	13%

ISIC Codes:
341. Paper and pulp products;
351. Industrial chemicals;
352. Other chemicals;
371. Iron and steel;
372. Non-ferrous metals;
300. Total manufacturing.
Source: STAN database (see OECD, 1992).

Where Em, *N*, *GDP* and P_E are, respectively, total carbon emissions, population, gross domestic product[6] and the average level of energy prices.[7] Student-t statistics are in parenthesis. This equation accounts relatively well for the cross-country variance of emissions per capita, and the estimated coefficients have high t-statistics and the expected signs. There is an approximate unitary elasticity between emissions per capita and income per capita and a negative relation between emissions and energy prices. The estimated coefficient of the EIS specialisation variable is significantly different from zero and has the expected sign. On average, a doubling in the share of EIS in total gross output would imply roughly 30 per cent higher emissions per capita.

This empirical evidence strengthens the argument that the EIS group should not be excluded from a carbon abatement policy. Indeed, for a given absolute target exemption of EIS will entail a serious efficiency loss because the rest of the economy has to bear the extra-burden of emission reduction.[8]

B2.2. Competitiveness and comparative advantage

Policy discussion is occasionally complicated by casual use of the notion of competitiveness. First, the most relevant concept for the analysis of the link between international trade in energy-intensive products and carbon emission abatement is comparative advantage rather than competitiveness. The confusion between competitiveness and comparative advantage often arises from the fact that the former should be defined in absolute terms, whereas the latter is a concept to be defined in relative terms.

For example, a country having an absolute cost advantage over all other countries in a given range of sectors can be said to be the most competitive. However, if its *relative* competitiveness is higher in some sectors than in others, the country has a comparative advantage only for the former sectors. Imposing a carbon tax shifts the comparative advantage in the country imposing an emission constraint away from energy-intensive industries to other sectors in the economy. Exempting energy-intensive industries from carbon taxation will shift the comparative advantage against non-energy intensive sectors. Environmental policy might well be aiming to induce a loss of competitiveness for some products and, in this way, create the right economic incentives for an overall decrease in environmentally damaging activities. However, this does not preclude the need for international co-ordination of environmental policies because emission or pollution spillovers among countries can affect the effectiveness of a unilateral policy. The leakage issue is an illustration of this point.

111

B3. Unilateral abatement policy and carbon leakages

The effectiveness of unilateral action to curb emissions can be affected by a phenomenon called "carbon leakages" or "offshore effects",[9] referring to changes in carbon emissions in non-participating regions induced by abatement efforts in the participating regions. These leakages may be driven by different mechanisms:

i) Changes in the trade structure; imposing an energy related tax will change the comparative advantage in the production of energy-intensive goods entailing changes in the location of their production.

ii) Changes in world energy prices; imposing a tax on carbon emissions (or energy) will reduce energy demand and thus depress world energy prices; this may stimulate energy demand in non-participating regions. It may also change the relative prices among different energy sources and induce inter-fuel substitution in non-participating regions and a change in their emissions.

iii) Regional terms of trade gains and losses due the carbon abatement policy; the changes in energy prices induce terms of trade losses or gains. The corresponding change in real income will lead to regional shifts in consumption and carbon emissions.

iv) Reduced income of energy-exporting regions; reduced rents for energy exporters entail reduction in their income, lower energy use and lower emissions.

These various mechanisms may work in opposite directions. The next sections will provide a quantitative assessment of these different leakage channels.

A leakage indicator can be defined as one minus the change in world emissions as a proportion of the domestic emission cut. This indicator will be positive (negative) if Rest of the World emissions increase (decrease) as a result of the domestic emission cut. The change in RoW emissions depends on the general equilibrium effects linking the domestic to the world economy. The increase in RoW emissions may even more than offset the domestic abatement effort. In that case, a country may actually worsen the environmental problem by implementing a unilateral abatement policy.[10] When implemented unilaterally, an effective abatement policy should then take into account these transborder ("offshore") effects.[11]

A quantification of the leakage effect requires a general equilibrium framework embodying a consistent and complete treatment of trade flows. An effective way to identify and gauge the main leakage mechanisms at work is to simulate a specific case and proceed to a sensitivity analysis around the base specification of the model.

B3.1. Leakage mechanisms: an illustrative case study with GREEN[12]

Given the many mechanisms at work it is convenient to analyse the effects of unilateral abatement action in the case of only one region. The EC countries' group was selected for illustrative purposes, though qualitatively similar results could be obtained with any other large OECD country or region.

Assume that the EC acts alone to stabilize its emissions at their 1990 levels, this abatement target being achieved by means of a carbon tax applied at the level of primary energy demand. The results for this policy experiment are given in Table B3: the *ex-ante* reduction in world emissions corresponds to the EC emission cut whereas the *ex-post* reduction is the net result incorporating all general equilibrium mechanisms represented in the model.

In this scenario, the net leakage rate in GREEN appears to be small, reaching a maximum of 6 per cent.[13] The leakage rate tends to decline throughout the period to become negative after 2030. The breakdown of the leakage rate by region helps to explain this time profile.

In Table B3 the twelve regions of GREEN are grouped according to their leakage profile. In the Energy-exporting LDCs,[14] the former-Soviet Union, China and India the leakage rate is negative (*i.e.* there is a net decrease in emissions in those regions in response to abatement action in the EC). Other regions, including OECD countries, are characterised by positive leakages in earlier periods which decrease progressively, therefore contributing to the fall in the total leakage rate. From a strict effectiveness viewpoint, the unilateral action should be extended to the regions where the leakages are positive, in this case the other OECD regions, DAEs and Brazil. In other regions, the emission spillover is already contributing to the reduction of world emissions through negative leakages.[15]

Table B3. **Leakage effect when the EC region stabilises emissions unilaterally** [1]

	1995	2000	2005	2010	2030	2050
Emissions in the EC – Baseline scenario [2]	893	961	1 001	1 030	1 213	1 530
Reductions in EC emissions or						
Ex-ante reductions in World Emissions [2]	–72	–137	–177	–206	–389	–707
Ex-post reductions in World Emissions [2]	–67	–129	–170	–203	–402	–718
Leakage rate (in%)	6	6	4	1	–3	–2
of which: OECD [3]	8	8	8	5	1	–1
DAEs, CEETs, Brazil and RoW	3	3	3	2	1	3
Energy-exporting LDCs	–1	–2	–2	–2	–2	0
Former Soviet Union, China and India	–4	–5	–5	–5	–4	–3

1. Emissions are stabilised at their 1990 levels.
2. In million tons of carbon.
3. Excluding Mexico.
Note: Figures may not add-up due to rounding.
Source: OECD GREEN Model simulations.

B3.1.1. Changes in trade flows

The changes in sectoral trade balances relative to the baseline scenario for four broad categories of goods are shown in Table B4: Agriculture, Energy, Energy-intensive goods and all Other Goods and Services. The direction and intensity of trade in Agricultural products is not much affected by the unilateral action of the EC. Not surprisingly, the main changes are in the energy and energy-intensive sectors.

Before 2030, the energy balance improves relative to the baseline because of the reduction of energy demand, however this trend is reversed subsequently. The reason is that after the phasing-out of carbon-based synthetic fuels the refined oil sector in the EC must rely relatively more on imported crude oil (see Table B5 below).[16]

The competitiveness losses incurred by energy-intensive sectors result in a deterioration of their trade balance in the EC. In counterpart, in all other regions the trade balance in energy-intensive industries improves relative to baseline. At the same time, this sectoral trade adjustment leads to an increased EC trade surplus in other goods & services[17] by the end of the period and a parallel decline for this sectoral trade balance in all other regions. This aspect is well-known in trade theory but is often neglected in the policy debate. In fact, inducing a loss of comparative advantage in energy-intensive sectors *necessarily* implies improving the comparative advantage in the rest of the economy.

These movements in trade flows illustrate a first channel creating carbon leakages but do not explain all the regional patterns observed in Table B3. Other channels are directly related to policy induced changes in world energy markets.

B3.1.2. Changes in world energy markets

The emission curtailment in the EC induces significant changes in world energy demands (Table B5). In the EC, there is a large fall in fossil-fuel consumption and an increased penetration of carbon-free energies. Between 1995 and 2030, crude oil demand in the EC declines relative to the baseline. After 2030, heavier reliance on crude oil reverses this trend.

The changes in the crude oil price relative to the baseline reflect these demand movements (see Figure B1) which have an interesting policy implication. For a large country (or country grouping) with potential to influence world energy prices, the welfare losses resulting from the imposition of a carbon tax may be partly offset by an improvement of its terms-of-trade (Figure B2).

These developments lead to two different negative leakage effects. First, the decrease in oil prices induces a *fuel substitution effect*, replacing coal and carbon-based synthetic fuels by less carbon-intensive oil products. A lower carbon content of energy demand results in reduced emissions. This effect is especially powerful in regions like China and India because they rely heavily on the use of coal.

Table B4. **Sectoral trade balances when the EC stabilises emissions unilaterally**

In billions of US$ 1985

	Baseline levels		Deviations relative to baseline				
	1985	2050	2000	2005	2010	2030	2050
Agriculture							
United States	10	85	0	0	0	0	0
Japan	−15	−182	0	0	0	0	−1
EC	−30	−220	−1	−2	0	0	6
Other OECD [1]	15	17	0	0	0	0	0
Energy-exporting LDCs	1	12	1	2	2	0	0
China	2	178	0	0	0	0	−1
Former Soviet Union	−5	−26	0	0	0	0	0
India	0	28	0	0	0	0	0
CEETs	1	3	0	0	0	0	0
DAEs	−3	−63	0	0	0	0	0
Brazil	4	18	0	0	0	0	0
RoW	20	148	0	0	0	0	−2
Energy							
United States	−39	−205	1	1	0	−2	13
Japan	−53	−125	0	0	0	−1	4
EC	−78	−183	8	13	17	10	−37
Other OECD [1]	6	−27	0	0	−1	0	2
Energy-exporting LDCs	158	755	−8	−12	−13	1	1
China	7	−79	0	0	−1	−2	6
Former Soviet Union	3	78	−1	−1	−1	−2	−4
India	−6	−47	0	0	0	0	1
CEETs	−19	−46	0	0	0	−1	0
DAEs	−20	−96	0	0	0	−1	3
Brazil	−7	−94	0	0	0	−1	4
RoW	48	69	0	0	0	0	7
Energy-intensive goods							
United States	−12	−46	1	2	2	3	4
Japan	6	9	1	1	1	2	3
EC	11	69	−7	−9	−9	−15	−22
Other OECD [1]	15	76	1	2	1	2	3
Energy-exporting LDCs	−20	−109	1	2	2	1	2
China	−11	−47	0	0	0	1	0
Former Soviet Union	−1	16	0	0	0	1	2
India	−3	−13	0	0	0	0	0
CEETs	1	−1	0	0	0	1	1
DAEs	−10	−120	0	0	0	0	1
Brazil	3	7	0	0	0	1	0
RoW	21	158	2	2	2	4	6
Other goods and services							
United States	−32	94	−2	−2	−1	−1	−17
Japan	110	346	−1	−1	0	0	−6
EC	111	348	0	−2	−6	5	53
Other OECD [1]	−23	−54	−1	−1	0	−2	−5
Energy-exporting LDCs	−109	−630	6	8	9	−1	−2
China	−29	−84	0	0	0	0	−5
Former Soviet Union	−27	−99	1	1	1	1	1
India	2	26	0	0	0	0	−1
CEETs	11	39	0	0	0	0	−1
DAEs	42	286	0	0	0	0	−4
Brazil	11	79	0	0	0	0	−3
RoW	−65	−351	−1	−2	−1	−3	−11

1. Excluding Mexico.
Source: OECD GREEN Model simulations.

Secondly, there is an *income effect* affecting the energy exporting regions. They lose revenues from lower energy exports, and these income losses slow their economic growth, their energy demand and ultimately their carbon emissions. This income effect appears in the Energy-exporting LDCs and in the Former-Soviet Union.

Table B5. **Changes in primary energy demands when the EC stabilises emissions unilaterally**

	Levels (in ExaJ)	% deviations relative to baseline				
	1985	2000	2005	2010	2030	2050
Coal and carbon-based backstop						
EC	10.1	−29.0	−37.4	−41.5	−63.0	−78.9
World	89.3	−2.9	−3.7	−4.0	−5.0	−4.4
Liquid fuels						
EC	18.9	−9.7	−11.0	−10.8	−15.7	−26.0
of which: crude oil	*16.8*	*−14.4*	*−15.2*	*−12.6*	*−5.0*	*46.1*
World	106.9	−1.4	−1.6	−1.5	−2.2	−3.8
Natural gas						
EC	8.6	−2.3	−3.6	−6.5	−15.7	−32.1
World	61.7	−0.3	−0.6	−1.1	−2.4	−4.9
Carbon-free energies						
EC	2.3	2.3	2.5	5.7	15.1	33.2
World	12.6	0.3	0.4	0.8	2.2	4.6

Source: OECD GREEN Model simulations.

Regarding the time profile of the net leakage rate, it tends to be higher in early periods because the unilateral emission cut puts downward pressure on the international oil price and induces some regions to become more energy intensive. The leakage rate is particularly high between 1995 and 2000 because the phase-in of negative leakages increases progressively with the fall in oil prices. After 2030, the rise in the oil price decreases the leakage rate by decreasing the overall energy demand.

B3.2. How sensitive are carbon leakages to alternative model specifications?

The results just described depend on the parameterisation of the model. Given the number of interacting parameters, sensitivity analysis with a large model like GREEN is not a easy task. Previous work with a reduced scale maquette[18] suggests several directions where the model's parameterisation could be tested:

- Determination of oil price (exogenous/endogenous).
- Armington elasticities ruling the substitution between domestic and imported goods.
- Supply elasticities of fossil-fuels.
- Elasticity of substitution between capital and energy.

The experiments implementing alternative parameterisations are shown in Figures B3*b* to B3*h*. In the first test, the *world oil price is exogenous*, *i.e.* the results exclude the mechanism whereby the reduction in energy demand in one region decreases the oil price and induces a substitution effect towards oil consumption in other regions. In the simulation presented in Figure B3*b*, where the oil price follows an exogenous path, both in baseline and in the policy scenarios,[19] the overall leakage rate is almost nil in early years. The positive leakages in OECD regions are roughly halved, implying that with the base specification the oil price channel accounts for roughly half of the leakage rate. The negative income effect in energy-exporting LDCs is also reversed after 2010.

The *role of the trade elasticities* is shown in Figures B3*c* and B3*d*. In Figure B3*c*, the elasticity of substitution between domestic and imported energy-intensive goods was raised from 3-4 to 15, a value extremely high compared with any available econometric estimate at this level of aggregation. In order to isolate the impact in European markets this change was implemented in the EC only. The overall leakage rate doubles from 6 to 12 per cent by 1995, but still declines afterwards.

In Figure B3*d* the trade elasticities were augmented in all regions. The competitiveness loss of European producers is now felt more intensively not only in domestic but also in foreign markets. As a result of this change, the leakage rate increases from 12 to roughly 16 per cent in 1995. With a very high price elasticity in the EIS trade, the leakage rate tends to increase again by 2050.

Figure B1. World oil prices when EC stabilises emissions unilaterally

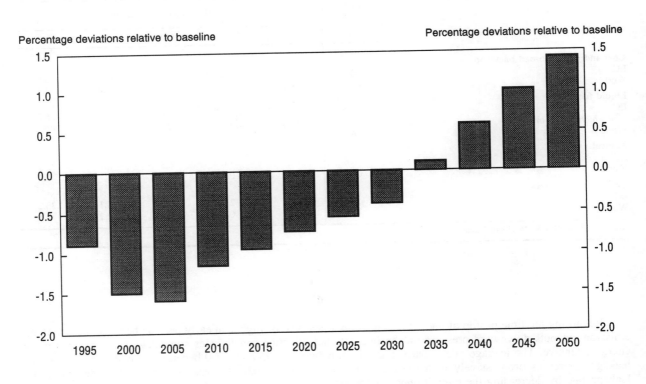

Percentage deviations relative to baseline

Percentage deviations relative to baseline

Figure B2. Terms of trade when EC stabilises emissions unilaterally

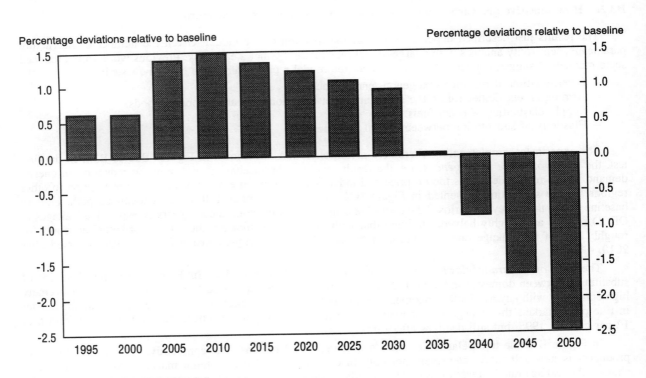

Percentage deviations relative to baseline

Percentage deviations relative to baseline

Source: OECD GREEN model simulations.

116

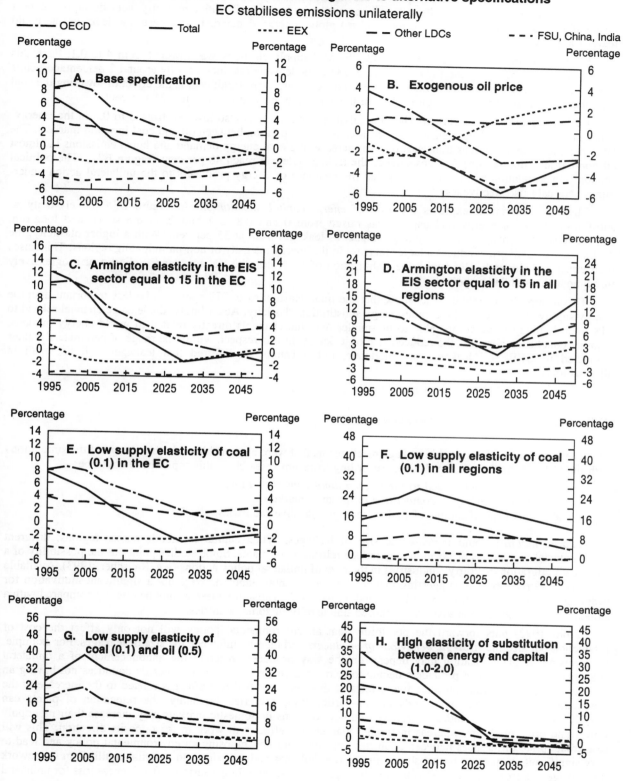

Figure B3. **Sensitivity of carbon leakage rate to alternative specifications**
EC stabilises emissions unilaterally

1. The carbon leakeage rate is defined in per cent of the EC emission reduction.
Source : OECD GREEN model simulations.

117

Regarding the *sensitivity with respect to the supply elasticity of fossil fuels*, a very inelastic supply implies that the price response to a demand shock will be very high. At the limit, with a perfectly inelastic supply there is no possibility of reducing (by a price mechanism) global energy demand. In this case, the leakage rate could reach 100 per cent.

In the experiment presented in Figure B3*e* the coal supply elasticity was lowered from 4 to 0.1. First, this change was implemented in the EC only (Figure B3*e*). The leakage rate increases by around 2 percentage points relative to base case a result of the increase of EC coal exports. More significant is the effect of lowering the coal supply elasticity in all regions (Figure B3*f*). In this case, the leakage rate reaches 25 per cent.

Leakages increase even further when the oil-supply elasticity is also lowered from 3 to 0.5 in the Energy-exporting LDCs.[20] Low supply elasticities create a fierce competition between oil and coal in world markets. The large decline in energy prices translates into an increase in global energy demand and boost emissions in almost all non-participating regions. In consequence the leakage rate can reach 40 per cent (Figure B3*g*). The political economy interpretation of this scenario is that the response of energy producers to the unilateral action undermines seriously its effectiveness.

The last experiment explores *the role of energy-capital substitution*. In Figure B3*h* the elasticity of substitution between energy and capital was raised from 0 and 0.8 to 1 and 2, in the short- and long-run, respectively. This change has a very large impact as leakages peak at 35 per cent. With a higher elasticity, the decline of world oil price induces a larger increase in the energy intensity of non-participating regions. This raises their emissions although, along with the stabilisation of oil prices, the leakages tend to disappear progressively throughout the simulation period.

To sum-up, the sensitivity tests show that the trade elasticities in EIS appear to be less important than the energy supply elasticities or the capital-energy substitution elasticity. Accordingly, the leakage channel related to EIS trade is likely to be comparable to or smaller than the channels directly related to world energy markets. Another conclusion concerns the reduced size of leakages. In this respect, within the range of parameters' values embodied in GREEN,[21] leakages are moderate, but it cannot be inferred that leakages will be small in all situations.

B3.3. Other possible leakage mechanisms

There are some other possible leakage mechanisms that were not considered in the context of the simulations with the GREEN model presented here. According to recent research in this topic those could be:

i) a leakage channel related to the *international capital mobility*;
ii) the effect of *imperfect competition* on product markets;
iii) alternative specifications of trade in energy-intensive industries.

Capital mobility could increase the size of leakages. When capital is mobile across regions, different environmental regulations or taxation may induce relocation of plants. Some studies point out the possibility of a significant migration of "dirty" industries in the case of unilateral policy actions (*e.g.* Rauscher, 1993). Available evidence is fairly robust in suggesting that tight environmental standards were not a significant motivation for firm migration (*e.g.* Barrett, 1993; and Low and Yeats, 1992). However, these cannot be directly compared with a situation where high carbon taxes are imposed unilaterally in some countries.

Ulph (1992) puts forward the possibility that an environmental policy will not only affect the cost of production but also the *strategic behaviour of producers* and thereby influence the size of leakages. For example, the decision of plant location may depend on the way producers react to the announcement of a unilateral abatement policy. Suppose producers decide to relocate their production units towards countries not having an emission constraint. Ulph considers two effects of this decision. A direct effect is related to the increase in the production of energy-intensive goods in non-participating countries. Secondly, the relocation of plants can modify market structures. Indeed, a reduced number of firms in domestic markets may increase their monopoly power and price mark-ups whereas in foreign markets the effect will work in the opposite direction. This will exacerbate price differences between countries imposing and not-imposing an environmental policy and lead to very significant changes in market shares, production volumes and emissions. In a partial equilibrium framework the leakage rate from this channel could reach 75 per cent thus entailing a serious effectiveness loss for unilateral abatement policies.

The Secretariat is not aware of any attempt to model, in a global general equilibrium framework, the impact of non-competitive behaviour on the size of the leakage effect. The net effect of all general equilibrium interactions could be smaller than the effect observed at the industry or firm level. However, this is still subject to further research (Horton, Rollo and Ulph, 1992).

Using the 12RT model, Manne (1993) provides an alternative assessment of the relative magnitude of the different leakage channels. In 12RT, the change in trade flows of energy-intensive goods is by and large the most important conduit for leakages whereas the channels related to energy markets are roughly comparable to GREEN.[22] Leakage rates in 12RT are usually in the range of 20-30 per cent. However, as Amano (1993) points out, the specification of EIS trade in 12RT raises some methodological problems. In 12RT only the EIS trade balance is endogenous. It depends directly on energy costs and a quadratic penalty imposed on deviations from trade patterns in the base year. EIS consumption is projected exogenously. Moreover, EIS products are assumed to be homogenous whatever their region of origin. 12RT illustrates the potential for a rapid phasing-out of EIS production in countries curtailing carbon emissions unilaterally, but is based on a speculative assessment of the limits for EIS trade. In contrast, the specification of GREEN is based on observed behaviour, but may have the disadvantage of imposing an overly rigid structure on future trade patterns.

B4. Carbon leakages in the context of an agreement involving FCCC – Annex 1 countries

The experiments discussed in the previous sections are illustrative. This section presents two policy scenarios related to on-going FCCC negotiations. Both simulate a stabilization of emissions at their 1990 levels in the group of Annex 1 countries.

In the first scenario, each Annex 1 country/region[23] stabilises emissions individually whereas in the second simulation the target is assigned to the Annex 1 group as a whole. The leakage rate and its regional breakdown in the two cases is given in Table B6. In both cases, the carbon leakage is virtually nil despite a large emission cut in the Annex 1 group (roughly 50 per cent relative to the baseline). However, there are significant changes in trade flows.

Table B6. **Leakage effect when the Annex 1 group stabilises emissions unilaterally**[1]

	1995	2000	2005	2010	2030	2050
Emissions in Annex 1 baseline scenario[2]	4 368	4 561	4 802	5 026	6 532	8 769
Emission stabilisation						
by Annex 1 countries individually:						
Reductions in Annex 1 emissions or						
Ex ante reductions in world emissions[2]	−298	−595	−821	−954	−2 314	−4 552
Ex post reductions in world emissions[2]	−294	−590	−818	−963	−2 350	−4 468
Leakage rate (in %)	1	1	0	−1	−2	2
of which: DAEs, Brazil and RoW	2	3	3	2	0	1
Energy-exporting LDCs	0	−1	−1	−2	−1	0
China and India	−1	−1	−1	−1	−1	0
Joint emission stabilisation						
by Annex 1 countries jointly:						
Reductions in Annex 1 emissions or						
Ex ante reductions in world emissions[2]	−166	−359	−617	−811	−2 313	−4 552
Ex post reductions in world emissions[2]	−165	−359	−616	−812	−2 316	−4 404
Leakage rate (in %)	1	0	0	0	0	3
of which: DAEs, Brazil and RoW	1	1	1	1	0	2
Energy-exporting LDCs	0	0	−1	−1	0	1
China and India	0	0	0	0	0	1

1. Emissions are stabilised at their 1990 levels.
2. In million tons of carbon.

Note: Figures may not add up due to rounding. Note that between 1995 and 2010, the emission reduction within the group of Annex 1 countries is higher when each country/region stabilises individually than when there is joint stabilisation. This is due to the fact that emissions in the former Soviet Union are already below 1990 levels in the baseline scenario.

Source: OECD GREEN Model simulations.

The changes in trade flows are illustrated in Table B7. There is a significant redistribution of trade deficits and surplus across regions. The surplus in energy sectors in the Energy-exporting LDCs falls as a counterpart of the cut in energy imports from the Annex 1 region. This decrease their revenues and lowers imports of Other

Table B7. Sectoral trade balances when each country/region in the Annex 1 group stabilises emissions unilaterally

Deviations relative to baseline in billion 1985 US$

	2000	2005	2010	2030	2050
Agriculture					
United States	−2	−2	−3	−3	3
Japan	−1	−1	−2	−1	5
EC	−2	−3	−3	−2	5
Other OECD[1]	−1	−2	−2	−2	0
Energy-exporting LDCs	6	8	10	4	−10
China	0	0	0	1	−2
Former USSR	1	1	1	2	5
India	0	0	0	0	−1
CEETs	0	0	0	1	3
DAEs	0	−1	−1	0	0
Brazil	0	0	0	1	−4
RoW	0	0	0	0	−3
Energy					
United States	8	12	14	5	−99
Japan	19	30	37	40	21
EC	11	16	20	10	−35
Other OECD[1]	1	1	2	4	−2
Energy-exporting LDCs	−35	−53	−61	−21	63
China	−1	−2	−3	−9	23
Former USSR	−4	−5	−5	−7	−9
India	0	0	0	−1	5
CEETs	0	0	0	−3	−17
DAEs	3	3	1	0	21
Brazil	0	0	0	−4	16
RoW	−3	−4	−5	−12	13
Energy-intensive goods					
United States	0	0	−2	0	9
Japan	−11	−15	−8	−16	−20
EC	−5	−6	−6	−9	−9
Other OECD[1]	1	1	−1	−2	−3
Energy-exporting LDCs	5	7	7	6	1
China	1	2	1	4	3
Former USSR	1	1	1	0	−5
India	0	0	0	1	0
CEETs	1	1	1	1	0
DAEs	0	1	0	1	2
Brazil	1	1	1	2	0
RoW	5	7	5	14	20
Other goods and services					
United States	−7	−10	−10	−2	87
Japan	−7	−14	−27	−23	−7
EC	−4	−8	−11	1	39
Other OECD[1]	−1	0	1	0	5
Energy-exporting LDCs	24	37	43	12	−54
China	0	0	2	4	−23
Former USSR	2	3	3	5	9
India	0	0	0	1	−5
CEETs	−1	−1	−1	2	14
DAEs	−3	−3	−1	0	−22
Brazil	−1	−1	0	1	−11
RoW	−2	−2	0	−2	−31

1. Excluding Mexico.
Source: OECD GREEN Model simulations.

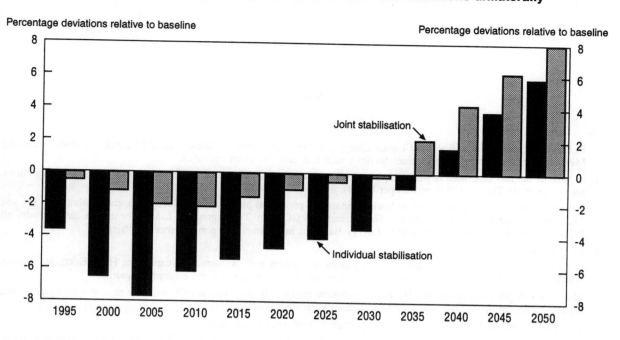

Figure B4. **World oil prices when Annex 1 stabilises emissions unilaterally**

Percentage deviations relative to baseline

Percentage deviations relative to baseline

Joint stabilisation

Individual stabilisation

Source: OECD GREEN model simulations.

Goods and Services; in turn, this translates into a lower surplus for that sector in OECD regions. Many of these patterns are reversed after 2030, because energy demand in Annex 1 regions must rely more heavily on imported crude oil after the phasing-out of coal and high-carbon synthetic fuels. In this way, unilateral action by Annex 1 countries has a large impact on the oil price, especially when each country/region stabilises individually (see Figure B4).

In the energy-intensive sectors the most salient fact is the change in the direction of trade observed for Japan, which becomes a net importer of energy-intensive goods (*cf.* Table B4 and B5). Shifts in trade balances are also specially marked for the RoW region. This displacement of trade flows may induce a sub-optimal allocation of resources at the world level. Assuming that the initial situation is at an optimum, the production of EIS may be displaced towards countries having a less efficient production process. Even though the carbon leakages involved appear to be minor, this resource (mis-)allocation effect also strengthens the case for international policy co-operation.

Notes

1. In the Framework Convention for Climate Change, Annex 1 countries comprise OECD Member countries (excluding Mexico), successor states to the former Soviet Union and east European countries.

2. In spite of the fact that there is weak empirical evidence on the link between environmental restrictions and trade flows, see for example Tobey (1993) or Klepper (1994).

3. Under this heading are grouped the following industries: paper and pulp products (ISIC 341), chemicals (ISIC 351 and 352), iron and steel (ISIC 371), and non-ferrous metals (ISIC 372). The aggregated EIS sector in IEA data includes all Paper and Chemical industries (see IEA, Energy Balances in member and non-member countries).

4. See CEC (1992).

5. For a more detailed test of the link between income per capita and emissions per capita see Holtz-Eakin and Selden (1993). On the other hand, that study did not incorporate energy prices into the estimated equations.

6. The GDP variable is expressed in 1985 US$. Estimation using GDP evaluated at PPP exchange rates was also carried out; the results do not differ significantly under such an alternative specification.

7. This price was calculated using a weighted average of coal, oil and gas prices.

8. This point was also illustrated in previously published simulation results with the GREEN model (see, Oliveira Martins, Burniaux and Martin, 1992).

9. The term "carbon leakages" was first introduced by Perroni and Rutherford (1993) and Rutherford (1992). Winters (1992) provides a survey on this topic.

10. This is particularly relevant in the case of an environmental problem of global dimension, because country specific benefits of emission abatement are small relative to global benefits.

11. This point can be illustrated in the case of a carbon tax. Consider the carbon tax (τ) defined as the shadow-price (or the marginal utility) of a constraint on domestic carbon emissions:

$$\tau = \frac{dW_d}{dE_d}$$

where W_d is a representative welfare indicator. However, as the environmental externality is related to world emissions (E_w) rather than exclusively domestic emissions (E_d), the optimal tax ($\overline{\tau}$) (should rather be defined as:

$$\overline{\tau} = \frac{dW_d}{dE_w} = \left(\frac{dW_d}{dE_d} \right) \bullet \left(\frac{dE_d}{dE_w} \right) = \tau \bullet \frac{dE_d}{dE_w}$$

The "leakage corrected" carbon tax will then be:

$$\overline{\tau} = \frac{\tau}{1 + \lambda_m}$$

where λ_m is the marginal leakage rate (Perroni and Rutherford, 1993). In the absence of leakages, the two taxes coincide, but if the leakages are positive the optimal tax should be lower than the tax based exclusively on domestic emissions.

12. See, Burniaux, Nicoletti and Oliveira Martins (1992) for a presentation of GREEN.

13. This leakage rate is somewhat lower than previously published comparable estimates derived from GREEN, (*e.g.* Martins, Burniaux and Martin, 1992). The reason for this difference is due to the different assumptions characterising the baseline scenario: the revised baseline assumes the phasing out of energy subsidies in all countries and higher output growth for China and India. Therefore, one has to bear in mind that the leakage rate may also depends on the baseline assumptions.

14. This group includes Mexico.

15. Of course, this is an *ex-ante* conjecture as the sign of the emission spillover could change if, for example, all countries in the OECD group participated in the agreement.

16. Recall that both crude oil or carbon-based backstops may enter as the production input for refined liquid fuels.

17. This result depends on the specific closure rule of the model (constant current balance in real terms). Other closures could complicate the picture, but would not invalidate these conclusions over the long run.

18. See Burniaux and Oliveira Martins (1993).

19. This path corresponds to a increase of $6.5 per barrel per decade until 2030 and thereafter the oil price stabilises at the price of the backstop, *i.e.* $50; all prices are constant 1985$.

20. All other oil producing regions are assumed to be price-takers in GREEN.

21. For a discussion of the parameterisation of GREEN, see Burniaux *et al.* (1992).

22. Manne and Oliveira Martins (1994) provide an overview of the two models and a comparison of results with respect to carbon leakages.

23. In the GREEN model the Annex 1 group maps into six countries/regions: the United States, Japan, the EC, Other OECD (excluding Mexico), NIS (the former-Soviet Union) and the eastern European countries (CEETs).

Bibliography

Amano, A. (1993), "Commentary to international trade: the impacts of unilateral carbon emission limits", proceedings of *OECD/IEA Conference: The Economics of Climate Change*, OECD, Paris.

Barrett, S. (1993), "Strategic environmental policy and international competitiveness", proceedings of *Environmental Policies and Industrial Competitiveness*, OECD, Paris.

Burniaux, J.-M. and Oliveira Martins, J. (1993), "Carbon leakages, trade and energy supply: evidence from a simplified maquette", mimeo.

Burniaux, J.M. *et al.* (1992), "GREEN – a multi-sector, multi-region general equilibrium model for quantifying the costs of curbing CO_2 emissions: a technical manual", *OECD Economics Department Working Papers,* No. 116.

Burniaux, J.M., Nicoletti, G. and Oliveira Martins, J. (1992), "GREEN: A global model for quantifying the costs of Policies to Curb CO_2 Emissions", *OECD Economic Studies*, No. 19 (Winter).

Commission of the European Communities (CEC) (1992), "The climate challenge: economic aspects of the Community's strategy for limiting CO_2 emissions", *European Economy*, No. 51 (May).

Holtz-Eakin, D. and Selden, T.M. (1993), "Stoking the fires? CO_2 emissions and economic growth", *NBER Working Papers*, No. 4248.

Horton, G., Rollo, J.M.C. and Ulph, A. (1992), "The implications for trade of greenhouse emission control strategies", *Environmental Economics Research Series*, UK Department of Trade and Industry.

Klepper, K. (1994), "Trade implications of environmental taxes", presented at *Workshop on Implementation of Environmental Taxes*, Paris, OECD.

Low, P. and Yeats, A. (1992), "Do 'dirty' industries migrate?", proceedings of *International Trade and Environment*, World Bank, Washington.

Manne, A. (1993), "International trade: the impacts of unilateral carbon emission limits", proceedings of *The Economics of Climate Change, proceedings of an OECD/IEA Conference*, OECD, Paris.

Manne, A. and Oliveira Martins, J. (1994), "Comparison of model structure and policy scenarios with GREEN and 12RT", *OECD Economics Department Working Papers,* (forthcoming).

OECD (1992), "STAN database for industrial analysis", OECD documents, Paris.

Oliveira Martins, J., Burniaux, J.-M. and Martin, J.P. (1992), "Trade and the effectiveness of unilateral CO_2-abatement policies: evidence from GREEN", *OECD Economic Studies*, No. 19 (Winter).

Perroni, C. and Rutherford, T. (1993), "International trade in carbon emission rights and basic materials: general equilibrium calculations for 2020", *Scandinavian Journal of Economics*, 95 (3).

Rauscher, M. (1993), "Environmental regulation and international capital allocation", *Fondazione ENI Enrico Mattei Working Papers*, No. 79.93.

Rutherford, T. (1992), "The welfare effects of fossil fuel carbon restrictions: results from a recursively dynamic trade model", *OECD Economics Department Working Papers,* No. 112.

Tobey, J. (1993), "The impact of domestic environmental policies on international trade", proceedings of *OECD Conference on Environmental Policies and Industrial Competitiveness*, OECD, Paris.

Ulph, A. (1992), "Environmental policy, plant location and government protection", presented at *The International Dimension of Environmental Policy*, Milan, Fondazione ENI Enrico Mattei.

Winters, L.A. (1992), "Trade and welfare effects of greenhouse gas abatement: a survey of empirical estimates", proceedings of *The Greening of World Trade Issues*, Harvester Wheatsheaf.

Annex C

CARBON SEQUESTRATION THROUGH BIOMASS USE

by

Dirk Pilat*

---

* This Annex is partly based on a consultancy report by Peter Read (Read, 1994).

TABLE OF CONTENTS

C1.   Introduction   129

C2.   Characteristics of Biomass   129
        C2.1.   Basic characteristics of biomass   129
        C2.2.   Technologies for sustainable biomass use   131

C3.   Costs and Benefits of Energy from Biomass   132

C4.   The Implementation of Biomass Energy Systems   134
        C4.1.   The need for preparations   134
        C4.2.   Policies required   135

Notes   136

Bibliography   137

C1. Introduction

Biological processes remove carbon dioxide from the atmosphere through photosynthesis. Enhancement of these processes, for instance by afforestation or growth of biomass, has become known as "carbon sequestration". Although attention is generally focused on afforestation, this has only limited potential to arrest global warming. Once the newly planted forests have matured, their net absorption of carbon from the atmosphere will slow down relative to the growth phase of the forest. More promising is growth of biomass as a source of fuel, which – by substituting for fossil fuels – can drastically reduce net carbon emissions. Biomass technologies are closer to large-scale commercial application than those of other renewable energy sources and fit more easily into existing systems of energy supply. Biomass is also fairly close to being competitive with coal, in particular if existing market distortions (including subsidies for food production and free carbon disposal in the atmosphere) are eliminated.

Large-scale implementation of biomass energy faces several constraints, in particular land requirements and some environmental uncertainties. To make a significant contribution to energy supply and mitigation of GHG emissions, hundreds of millions of hectares of land would be required. However, substantial amounts of agricultural land are currently not used in industrial countries and, deforestation in developing countries also has produced large degraded areas which could be used for biomass production. Many of the environmental uncertainties are similar to those of (intensive) agriculture and could be mitigated by careful management. Biomass is generally seen as a medium term transitory option which may be replaced in later years by other renewable sources of energy, such as those based on photovoltaic power.

Growth of trees can remove carbon from the atmosphere for long periods, in particular if the wood is eventually harvested and used for building materials or other long-term structural purposes. Afforestation may be a desirable policy in itself and can contribute to controlling the rise in GHG concentrations.[1] However, afforestation does not arrest the growth of gross carbon emissions, as it does not replace the use of fossil fuels in energy supply. In addition, there is a limit to the amount of land which can be used for afforestation and therefore to the amount of carbon that can be sequestered permanently.

The potential of the biomass option in mitigating net carbon emissions is discussed in this annex. First, the types and available technologies for biomass production are reviewed. Next, the costs and benefits of energy supply from biomass are examined. Finally, desirable policies to implement the biomass option are discussed.

C2. Characteristics of Biomass

C2.1. Basic characteristics of biomass

All living plants absorb carbon dioxide but most plants only store it for a short time. Overlapping rotations of trees and shrubs provide long lived standing storage of carbon, and therefore forestry provides a technology for sequestration. Roots and in-soil carbon are a substantial fraction of this permanent storage. Techniques for enhanced sequestration include improved management of low grade forest, improved timber harvesting with selective logging, reduced deforestation, reforestation of former forest land, agro-forestry and plantation forestry.

Apart from *in situ* storage, commercial forest activity leads to sequestration in the products. Depending on the type of product (structural timber, furniture, paper pulp, etc.) such sequestration will be long, medium or short term, with eventual decay to carbon dioxide in the atmosphere by fire or by fungal/microbial attack. Use of structural timber might also replace some energy-intensive materials, such as cement, steel and aluminium.

Most significant from a policy perspective is the commercial production of biomass for burning as bio-fuel. Carbon emissions of different electricity generation technologies are shown in Table C1. Net emissions of energy systems based on biomass, if operating on a sustainable basis, can be negative since bi-annual woody crops

Table C1. Carbon emissions of electricity generation technologies [1]

Tons of CO_2/Gigawatthour

Conventional coal plant	964.0
Oil fired plant	726.2
Gas fired plant	484.0
Boiling water reactor (nuclear)	7.8
Geothermal steam	56.8
Large hydropower	3.1
Wind energy	7.4
Photovoltaics	5.4
Wood (sustainable harvest)	−159.9 [2]

1. Carbon emissions include emissions during fuel extraction, plant construction and plant operation.
2. Sustainable biomass may have negative carbon emissions, since roots and other unharvested parts of biomass remain in place. Carbon emissions from fertilizers, pesticides and fossil fuels during the production stage are included in the analysis (see San Martin, 1989).

Source: IEA/OECD (1991).

sequester carbon not only in the parts which are used as fuel, but also in roots and soil.[2] This is true even if carbon emissions from use of fertilizers and fossil fuels in the production process (harvesting, etc.) are included.

Substantial amounts of biomass are currently produced as waste materials. These include crop and forest residues, dung and municipal wastes. Table C2 shows the potential contribution of these residues to energy supply, based on the assumption that 25 per cent of available residues are used. The contribution could be substantial in developing countries, and at the global level about 7 per cent of current energy needs could be covered by use of only 25 per cent of these available residues. In 1992, US power plants fuelled primarily by such waste products accounted for some 1.3 per cent of total electricity generated (U.S. Department of Energy, 1993). Use of biomass residues can help to reduce waste, replaces some fossil fuel use and can contribute to the commercial development of sustainable biomass technologies. However, since this option is not based on a closed biomass loop its contribution to reducing GHG cumulation is typically smaller than that of sustainable biomass.

Table C2. Potential contribution of biomass residue resources to energy supply

	Energy content of potentially harvestable residues (10^6 GJ)				Energy consumption in 1990 (10^6 GJ)	Per cent of energy use potentially provided [1]
	Crops	Forest	Dung	Total		
Developing countries	21 510	16 671	13 328	51 509	86 160	15
Africa	1 947	3 880	2 528	8 355	11 845	18
Central America	1 283	563	669	2 514	5 992	10
South America	3 114	3 036	2 719	8 870	10 748	21
Asia	15 143	9 099	7 390	31 632	57 409	14
Oceania	23	93	21	137	167	21
Industrialised countries	16 528	18 802	6 295	41 626	238 351	4
North America	6 598	8 789	1 542	16 929	92 955	5
Europe	5 347	4 534	2 112	11 993	65 441	5
USSR	3 568	4 710	1 796	10 074	58 620	4
Asia	381	376	162	919	17 112	1
Oceania	635	394	682	1 711	4 223	10
World	38 038	35 473	19 623	93 135	324 511	7

1. Assuming that only 25 per cent of the potentially harvestable residues are used commercially.

Source: Read (1994).

To make a further contribution to energy supply, biomass would have to grown specifically for fuel production. In broad terms the production choices are:

– conventional timber product oriented forestry (medium to long rotation);
– bio-fuel product oriented forestry (short rotation, mainly woody crops);
– herbaceous cropping for bio-fuel products (sugar cane, oil seeds, maize).

To make a significant impact on GHG emissions, any of these technologies will imply substantial demands for land.

Comparison of these options has shown that the second optimizes sustainable biomass from the point of view of carbon sequestration over time, while requiring the smallest land area (Hall, 1994). This technology would most likely be based on woody crops with three- to seven-year rotation cycles, depending on the species selected, climatic and soil conditions. The crops could be coppiced, where part of the three would remain standing. This type of cultivation could also produce several by-products. For instance, some trees could remain for longer periods to produce other wood products (willow wands, paper pulp).

C2.2. Technologies for sustainable biomass use

Various technologies are available to retrieve marketable fuels from biomass (Figure C1). It can be burned directly to produce heat, burned in power plants to produce electricity (and in combined heat and power plants to produce both heat and electricity) or converted through various chemical and biological processes to liquid (ethanol, methanol) or gaseous fuels, which subsequently can be used for production of electricity or used for transportation purposes. All applications are currently in use. Direct combustion for heat is primarily in use in developing countries for domestic heating and cooking. Here, such "traditional" biomass provides more than 20 per cent of primary energy needs (Rosillo-Calle and Hall, 1992), and in some areas up to 90 per cent of energy needs are met by such fuels. Estimates of the recent contribution of such "traditional" biomass to primary energy supply are provided in Table C3.[3] This traditional use of biomass has significant negative environmental effects, however, and further extension of this option is not considered desirable.

Figure C1. **Converting biomass**

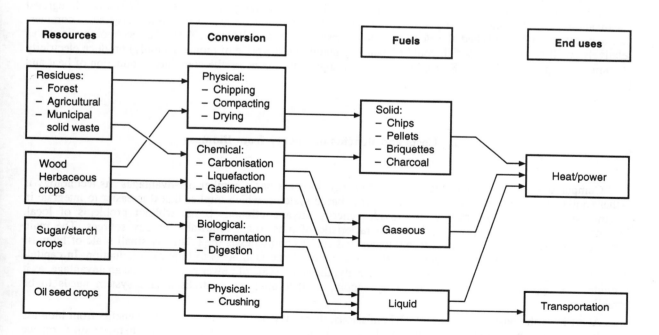

Source: Shell briefing service (1994).

Table C3. **Contribution of biomass to energy supply, 1988**

	Commercial energy consumption (10⁶ GJ)	Fuelwood (10⁶ GJ)	Biomass[1] (10⁶ GJ)	Total energy[2] (10⁶ GJ)	Contribution to total energy use	
					Fuelwood	Biomass[1]
					In per cent	
Developing countries	70 430	16 272	n.a.	86 702	18.8	n.a.
Africa	7 363	4 688	n.a.	12 052	38.9	n.a.
Central America	5 488	521	n.a.	6 009	8.7	n.a.
South America	8 328	2 497	n.a.	10 825	23.1	n.a.
Asia	49 146	8 501	n.a.	57 648	14.7	n.a.
Oceania	105	64	n.a.	169	37.9	n.a.
Industrialised countries	236 338	2 955	6 689	239 293	1.2	2.7
North America	91 636	1 338	4 022	92 974	1.4	4.2
Europe	65 029	613	1 050	65 643	0.9	1.6
USSR	58 376	965	1 617	59 341	1.6	2.7
Asia	17 106	6	n.a.	17 112	0.0	n.a.
Oceania	4 192	32	n.a.	4 224	0.8	n.a.
World	306 768	19 227	6 689	325 995	5.9	n.a.

1. Alternative estimate for selected industrialised regions only. Includes fuelwood.
2. Commercial energy consumption and fuelwood.
Source: Rosillo-Calle and Hall (1992).

Brazil's "Proalcool" programme derives liquid fuels from sugar cane, providing more than 50 per cent of automotive fuels in the country. This programme has been heavily subsidised, and the fuels have less environmental benefits than other modern biomass applications. Overcropping of such biofuel crops can, for instance, impoverish the soil. In addition, land requirements are much larger for this type of biomass than in the case of woody crops.

Currently, the most promising option economically appears to be biomass production for electricity generation. Most interest seems to be focused on gasification of biomass in highly efficient BIG-GT (Biomass Integrated Gasification – Gas Turbine) power plants. Although this technology is not yet available for large-scale commercial application, it has reached the demonstration phase (Elliott and Booth, 1993). This technology involves relatively small power plants which could (depending mainly on the price of biomass supply) produce electricity at competitive prices (4-5 cents/Kwh). Other possible applications concern the combined production of heat and power (IEA/OECD, 1993).

C3. Costs and Benefits of Energy from Biomass

Compared with other renewable sources of energy, biomass has a number of advantages. Its technology is rather similar to the currently dominating fossil fuel-based systems, which implies that it is easier to integrate in existing systems of energy supply. It provides energy on a continuous basis, without problems of local, intermittent or periodic supply, which are characteristic of most other renewable energy sources. The main difference between existing biomass technologies and coal technologies is the relatively small scale of biomass power plants, which is due to the impracticality of devoting large land areas to biomass production. In capital-poor developing countries with low population density, the small scale of power plants may be an advantage, as it provides the opportunity for local electricity supply, so that no large centralised grid system needs to be established.

Apart from the positive effect on GHG emissions, there may be other environmental benefits from biomass use. In particular in degraded areas it may help to reduce soil erosion, improve soil characteristics, reduce pressures on natural forests and even lead to increased bio-diversity. Biomass produced from waste products avoids landfills and may help to reduce methane emissions from such landfills.[4] The establishment of so called "dedicated" biomass supply may also reduce pressures on existing forests by reducing the demand for fuelwood from these forests.[5]

One of the main constraints to the biomass option is the major surface area needed. For a given sequestration target, land requirements would be greatest for long-term sequestration in trees or for annual bio-fuel crops, but even for short-rotation woody crops, substantial land areas would be required (Hall, 1994). As population pressures are mounting in many developing countries, diverting large areas to production of energy crops instead of food supply may appear unrealistic. However, there are a number of reasons to think that fairly large areas may be available for biomass production. First, in industrialised countries large agricultural areas are currently not used. In the United States, at least 30 million hectares (300 000 square kilometres) are under set-aside and conservation programs. In Europe, trends also indicate that the need for agricultural land is shrinking and up to 40 million hectares may be available here as well (Hall, 1994). Although not all of these areas may be suitable for biomass production, such production may enhance the economic value of these areas, by offering a commercial alternative to food production. Second, in particular in developing countries, deforestation has led to the degradation of large areas which are threatened by soil erosion. Biomass could help in restoring and protecting such areas. In the long run, population growth may nevertheless lead to increased pressure on land which may reduce land availability for energy production. In this case, biomass could be a medium term transitory source of energy, as in the long run photovoltaic power or other renewable energy systems could take over.

Some estimates of available land are provided in Table C4. The range of estimates is very wide but suggests that globally at least 300 million hectares are available for biomass production. The contribution of such an area to energy supply depends mainly on land productivity. The species selected for growing, water supply, soil characteristics and biomass management are critical elements in determining productivity.

Assuming an average yield per hectare of 12 (dry) tons of biomass and a heating value of 20 Gigajoules per ton (Rosillo-Calle and Hall, 1992), the 300 million hectares of biomass quoted above could produce 72 Exajoules of energy.[6] Supposing these 300 million hectares could be committed to energy supply by 2020, the global contribution of biomass to baseline primary supply in 2020 could be about 14 per cent.[7] If, as is likely, biomass would displace coal, net carbon emissions could fall (compared with the baseline) by some 1.8 GtC, or more than 20 per cent of total 2020 emissions. Several recent scenario studies (Lazarus, 1993; Edmonds, et al., 1994) show contributions of biomass to energy supply of 20 per cent or more before the middle of the next century.

Biomass may primarily be a regional option, and could in particular be attractive to land-abundant developing countries in Latin America and Africa. In these areas (as well as some areas in south-east Asia), deforestation has led to the degradation of land and made significant land surfaces available for biomass production. These tropical areas are also those where the process of photo-synthesis is most efficient and carbon sequestration per hectare could be highest. In several countries in these areas, electricity distribution systems are currently poorly developed. Biomass could reduce the need for a large, centralised grid, and thus reduce the cost of electricity.

The second major constraint to the large scale use of biomass energy concerns environmental uncertainties. Alongside the environmental benefits of biomass discussed above are some potentially serious environmental risks. Much depends on how and where biomass energy systems are implemented (Hall, 1994). If biomass

Tableau C4. **Alternative estimates of potentially available land for biomass production**

Millions of hectares

Source	Land area estimate	Remarks
Houghton and Woodwell (1989)	850	
Grainger (1988)	758	Of which 203 fallow forests, 137 logged forests, 87 deforested watersheds and 331 desertified drylands
Myers (1989)	300	Primarily areas which urgently require reforestation
Massoud (1979)	1 000	
Alpert et al. (1992)	952	
Bekkering (1992)	385	Only 11 countries
Nakicenovic et al. (1993)	265	
Read (1994)	1 266	Of which 738 estimated deforested areas in the period 1970-2000, 267 (fallow) agricultural land and 261 grasslands

Source : For a complete list of references see Read (1994).

Figure C2. **Typical electricity generation costs**

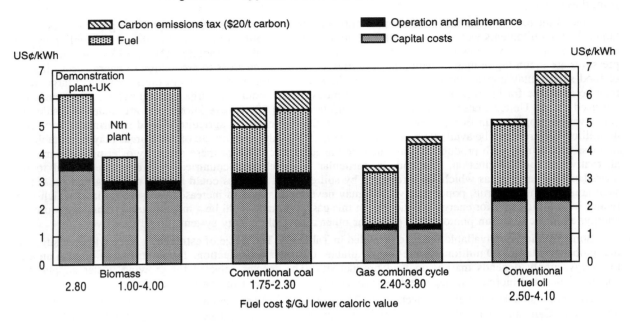

Note: With the exception of biomass, the fuel cost ranges are representative for crude oil prices in the range US$ 15-25 per barrel.

Source: Elliott and Booth (1990).

plantations displace natural forests, the adverse environmental effects would be serious. Large mono-cultures could lead to loss of bio-diversity, although biomass could be more biologically diverse than agricultural mono-cultures. Intensive biomass production may contribute to erosion, to pollution caused by fertilizer and pesticide use and may lead to water shortages. Many of these environmental concerns are similar to those expressed regarding (intensive) agricultural production, some of which might be overcome by careful planning and management, for example by matching biomass species to the location selected[8] and by paying attention to the long-term fertility of the soil.[9]

Biomass-based technologies are currently already close to being competitive with conventional power plants based on fossil fuels. Technical progress and expansion of the application of biomass for energy production are expected to lead to a further decrease in unit costs. The range of electricity generation costs for biomass and fossil fuels is shown in Figure C2. Biomass may be close to being competitive with coal and may also become competitive with gas if fossil fuel prices would rise from their current levels. The precise costs of electricity from biomass depend to a large extent on regional variations in the production costs of biomass, which are related to land productivity, species selected and the potential availability of waste material. This picture would look even better if the negative external effects from burning fossil fuels were included in their prices. A carbon tax could adjust for this, making biomass fuels more competitive compared with these fuels. A further barrier is due to biomass' competition with agricultural production. Since most OECD countries subsidise the production of agricultural commodities, this drives up land prices and constitutes a barrier to the commercially viable expansion of biomass production.

C4. The Implementation of Biomass Energy Systems

C4.1. The need for preparations

Some experience with modern biomass energy systems has emerged in the past two decades. Progress is being made in the commercialisation of technologies and as the market grows, costs are likely to fall. The US

Department of Energy foresees a considerable growth in biomass use, and in Europe prospective growth is also substantial. In this respect, it is not clear if much needs to be done to promote biomass. The private sector seems to become aware of its possibilities, and if a carbon tax were implemented or a net carbon emission constraint appeared, many utility companies might switch to biomass feedstock. However, such decisions should preferably be made by the utility companies (in case of electricity production) or other producers of primary energy, on the basis of relative price signals, rather than being forced on the market by government regulation.

From an insurance perspective (discussed in greater detail in Part 4 of the main paper) however, some R&D and pilot projects could be further required to explore the costs and benefits of the biomass option. Although part of this could be privately financed, some government involvement might be needed with regard to basic R&D. Such R&D would, in particular, concern the selection of biomass species which are optimal for the different areas considered. Much of this research would need to be regional to determine local soil and climate characteristics to facilitate optimal species choice. Some further research, development and demonstration (RD&D) might also be required with regard to technologies for electricity generation from biomass. The initial implementation of biomass energy can be based on residues, which already provides a substantial contribution to energy supply and has a significant additional potential for a further contribution. In the long run, sustainable energy crops are likely to have much larger environmental benefits.[10]

C4.2. Policies required

Removal of existing market imperfections could provide a powerful stimulus to the biomass option. Reduction of agricultural subsidies, a critical review of regulatory barriers, for instance restrictions with regards to the use of municipal waste and the use of set-aside agricultural areas (U.S. Department of Energy, 1993), as well as the inclusion of negative externalities in prices of fossil fuels are important elements in this respect. Along these lines, the implementation of either a carbon tax or a system of tradeable emission permits could also provide a major stimulus.

Biomass may have not only neutral, but negative effects on net carbon emissions over its life time (San Martin, 1989). As it initially sequesters some carbon, which is not harvested for fuel, in roots, soil and standing parts (coppiced biomass could leave part of the tree standing), it can be argued that biomass production should receive an initial (start-up) subsidy if a carbon tax were introduced, in order to secure a "level playing field" with respect to the tax treatment of net emissions. This subsidy should be the same per unit of carbon as that for afforestation, but since afforestation has much higher net sequestration rates per unit of land, the subsidy per hectare would be much smaller for biomass than for afforestation. Such a small initial subsidy would make biomass even more competitive with existing fuels. For practical purposes, such a subsidy may be less relevant, as it is difficult to measure the amount of carbon sequestered, and to monitor whether the biomass is actually being grown or not.

Notes

1. Reducing deforestation is sometimes also included among sequestration options. Deforestation and land-use changes contributed over 17 per cent to global anthropogenic carbon emissions in 1990 (see Table 3.4 in the main paper).

2. Modern applications of biomass should not be confused with traditional applications, such as the burning of wood in open stoves. In the latter case biomass is often not exploited on a sustainable basis: typically insufficient biomass is grown to replace the burned wood. Traditional biomass applications are also a major contributor to emissions of other GHGs, for instance carbon monoxide and NO_x, as Table 3.4 of the main paper shows.

3. The 6 per cent estimate of biomass' contribution to global energy supply is likely to be on the low side. Biomass use is poorly documented and mainly takes place in the informal sector in developing countries. An estimate by Rosillo-Calle and Hall (1992) mentions a 35 per cent contribution of biomass to primary energy supply in developing countries and a 14 per cent contribution to global supply.

4. Methane emissions from landfills make a significant contribution to global warming. Some 10 per cent of anthropogenic emissions of methane are estimated to be from landfills (see Table 3.4 in the main paper).

5. ''Dedicated'' biomass is grown specifically for its contribution to energy supply.

6. Estimates of production per hectare range from 10-15 tons of biomass. Yields are generally lower in temperate areas compared with tropical areas.

7. Based on GREEN's baseline scenario.

8. The species selected should fit water availability, soil characteristics, and be resistant to possible pests and diseases.

9. This involves good soil management, for instance by recovering nutrients, as well as the selection of some nitrogen-fixing species, which can be grown mixed with energy crops.

10. Further developments in biomass technologies could make more ''exotic'' technologies available for application, such as production of ocean biomass or photobiology (Hall, 1994). The latter technology can produce biomass (algae) which sequesters carbon directly from flue gases from power plants. Such technologies could be integrated with current fossil fuel uses.

Bibliography

Edmonds, J., Wise, M. and MacCracken, C. (1994), "Advanced energy technologies and climate change – an analysis using the Global Change Assessment Model (GCAM)", Pacific Northwest Laboratory, Washington DC, mimeo.

Elliott, P. and Booth, R. (1990), "Sustainable biomass energy", Selected Papers, Shell, London.

Elliott, P. and Booth, R. (1993), "Brazilian biomass power demonstration project", Special Project Brief, Shell, London.

Hall, D. (1994), "Biomass energy options in W. Europe (OECD) to 2050", in IEA/OECD, *Energy Technologies to reduce CO_2 emissions in OECD Europe: Prospects, Competition, Synergy*", Paris.

IEA/OECD (1991), *Greenhouse Gas Emissions – The Energy Dimension*, Paris.

IEA/OECD (1993), *Electric Power Technologies: Environmental Challenges and Opportunities*, Paris.

Lamarre, L. (1994), "Electricity from whole trees", *EPRI Journal*, Vol. 19, No. 1, pp. 17-24.

Lazarus, M., *et al.* (1993), *Towards a Fossil Free Energy Future*, Stockholm Environment Institute, Boston Center, Boston.

Patterson, W. (1994), *Power from Plants – The Global Implications of New Technologies for Electricity from Biomass*, Royal Institute of International Affairs, London.

Read, P. (1994), "Carbon sequestration in forests – Bio-fuel as the core technology in an effective response strategy", Massey University, mimeo.

Rosillo-Calle, F. and Hall, D.O. (1992), "Biomass energy, forests and global warming", *Energy Policy*, February, pp. 124-136.

San Martin, R.L. (1989), "Environmental emissions from energy technology systems: the total fuel cycle", in IEA/OECD, *Energy Technologies for Reducing Emissions of Greenhouse Gases*, Paris.

Shell Briefing Service (1994), *Renewable Energy*, Number 1, London.

U.S. Department of Energy (1993), *Electricity from Biomass – National Biomass Power Program Five Year Plan (FY 1994 – FY 1998)*, Washington DC.

Bibliography

Annex D

UNCERTAINTIES IN CLIMATE POLICY DESIGN

by

Dirk Pilat*

---

* This Annex is largely based on a study by Jacoby and Prinn (1994), which provides more detailed information.

TABLE OF CONTENTS

D1. Introduction 143

D2. The Greenhouse Effect 144

D3. Emissions of GHGs: Current and Future Uncertainties 145

D4. Changes in GHG Concentrations 148

D5. Climate Change 150

D6. Economic and Ecological Impacts of Climate Change 151

D7. Summary 153

Notes 154

Bibliography 155

D1. Introduction

This paper provides a concise overview of the uncertainties which arise when attempting to determine the damages caused by future climate change. These uncertainties can be classified into four areas, pertaining to the various links in the causal loop describing the interaction between economic activity and the global climate (Figure D1):

- What are current (anthropogenic) emissions of GHGs, and what are future emissions likely to be?
- How do these emissions change the atmospheric concentrations of the GHGs?
- What is the relation between the rise in atmospheric concentrations and climate change?
- What are the impacts of climate change on economic and ecological systems?

All four causal links underlying these questions are characterised by major uncertainties, partly linked to the long-term nature of the global warming problem. A fundamental fifth problem is that there may be limits to man's ability to predict climate change, partly because elements of the climate system may be chaotic.

The next section briefly outlines the greenhouse effect; subsequently the five areas of uncertainty are discussed. The final section of this paper draws some conclusions from these uncertainties for the policy response to the risk of global warming.

Figure D1. **Climate change feedback loop**

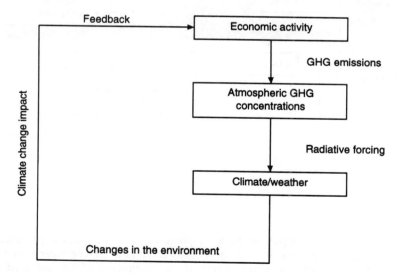

Source: OECD.

D2. The Greenhouse Effect

The greenhouse effect itself is a natural phenomenon. Without it, the world would not be habitable, as surface temperatures would be some 33 °C below current levels (IPCC, 1992). The present concern with global warming reflects the fact that economic activity is distorting the natural balance, leading to climate change with unknown economic and ecological impacts.

The greenhouse effect basically works as follows (IPCC, 1990, 1992). Incoming solar radiation is absorbed by the earth, mainly at the surface. Some of the energy is radiated back to space at longer (thermal/infrared) wavelengths. Some of this radiation is absorbed and re-radiated by GHGs in the atmosphere, mainly water vapour, clouds, CO_2 (carbon dioxide), CH_4 (methane), N_2O (nitrous oxide) and CFCs (chlorofluorocarbons). The result of this re-radiation is that the earth's surface receives radiant energy from the atmosphere above as well as directly from the sun, thus raising average surface temperatures (Figure D2).

Figure D2. A simplified diagram illustrating the greenhouse effect

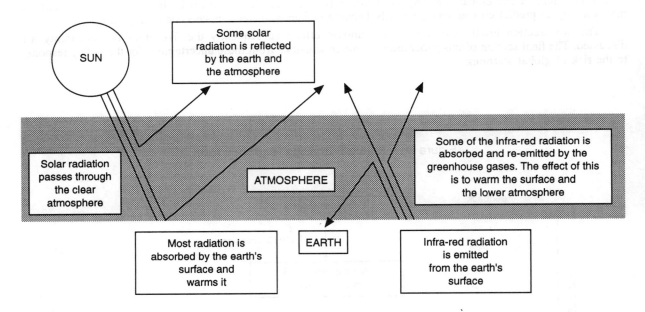

Source: IPCC (1992).

With the exception of CFCs, all major GHGs appear in the atmosphere as a result of natural processes, but anthropogenic emissions of GHGs are reputed to distort the natural balance and add to GHG concentrations, thus increasing the natural greenhouse effect. The qualitative mechanism of the greenhouse effect and most of the processes involved are well known. Problems arise because the exact magnitudes, variation and details of the processes are highly uncertain.

The main result of the greenhouse effect is an increase in average world temperatures. Other possible effects are changes in precipitation, wind patterns and cloud formation. These impacts can also show great regional variation. Each of these effects has potentially major impacts on environment and the economy.

D3.   Emissions of GHGs: Current and Future Uncertainties

The first major uncertainty concerns (anthropogenic) emissions of GHGs, both current and in the future. How large are current man-made emissions and how will these emissions change over time?

Table D1 presents the basic characteristics of the major long-lived GHGs (*i.e.* gases other than the major short-lived GHG, water vapour). The first column shows the estimated volume of emissions of the major gases in 1990. CO_2 dwarfs the other long-lived GHGs in this respect. The second column shows the average atmospheric lifetime of the gases. After a certain period, gases are either broken down by chemical processes into other compounds, or they are sequestered from the atmosphere in "sinks". The third column shows the direct radiative forcing of the gases, expressed relative to CO_2. This figure measures the direct contribution of each gas to global warming per unit of mass change relative to present concentrations. The fourth column integrates the direct contribution to radiative forcing over time, and therefore accounts for the different atmospheric lifetimes of the gases; this characteristic is known as the "Global Warming Potential" (GWP).[1] The GWPs of the different GHGs are all expressed relative to the effect of CO_2. The GWPs of CFCs, in particular, are very high compared to CO_2. Caution is required in interpreting these numbers, however, because the GWPs are in general dependent on the time horizon (100 years in Table D1), and indirect effects can substantially alter their value (in some cases by a factor of 2 or more).

Column five shows the total contribution to global warming of 1990 emissions from the various GHGs, which is based on the volume of annual emissions and the GWP index.[2] The predominant role of CO_2 is quite clear from this column, but so are the effects of the relatively small emissions of CFCs. The second IPCC assessment (IPCC, 1992) paid less attention to CFCs than the first assessment (IPCC, 1990), partly because their role in breaking down stratospheric ozone was seen as counteracting much of the direct effects of CFCs on greenhouse forcing.[3] CH_4 and N_2O are also important contributors to global warming. The bottom part of Table D1 shows some GHGs which have an indirect effect on radiative forcing. Apart from its direct effect, methane also has an indirect effect, which could double its GWP index. This indirect effect results from methane's ability to deplete the chemical compound responsible for its destruction in the atmosphere. The final column shows the main anthropogenic sources of the various gases.

Current man-made emissions of GHGs are measured with varying degrees of precision. CO_2 is the main GHG contributing to global warming and is primarily the result of combustion of fossil fuels and land-use changes, in particular deforestation. Knowledge of the current volume of CO_2 emissions from fossil fuels is relatively certain as they can be directly related to fuel consumption. In 1990 emissions were estimated to be 5.5 GtC, with an error margin of 0.5 GtC. More uncertainty surrounds emissions from deforestation and related land-use changes, which are estimated at 1.3 GtC in 1990, with an uncertainty margin of 1.3 GtC (*i.e.* estimates vary from zero to 2.6 GtC).

Current emissions of CFCs and other halocarbons are all of industrial origin and can therefore be measured with high accuracy. Much more uncertainty surrounds the two other major GHGs, methane and N_2O. Both gases have a wide range of anthropogenic sources of emissions, with highly uncertain magnitudes. Tables D2 and D3 show the major sources of these two gases and the available estimates of emissions. Estimated emissions of methane vary by a factor of 2, while the variation in estimated emissions of N_2O is even larger.

Climate change is a long-term process, and several GHGs have a long residence time in the atmosphere. CO_2, N_2O and some CFCs have estimated atmospheric lifetimes of more than a 100 years. Understanding and forecasting climate change therefore requires emission scenarios for the major GHGs covering long time periods.

Table D4 shows six emission scenarios of the 1992 assessment by the Intergovernmental Panel on Climate Change (IPCC, 1992).[4] For the most important GHG, CO_2, estimated emissions in 2025 vary between 8.8 and 15.1 GtC. For 2100, the uncertainty is much larger, with estimated emissions between 4.6 and 35.8 GtC. Carbon emissions from fossil fuels are determined by the rate of economic growth, the availability of fossil fuel reserves, substitutions between fossil fuels with different carbon contents and between carbon-free energy sources and fossil fuels, structural change, the development of carbon-removal technologies and several other developments. Carbon emissions from deforestation are also highly uncertain, as they are determined by population and income growth in developing countries and the resulting changes in land requirements. Development of property rights and policies that promote sustainable logging practices can also affect future emissions from this source.

For CH_4 and N_2O the scenarios show only small differences, but this mainly reflects the limited knowledge about the origins and atmospheric behaviour of these gases, and the difficulty of predicting future emissions of these gases on the basis of economic growth scenarios. Emissions are related to future energy consumption, but also the size and intensity of agriculture and the characteristics of farming technology. CFCs will most probably be phased out completely in response to the Montreal Protocol and its London Amendments, which reduces the

Table D1. Characteristics and sources of major greenhouse gases

	Anthropogenic emissions in 1990 (million tons)	Atmospheric lifetime (years)[1]	Direct radiative forcing relative to CO_2	Global warming potential (GWP) (over 100 years)	Total effect on radiative forcing of 1990 emissions[2]	Main anthropogenic sources of emissions
Greenhouse gases with direct effect on radiative forcing						
CO_2	26 000	120	1	1	64.2%	Energy use (80%), changing land use (mainly deforestation) (17.3%), cement production (2.7%)
CH_4	300	10.5	58	11	19.3%	Energy production and use (25.9%), enteric fermentation (23.9%), rice paddies (17%), wastes (7.4%), landfills (10.8%), biomass burning (8%), domestic sewage (7.1%)
N_2O	6	132	206	270	4.0%	Combustion of fossil fuels (8.7%), fertilised soils (47.8%), land clearing (17.4%), acid production (15.2%), biomass burning (10.9%)
CFC-11	0.3	55	3 970	3 400	2.5%	Industrial (100%), primarily refrigeration, aerosols, foam blowing, solvents
CFC-12	0.4	116	5 750	7 100	7.0%	Industrial (100%), primarily refrigeration, aerosols, foam blowing, solvents
Other halocarbons[3]	1.2	various	various	various	2.9%	Mostly industrial, similar uses as CFCs, also aluminium production
Greenhouse gases with indirect effects on radiative forcing						
CO	200	months	–	–	–	Incomplete combustion of fossil fuels (30.4%), biomass burning (69.6%)
NO_x	66	days	–	–	–	Combustion of fossil fuels (73.5%), biomass burning (26.5%)
Non-methane hydrocarbons	20	days to months	–	–	–	Biomass burning, solvents and fossil fuel combustion

1. The atmospheric lifetime is the ratio of the atmospheric content to the rate of removal. For CO_2 it represents the time it would take for CO_2 concentrations to adjust to changes in emissions (see IPCC, 1990).
2. Calculated as the share of each GHG in the total volume of emissions (column 1) times the GWP index (column 4). Only direct effects are included.
3. See IPCC (1992) for more detail on these gases.

Sources: Columns 1 and 5 from IPCC (1990), Table 2.9; Column 2 and top part Column 4 from IPCC (1992), Table A2.1; bottom part Column 4 from IPCC (1992), Table A2.1; Column 3 from IPCC (1990), Table 2.3; Column 6 from IPCC (1992), Table A3.12.

Table D2. Estimated sources and sinks of methane
In million tons of CH_4

	Best estimate	Range of estimates
Sources:		
Natural:		
Wetlands	115	(100-200)
Termites	20	(10-50)
Ocean	10	(5-20)
Freshwater	5	(1-25)
CH_4 hydrate	5	0-5)
Anthropogenic:		
Coal mining, natural gas and petroleum industry	100	(70-120)
Rice paddies	60	(20-150)
Enteric fermentation	80	(65-100)
Animal wastes	25	(20-30)
Domestic sewage treatment	25	?
Landfills	30	(20-70)
Biomass burning	40	(20-80)
Sinks:		
Removal by atmospheric reactions	470	(420-520)
Removal by soils	?	?
Increase in atmospheric concentrations	32	(28-37)

Source: Prinn (1994).

uncertainty about future emissions. It is less clear, however, to what extent CFCs will be replaced by HCFCs and HFCs, some of which also have relatively long atmospheric lifetimes and relatively high GWPs.

Table D4 also shows a scenario for SO_x (sulphur oxides). Sulphur emissions help to create sulphate aerosols, which have a cooling effect on the world's atmosphere by reflecting incoming solar radiation back into space. Sulphate aerosols also have an effect on cloud formation by providing cloud condensation nuclei and provide an

Table D3. Estimated sources and sinks of nitrous oxide
In million tons of N

	Range of estimates
Sources :	
Natural:	
Oceans	1.4-2.6
Tropical soils	3.8-4.8
Wet forests	2.2-3.7
Dry savannas	0.5-2.0
Temperate soils	−0.6
Forests	0.05-2.0
Grasslands	?
Anthropogenic:	
Cultivated soils	0.03-3.0
Biomass burning	0.2-1.0
Stationary combustion	0.1-0.3
Mobile sources	0.2-0.6
Adipic acid production	0.4-0.6
Nitric acid production	0.1-0.3
Sinks:	
Removal by soils	?
Photolysis in the stratosphere	7-13
Increase in atmospheric concentrations	3-4.5

Source: Prinn (1994).

Table D4.   Results of six IPCC greenhouse gas emission scenarios
Annual emissions

Scenario/reporting year	CO$_2$ (GtC)	CH$_4$ (million tons)	N$_2$O (Million tons N)	CFCs (kt)	HCFCs/ HFCs (kt)	Other halocarbons (kt)	SO$_x$ (million ton S)
1990	*7.4*	*506*	*12.9*	*827*	*143*	*864*	*98*
IS92a							
2025	12.2	659	15.8	217	1 335	121	141
2100	20.3	917	17.0	3	2 897	0	169
IS92b							
2025	11.8	659	15.7	36	1 380	3	140
2100	19.1	917	16.9	0	2 898	0	164
IS92c							
2025	8.8	589	15.0	217	1 335	121	115
2100	4.6	546	13.7	3	2 897	0	77
IS92d							
2025	9.3	584	15.1	24	1 380	3	104
2100	10.3	567	14.5	0	2 764	0	87
IS92e							
2025	15.1	692	16.3	24	1 380	3	163
2100	35.8	1 072	19.1	0	2 764	0	254
IS92f							
2025	14.4	697	16.2	217	1 335	121	151
2100	26.6	1 168	19.0	3	2 897	0	204

Source: IPCC (1992).

additional cooling effect by making clouds more reflective. Anthropogenic emissions of sulphur dioxide are primarily due to the combustion of fossil fuels and are therefore as uncertain as emissions of CO$_2$. Unlike CO$_2$, however, procedures are already available and in use to "scrub" SO$_x$ from flue gases, so that more restrictive pollution laws may also have a great impact on future emissions of sulphur, decoupling them from CO$_2$ emission levels.

D4.   Changes in GHG Concentrations

The relation between changes in emissions and changing concentrations of GHGs in the atmosphere is not straightforward. After a certain period, GHGs are broken down in the atmosphere by chemical processes into other compounds, or they are sequestered in sinks. For instance, CO$_2$ is absorbed in forests, oceans and soils, and CFCs are slowly broken down by photolysis in the stratosphere (IPCC, 1990, 1992). The major uncertainties in this area concern the limited understanding of sinks and removal processes, as well as the complicated interactions between gases in the atmosphere, for instance with regard to the formation of ozone. Partly due to our limited understanding of removal processes, the atmospheric lifetime of the different gases, which influences the rate of change in concentrations, is not known with certainty. The uncertainty about atmospheric lifetimes in its turn implies that the GWP index for the various GHGs, presented in Table D1, is also surrounded by considerable uncertainty.

Anthropogenic emissions of CO$_2$, the main long-lived GHG, add to flows of the natural carbon cycle. A simple schematic presentation of this cycle is shown in Figure D3. Carbon flows between the atmosphere, oceans (surface and deep layers), ocean biota (algae) and land biota (forests and plants) and soils. The natural flows, which are difficult to measure and therefore very uncertain, are based on photosynthesis (land and ocean biota – atmosphere), oxidation of carbon (soil – atmosphere) and partial pressure differences in CO$_2$ (ocean and atmosphere). Of the estimated 1990 annual emissions of approximately 7 GtC, about 3.4 GtC was added to atmospheric concentrations and about 2 GtC (+ or – 0.6 GtC) was probably sequestered by the ocean. The sink

Figure D3. **The carbon cycle**
Numbers in gigatons of carbon

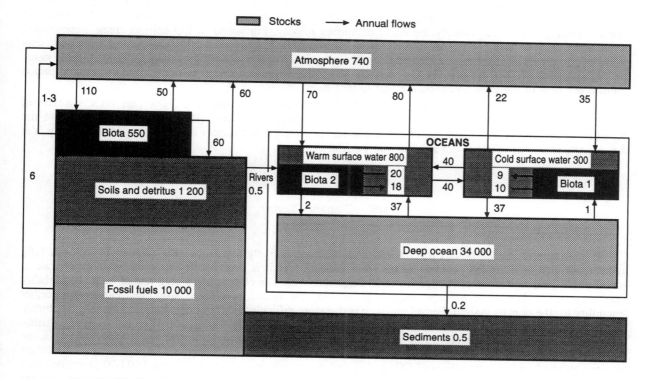

Source: Edmonds *et al.* (1993).

responsible for the remainder of 1.6 GtC is likely terrestrial (biota) and probably located in the Northern hemisphere. It is possible, for instance, that increased CO_2 in the atmosphere has a "fertilising" effect on plants, leading to increased photosynthesis and more carbon sequestration. The uncertainty about the long-term sequestration potential of these terrestrial sinks is large, as climate change may influence the absorption capacity of the terrestrial sink.

Other GHGs are influenced by different removal mechanisms, and are generally broken down in the atmosphere. N_2O may be removed by soils, but its primary removal mechanism is destruction by ultraviolet radiation in the atmosphere. Removal by soils can be influenced by climate change and is therefore uncertain in the long term. The sink for CFCs is photolysis in the stratosphere, and the primary sink for other halocarbons is reaction with the OH (hydroxyl) radical (see below).

The most uncertain removal mechanism among other GHGs is that for methane. Methane is mainly removed by reaction with the OH radical, which converts it, first to CO (carbon monoxide), and then to CO_2. The long-term sink potential of methane depends therefore on the availability of the short-lived OH radical. Human air pollution, in particular NO_x (nitrogen oxide), helps to generate OH, which implies that the removal rate of methane is strongly influenced by the location and magnitude of NO_x emissions. This process is further complicated by reactions with SO_x, ozone and CO.[5] The nature of these processes is relatively well known, but their effects and magnitudes are uncertain in the long term, due to the complexity of interactions and the influence of several anthropogenic gases.

GHGs can have long residence times in the atmosphere, which implies that current emissions of GHGs can have impacts on climate in a distant future. Methane is broken down in the atmosphere in about 11 years (IPCC, 1992). This implies that only a relatively small reduction (15-20 per cent) from current annual emissions would be needed to stabilise current concentrations in the atmosphere. For long-lived GHGs, such as CFCs, CO_2 and

N_2O, which all have atmospheric lifetimes in excess of 100 years, much larger cuts, of 60-80 per cent of current annual emissions, would be required to stabilise atmospheric concentrations at present levels (IPCC, 1990).

CO_2, methane, N_2O and CFCs are all powerful GHGs which have an direct effect on greenhouse warming, while anthropogenic emissions of other gases have an indirect effect on global warming. Most influence complex processes in the atmosphere which help to create tropospheric ozone (O_3), which is an important contributor to global warming, and is not directly the result of human activity. Emissions of CO help to create tropospheric ozone and CO_2. NO_x also contributes to the creation of tropospheric ozone and NMHCs (non-methane hydrocarbons) help to create tropospheric ozone and CO_2. The magnitude of the indirect greenhouse effects of these gases are highly uncertain, but the first IPCC report (IPCC, 1990) suggested that emissions of NO_x had contributed about 6 per cent to the total greenhouse effect to that date.

A final complicating factor is the impact of CFCs on ozone concentrations. The first IPCC assessment (IPCC, 1990) stressed CFCs as a major GHG, but its second assessment (IPCC, 1992) suggested that the depletion of ozone by CFCs might well compensate for the strong direct impact of CFCs on global warming. Yet the magnitude of this offset is not known with certainty.

D5. Climate Change

If atmospheric concentrations of GHGs change, climate is likely to change. The relation is far from fully understood, however. A first problem arises from the fact that it is difficult to determine whether climate is actually changing as a result of changes in GHG concentrations. The climate has a high rate of natural variability over short to medium-term periods. Exogenous shocks, for instance volcanic eruptions, can create further instability for the climate system. For scientists, it is therefore difficult to differentiate between signal (the climate is actually changing) and noise (natural/random disturbances). Unequivocal detection of global warming attributable to GHG changes can therefore still not be extracted from data collected over the past 200 years, despite the significant increase in atmospheric CO_2 concentrations over that period.[6] Figure D4 depicts the correlation between atmospheric concentrations of CO_2 and global mean temperatures over the past 160 000 years, deduced from analysis of Antarctic icecores, but it is not at all clear whether CO_2 changes forced the temperature changes or if temperature variations caused the CO_2 changes.

Climate modellers attempt to forecast climate change. One indicator used in their models is that of climate sensitivity, which estimates the change in mean world temperature between hypothetical present and future equilibrium states, as the result of a change in GHG concentrations, for instance a doubling of CO_2 compared to pre-industrial concentrations. The IPCC (1992) suggested that the change in global mean temperature's in response to a doubling of CO_2 concentrations was likely to fall inside the range of 1.5 to 4.5 °C. Although the best guess reported by IPCC (1990) was given as 3 °C, there is no analytical basis for preferring any estimate in this range above another (Jacoby and Prinn, 1994). Even though such calculations are surrounded by major uncertainties, the climate sensitivity index itself is a very rough measure. It refers to equilibrium states that may never actually occur, and temperature change is only one aspect of climate change, and its distribution over the globe can be highly varied. In addition, other important climate variables, such as changes in precipitation, soil moisture, cloud formation and wind patterns are not covered by the indicator.

There are three major feedback effects involving the atmosphere and the surface, that influence the climate impact of changing GHG concentrations. The best understood of these is albedo (whiteness) of the planet. Albedo is a measure for the reflection of sunlight from the earth and is particularly sensitive to changes in the area covered by snow and ice. As temperatures rise, ice fields (both on land and on sea) may retreat, leading to lower albedo, less reflection and higher absorption, thus reinforcing greenhouse warming. Clouds and aerosols can also affect albedo (see below).

The second feedback results from water vapour. Water vapour is the major natural contributor to the greenhouse effect. Higher temperatures will lead to more evaporation from both ocean and land surface and a warmer atmosphere will hold more water vapour, thus increasing the greenhouse effect. Both surface albedo and water vapour are therefore positive feedback mechanisms. One main uncertainty concerns the magnitude of this effect.

The third feedback mechanism is the least well understood and potentially the most important: the role of clouds, which play a dual role. One is to reflect solar radiation, thus leading to a cooling effect, the other is to block thermal radiation from the Earth, thus leading to a warming effect. It is not absolutely clear which is the dominant effect, and therefore whether clouds form a positive or a negative feedback process. Long term

Figure D4. Correlation of atmospheric carbon dioxide concentrations and global average surface temperature

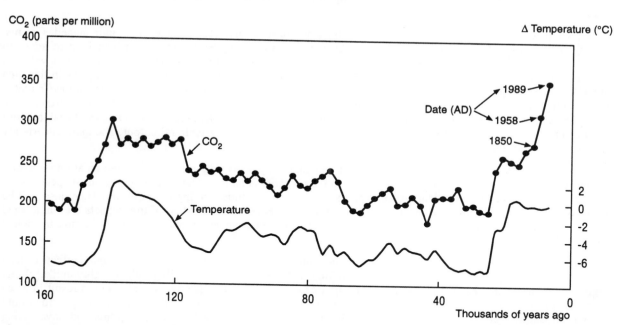

Source: C. Lorius, J. Jouzel, D. Reynaud, J. Hansen and H. Le Treut, "Greenhouse Warming, Climate Sensitivity and Ice Core Date", *Nature*, June 1990.

predictions are even more uncertain, as cloud formation is highly variable in space and time. Cloud processes might change as the result of changes in global and regional temperatures, of changes in atmospheric moisture, quantities of atmospheric dust and wind patterns. The total effect of these three feedback mechanisms increases the uncertainty in the climate sensitivity index from around 30 per cent for the direct radiation effects to a factor of at least 3.

A further major complicating factor, and source of uncertainty, is the ocean. The ocean works as a "thermal" buffer, which absorbs heat from the sun and the atmosphere. The whole surface of the earth potentially works in this way, but the ocean is much more efficient than the land as ocean currents can carry the warm surface waters to the deep ocean, which has a very large heat storage capacity. Ocean dynamics, however, are poorly understood and are difficult to model, because of lack of data, the scale of the problem and the local character of many phenomena. This heat absorption process influences the timing and extent of warming. So even if the equilibrium effect of a doubling of GHG concentrations on average world temperature were known with certainty, the speed with which the new equilibrium temperature will be reached once GHG concentrations have doubled is highly uncertain, ranging between a minimum of a few decades (if only the heating of upper ocean layers is included) to as much as 1 000 years if deep ocean warming is included as well.

A final complicating factor are biogeochemical processes. Emissions of methane and NO_x are partly the result of natural causes. Changes in climatic conditions, in particular temperature and soil moisture may influence these emissions and thus provide an additional feedback process.

D6. Economic and Ecological Impacts of Climate Change

Not only the process of climate change is poorly understood and magnitudes as well as speeds of change are difficult to predict, but little is known about the effects of climate change on economic and ecological systems as well. A rational climate policy would require knowledge about the costs of possible climate change in economic terms. Some areas can be identified where climate change could lead to serious damages. However, the problems of more precise quantification are immense. There is a need to catalogue potential impacts, to quantify them, and finally, and perhaps the most difficult, to value the effects in economic terms. Only after all of these steps are taken, can the costs of climate change be ascertained.

Two main areas of potential impacts can be distinguished, namely managed and unmanaged systems. Managed systems are those that are under human control, which implies human action can help to adapt to climate change and avoid direct damages. In addition, impacts on managed systems usually have a value in economic terms, as there is frequently a market price attached to them. Most of the expected impacts in this area are related to the primary sector (agriculture, forestry) or to sectors with a dependency on climate patterns (construction, tourism, water supply). Climate effects do not need to be damaging, however. Up to a certain level, increased CO_2 concentrations may have a fertilizing effect on plants, leading to higher agricultural output.[7] Changed rainfall or temperatures may in certain areas also help to boost agricultural output. The main uncertainty here is the overall balance of climate change.

Less is known about the potential impacts on unmanaged systems. These are systems which are not directly under human control, which implies their only adaptive potential is natural. Damages in the areas of species loss, migration of forests and desertification are expected but their magnitudes are highly uncertain. There also will be some systems with net gains due to CO_2 fertilization and increased rainfall. Most of the impacts on unmanaged systems will be ecological, which often implies there is no market value attached, making valuation in money terms difficult.

A major source of concern is the possibility that climate change may have certain catastrophic effects or lead to extreme weather patterns. Catastrophic events (Cline, 1992) include the possibility (albeit highly unlikely) that higher temperatures might lead to the disintegration of the West Antarctic ice fields, which could result in a sea level rise of up to six meters. Another scenario is that the melting of polar ice and increased precipitation could change the salinity of the sea water in the North Atlantic, which could affect ocean currents and have strong impacts on climate patterns, in Northern Europe in particular. Extreme weather patterns, such as severe storms, could also result from climate change. However, small-scale phenomena, such as hurricanes and thunderstorms, cannot yet be analysed by current climate models, making the likely occurence of such events much more uncertain than that of general patterns of climate change, such as changes in global mean temperatures.

Some rise in the sea-level is likely to be the result of global warming. There are two main effects here: higher temperatures could lead to the melting of snow and ice cover, and would also lead to some thermal expansion of ocean water. The first effect could partly be compensated by increased precipitation in polar areas. Given a change in global mean temperatures, the uncertainty concerning changes in the sea level are relatively small compared to the uncertainty concerning changes in temperature. For a 3 °C rise in global mean temperatures, the estimated rise in sea levels ranges from 9 to 30 cm (IPCC, 1990).

The effects of climate change will show great regional variation. Agricultural areas in Northern latitudes may perhaps benefit from higher temperatures and increased precipitation, but other areas may become too hot and arid. A sea-level rise could have grave impacts on some small islands, and on some low-lying delta areas, for instance in Egypt and Bangladesh.

The impacts of climate change may be very different depending on whether it occurs in a short period or is spread over centuries. Some natural adjustment, of both managed and unmanaged systems, could take place in the latter case.[8] Another concern is that the transition from one equilibrium climate pattern to another may not be smooth, or even monotonic and the final state may be path dependent due to chaotic and other effects.. These issues introduce additional uncertainty in the prediction of the impact of climate change.

There have been several estimates of the economic damages of climate change (Cline, 1992; Titus, 1992; Nordhaus, 1993. Fankhauser, 1993). It is no surprise that these are highly controversial. They have little or no basis in empirical research on natural eco-systems (where the greatest uncertainties lie) and do not reflect the great range of uncertainty on damages. Table D5 summarises some of the estimates. Those of Nordhaus, Cline and Titus are only available for the United States. In addition, most estimates in Table D5 only show damages corresponding to a doubling of CO_2 concentrations, which represents a relatively limited increase in atmospheric concentrations and global warming. For these scenarios, annual costs in terms of GDP are between 1 and 2.4 per cent. Fankhauser's estimate of global costs also shows only 1.5 per cent of GDP as the annual costs of global warming. However, Cline (1992) estimates the damages for the United States of extreme (10 °C) warming, and finds this to be around 6 per cent of GDP annually. These estimates also depend on the speed of climate change, the degree to which adaptation can take place, the discount rate used, and the valuation of the impacts on unmanaged systems, which have no market price attached to them.

Table D5. **Estimated annual damages of global warming**

In billions of 1988 US$[1]

| | Damages under CO_2 doubling (2.5 °C increase in temperature) | | | | | Long term warming (10 °C increase in temperature) United States Cline (1992) |
| | United States | | | | World Fankhauser (1993) | |
	Nordhaus (1993)	Cline (1992)	Fankhauser (1993)	Titus[2] (1992)		
Heavily affected sectors:						
Agriculture	1.0	15.2	7.4	1.0	39.1	82.5
Coastal areas	10.7	2.5	2.3	2.0	15.1	30.2
Energy	0.5	9.0	0.0	–	0.0	54.6
Other sectors:	38.1	26.7	57.2	118.7	231.0	123.7
Total	50.3	53.4	66.9	121.7	285.2	291.0
In per cent of 1988 GDP	*1.0*	*1.1*	*1.3*	2.4	*1.5*	6.0

1. Estimates have different base years, but are rebased to 1988.
2. Titus assumes a rise in global mean temperatures at 4 °C under CO_2 doubling. See also Cline (1994).
Source: Cline (1992), Nordhaus (1993) and Fankhauser (1993).

D7. Summary

In the light of the uncertainty concerning major aspects of climate change, an optimal policy response is not easy to formulate. We do know:

- that anthropogenic emissions of GHGs are adding to atmospheric concentrations;
- that higher atmospheric concentrations of GHGs have the potential to raise global temperatures and change climate;
- that climate change can have serious impacts on the economy and ecology.

We are less sure about:

- the amount of future GHG emissions;
- the exact sources and sinks of most GHGs;
- the exact effect of these gases on global warming;
- several feedback effects, which may either compensate for or strengthen global warming.

And we know little about:

- the ocean circulation and its effects on the timing, magnitude and patterns of climate change;
- the effects and associated costs of climate change on economy and ecology.

The physical, biological and chemical processes of the climate system interact in complicated ways, which are difficult to capture in climate models. The current climate models, which couple ocean and atmosphere, can not even reproduce present climate conditions, using current concentrations of CO_2, indicating major uncertainties about their ability to forecast future climate conditions. Climate models already push the limits of current supercomputers, but are still rough compared to the phenomena studied and the local character of several important phenomena.

Some of the uncertainties may be resolved by further research, but there may be limits to the extent to which climate change can be predicted. Some of the uncertainties mentioned above may prove difficult to remove. In addition, new research may also increase uncertainty, by showing that previous understandings of the climate system were not correct. It is possible that certain elements of the climate system are not predictable, but are essentially chaotic. Even with a much more extensive climate observation network, the complete climate system can only be observed with a limited degree of accuracy. If the system is chaotic, changes in initial values for predicted variables smaller than the accuracy of current measurements may lead to large changes in predicted future climate conditions. Even with perfect climate models, predictions could then prove false. It is also possible

153

that additional research may show that the climate system is much more complex than it is presently assumed to be, thereby not reducing but increasing uncertainty.[9]

To sum up, there is a distinct possibility that an unfettered increase in GHG emissions can have serious – some say catastrophic – consequences. In addition, many of the consequences of climate change are irreversible. Policy choices must therefore be made in view of both the large stakes involved and the all-pervasive uncertainty. If research could reduce all or most of the uncertainties, policies might wait for more information, allowing some additional build-up of concentrations in the atmosphere. However, although some uncertainties may be reduced over time, there are limits to the degree to which climate change and its consequences can be predicted.

Notes

1. See IPCC (1990) for the mathematical expression of the GWP index.
2. As these figures are based on a GWP index for a 100-year period, column five measures the contribution of 1990 emissions to global warming over the period 1990-2090.
3. This is one of the important indirect effects mentioned above.
4. See Panel B of Table 2.1 in the main paper for further details concerning the underlying assumptions.
5. See Jacoby and Prinn (1994) for more detail.
6. Pre-industrial concentrations of CO_2 were approximately 280 ppmv (parts per million by volume). In 1960 concentrations had risen to 316 ppmv and in 1990 the level was already 354 ppmv (IPCC, 1990).
7. On the other hand, changes in rainfall or soil humidity might offset this effect (see Rosenzweig, 1994).
8. Farming in developed countries may be able to adapt quite rapidly to changed climate conditions.
9. Some disturbing evidence in this respect was recently gathered by scientists studying past climate change by analyzing the Greenland ice core. They (Dansgaard, et al., 1993; Anklin, et al., 1993) found evidence that during the relatively stable Eemian period (115.000-125.000 years ago), large fluctuations (10 °C) in temperature could occur within a few decades, probably caused by changes in deep-ocean circulations.

Bibliography

Anklin, M., *et al.* (1993), ''Climate instability during the last interglacial period recorded in the GRIP ice core'', *Nature*, Vol. 364, July, pp. 203-207.

Cline, W.R. (1992), *The Economics of Global Warming*, Institute for International Economics, Washington DC.

Cline, W.R. (1994), ''Costs and benefits of greenhouse abatement: a guide to policy analysis'', in: OECD/IEA, *The Economics of Climate Change*, pp. 87-105.

Dansgaard, *et al.* (1993), ''Evidence for general instability of past climate from a 250-kyr ice-core record'', *Nature*, Vol. 364, July, pp. 218-220.

Edmonds, Jae, David W. Barns, Marshall Wise, My Ton (1993), ''Carbon coalitions (the cost and effectiveness of energy agreements to alter trajectories of atmospheric carbon dioxide emissions), typescript, Pacific Northwest Laboratories, Washington DC.

Fankhauser, S. (1993), ''The economic costs of global warming: some monetary estimates'', in: Kaya, Y., Nakicenovic, N., Nordhaus, W.D. and Toth, F.L. (eds.), *Costs, Impacts, and Benefits of CO_2 Mitigation*, IIASA, Laxenburg.

IPCC (1990), *Climate Change – The IPCC Scientific Assessment*, Cambridge University Press, Cambridge.

IPCC (1992), *Climate Change 1992 – The Supplementary Report to the IPCC Scientific Assessment*, Cambridge University Press, Cambridge.

Jacoby, H.D. and Prinn, R. (1994), ''Uncertainty in climate change prediction'', MIT Joint Program on the Science and Policy of Global Change, Report No. 94-1, Cambridge, MA.

Nordhaus, W.D. (1993), ''Reflections on the economics of climate change'', *Journal of Economic Perspectives*, Vol. 7, No. 4, Fall, pp. 11-26.

OECD (1994), *Global Change of Planet Earth*, Paris.

Prinn, R. (1994), ''The interactive atmosphere: global atmospheric-biospheric chemistry'', *Ambio*, Vol. 23, pp. 50-61.

Rosenzweig, C. and Hillel, D. (1993), *Agriculture in a Greenhouse World*, National Geographic Research and Exploration, Vol. 9, No. 2, pp. 208-221.

Titus, J. (1992), ''The cost of climate change to the United States'', in: Majumdar, S.K. *et al.* (eds.), *Global Climate Change: Implications, Challenges and Mitigation Measures*, Pennsylvania Academy of Sciences.

MAIN SALES OUTLETS OF OECD PUBLICATIONS
PRINCIPAUX POINTS DE VENTE DES PUBLICATIONS DE L'OCDE

ARGENTINA – ARGENTINE
Carlos Hirsch S.R.L.
Galería Güemes, Florida 165, 4° Piso
1333 Buenos Aires   Tel. (1) 331.1787 y 331.2391
Telefax: (1) 331.1787

AUSTRALIA – AUSTRALIE
D.A. Information Services
648 Whitehorse Road, P.O.B 163
Mitcham, Victoria 3132   Tel. (03) 873.4411
Telefax: (03) 873.5679

AUSTRIA – AUTRICHE
Gerold & Co.
Graben 31
Wien I   Tel. (0222) 533.50.14

BELGIUM – BELGIQUE
Jean De Lannoy
Avenue du Roi 202
B-1060 Bruxelles   Tel. (02) 538.51.69/538.08.41
Telefax: (02) 538.08.41

CANADA
Renouf Publishing Company Ltd.
1294 Algoma Road
Ottawa, ON K1B 3W8   Tel. (613) 741.4333
Telefax: (613) 741.5439
Stores:
61 Sparks Street
Ottawa, ON K1P 5R1   Tel. (613) 238.8985
211 Yonge Street
Toronto, ON M5B 1M4   Tel. (416) 363.3171
Telefax: (416)363.59.63
Les Éditions La Liberté Inc.
3020 Chemin Sainte-Foy
Sainte-Foy, PQ G1X 3V6   Tel. (418) 658.3763
Telefax: (418) 658.3763

Federal Publications Inc.
165 University Avenue, Suite 701
Toronto, ON M5H 3B8   Tel. (416) 860.1611
Telefax: (416) 860.1608
Les Publications Fédérales
1185 Université
Montréal, QC H3B 3A7   Tel. (514) 954.1633
Telefax : (514) 954.1635

CHINA – CHINE
China National Publications Import
Export Corporation (CNPIEC)
16 Gongti E. Road, Chaoyang District
P.O. Box 88 or 50
Beijing 100704 PR   Tel. (01) 506.6688
Telefax: (01) 506.3101

CZECH REPUBLIC – RÉPUBLIQUE TCHÈQUE
Artia Pegas Press Ltd.
Narodni Trida 25
POB 825
111 21 Praha 1   Tel. 26.65.68
Telefax: 26.20.81

DENMARK – DANEMARK
Munksgaard Book and Subscription Service
35, Nørre Søgade, P.O. Box 2148
DK-1016 København K   Tel. (33) 12.85.70
Telefax: (33) 12.93.87

EGYPT – ÉGYPTE
Middle East Observer
41 Sherif Street
Cairo   Tel. 392.6919
Telefax: 360-6804

FINLAND – FINLANDE
Akateeminen Kirjakauppa
Keskuskatu 1, P.O. Box 128
00100 Helsinki
Subscription Services/Agence d'abonnements :
P.O. Box 23
00371 Helsinki   Tel. (358 0) 12141
Telefax: (358 0) 121.4450

FRANCE
OECD/OCDE
Mail Orders/Commandes par correspondance:
2, rue André-Pascal
75775 Paris Cedex 16   Tel. (33-1) 45.24.82.00
Telefax: (33-1) 49.10.42.76
Telex: 640048 OCDE
Orders via Minitel, France only/
Commandes par Minitel, France exclusivement :
36 15 OCDE

OECD Bookshop/Librairie de l'OCDE :
33, rue Octave-Feuillet
75016 Paris   Tel. (33-1) 45.24.81.67
(33-1) 45.24.81.81

Documentation Française
29, quai Voltaire
75007 Paris   Tel. 40.15.70.00

Gibert Jeune (Droit-Économie)
6, place Saint-Michel
75006 Paris   Tel. 43.25.91.19

Librairie du Commerce International
10, avenue d'Iéna
75016 Paris   Tel. 40.73.34.60

Librairie Dunod
Université Paris-Dauphine
Place du Maréchal de Lattre de Tassigny
75016 Paris   Tel. (1) 44.05.40.13

Librairie Lavoisier
11, rue Lavoisier
75008 Paris   Tel. 42.65.39.95

Librairie L.G.D.J. - Montchrestien
20, rue Soufflot
75005 Paris   Tel. 46.33.89.85

Librairie des Sciences Politiques
30, rue Saint-Guillaume
75007 Paris   Tel. 45.48.36.02

P.U.F.
49, boulevard Saint-Michel
75005 Paris   Tel. 43.25.83.40

Librairie de l'Université
12a, rue Nazareth
13100 Aix-en-Provence   Tel. (16) 42.26.18.08

Documentation Française
165, rue Garibaldi
69003 Lyon   Tel. (16) 78.63.32.23

Librairie Decitre
29, place Bellecour
69002 Lyon   Tel. (16) 72.40.54.54

GERMANY – ALLEMAGNE
OECD Publications and Information Centre
August-Bebel-Allee 6
D-53175 Bonn   Tel. (0228) 959.120
Telefax: (0228) 959.12.17

GREECE – GRÈCE
Librairie Kauffmann
Mavrokordatou 9
106 78 Athens   Tel. (01) 32.55.321
Telefax: (01) 36.33.967

HONG-KONG
Swindon Book Co. Ltd.
13–15 Lock Road
Kowloon, Hong Kong   Tel. 2376.2062
Telefax: 2376.0685

HUNGARY – HONGRIE
Euro Info Service
Margitsziget, Európa Ház
1138 Budapest   Tel. (1) 111.62.16
Telefax : (1) 111.60.61

ICELAND – ISLANDE
Mál Mog Menning
Laugavegi 18, Pósthólf 392
121 Reykjavik   Tel. 162.35.23

INDIA – INDE
Oxford Book and Stationery Co.
Scindia House
New Delhi 110001   Tel.(11) 331.5896/5308
Telefax: (11) 332.5993
17 Park Street
Calcutta 700016   Tel. 240832

INDONESIA – INDONÉSIE
Pdii-Lipi
P.O. Box 4298
Jakarta 12042   Tel. (21) 573.34.67
Telefax: (21) 573.34.67

IRELAND – IRLANDE
Government Supplies Agency
Publications Section
4/5 Harcourt Road
Dublin 2   Tel. 661.31.11
Telefax: 478.06.45

ISRAEL
Praedicta
5 Shatner Street
P.O. Box 34030
Jerusalem 91430   Tel. (2) 52.84.90/1/2
Telefax: (2) 52.84.93
R.O.Y.
P.O. Box 13056
Tel Aviv 61130   Tél. (3) 49.61.08
Telefax (3) 544.60.39

ITALY – ITALIE
Libreria Commissionaria Sansoni
Via Duca di Calabria 1/1
50125 Firenze   Tel. (055) 64.54.15
Telefax: (055) 64.12.57
Via Bartolini 29
20155 Milano   Tel. (02) 36.50.83
Editrice e Libreria Herder
Piazza Montecitorio 120
00186 Roma   Tel. 679.46.28
Telefax: 678.47.51
Libreria Hoepli
Via Hoepli 5
20121 Milano   Tel. (02) 86.54.46
Telefax: (02) 805.28.86
Libreria Scientifica
Dott. Lucio de Biasio 'Aeiou'
Via Coronelli, 6
20146 Milano   Tel. (02) 48.95.45.52
Telefax: (02) 48.95.45.48

JAPAN – JAPON
OECD Publications and Information Centre
Landic Akasaka Building
2-3-4 Akasaka, Minato-ku
Tokyo 107   Tel. (81.3) 3586.2016
Telefax: (81.3) 3584.7929

KOREA – CORÉE
Kyobo Book Centre Co. Ltd.
P.O. Box 1658, Kwang Hwa Moon
Seoul   Tel. 730.78.91
Telefax: 735.00.30

MALAYSIA – MALAISIE
University of Malaya Bookshop
University of Malaya
P.O. Box 1127, Jalan Pantai Baru
59700 Kuala Lumpur
Malaysia   Tel. 756.5000/756.5425
Telefax: 756.3246

MEXICO – MEXIQUE
Revistas y Periodicos Internacionales S.A. de C.V.
Florencia 57 - 1004
Mexico, D.F. 06600   Tel. 207.81.00
Telefax : 208.39.79

NETHERLANDS – PAYS-BAS
SDU Uitgeverij Plantijnstraat
Externe Fondsen
Postbus 20014
2500 EA's-Gravenhage   Tel. (070) 37.89.880
Voor bestellingen: Telefax: (070) 34.75.778

NEW ZEALAND
NOUVELLE-ZÉLANDE
Legislation Services
P.O. Box 12418
Thorndon, Wellington   Tel. (04) 496.5652
                          Telefax: (04) 496.5698

NORWAY – NORVÈGE
Narvesen Info Center – NIC
Bertrand Narvesens vei 2
P.O. Box 6125 Etterstad
0602 Oslo 6   Tel. (022) 57.33.00
                  Telefax: (022) 68.19.01

PAKISTAN
Mirza Book Agency
65 Shahrah Quaid-E-Azam
Lahore 54000   Tel. (42) 353.601
                  Telefax: (42) 231.730

PHILIPPINE – PHILIPPINES
International Book Center
5th Floor, Filipinas Life Bldg.
Ayala Avenue
Metro Manila   Tel. 81.96.76
                  Telex 23312 RHP PH

PORTUGAL
Livraria Portugal
Rua do Carmo 70-74
Apart. 2681
1200 Lisboa   Tel.: (01) 347.49.82/5
                  Telefax: (01) 347.02.64

SINGAPORE – SINGAPOUR
Gower Asia Pacific Pte Ltd.
Golden Wheel Building
41, Kallang Pudding Road, No. 04-03
Singapore 1334   Tel. 741.5166
                    Telefax: 742.9356

SPAIN – ESPAGNE
Mundi-Prensa Libros S.A.
Castelló 37, Apartado 1223
Madrid 28001   Tel. (91) 431.33.99
                  Telefax: (91) 575.39.98

Libreria Internacional AEDOS
Consejo de Ciento 391
08009 – Barcelona   Tel. (93) 488.30.09
                       Telefax: (93) 487.76.59

Llibreria de la Generalitat
Palau Moja
Rambla dels Estudis, 118
08002 – Barcelona
       (Subscripcions) Tel. (93) 318.80.12
       (Publicacions) Tel. (93) 302.67.23
                Telefax: (93) 412.18.54

SRI LANKA
Centre for Policy Research
c/o Colombo Agencies Ltd.
No. 300-304, Galle Road
Colombo 3   Tel. (1) 574240, 573551-2
               Telefax: (1) 575394, 510711

SWEDEN – SUÈDE
Fritzes Information Center
Box 16356
Regeringsgatan 12
106 47 Stockholm   Tel. (08) 690.90.90
                      Telefax: (08) 20.50.21

Subscription Agency/Agence d'abonnements :
Wennergren-Williams Info AB
P.O. Box 1305
171 25 Solna   Tel. (08) 705.97.50
                  Téléfax : (08) 27.00.71

SWITZERLAND – SUISSE
Maditec S.A. (Books and Periodicals - Livres
et périodiques)
Chemin des Palettes 4
Case postale 266
1020 Renens VD 1   Tel. (021) 635.08.65
                      Telefax: (021) 635.07.80

Librairie Payot S.A.
4, place Pépinet
CP 3212
1002 Lausanne   Tel. (021) 341.33.47
                   Telefax: (021) 341.33.45

Librairie Unilivres
6, rue de Candolle
1205 Genève   Tel. (022) 320.26.23
                 Telefax: (022) 329.73.18

Subscription Agency/Agence d'abonnements :
Dynapresse Marketing S.A.
38 avenue Vibert
1227 Carouge   Tel.: (022) 308.07.89
                  Telefax : (022) 308.07.99

See also – Voir aussi :
OECD Publications and Information Centre
August-Bebel-Allee 6
D-53175 Bonn (Germany)   Tel. (0228) 959.120
                            Telefax: (0228) 959.12.17

TAIWAN – FORMOSE
Good Faith Worldwide Int'l. Co. Ltd.
9th Floor, No. 118, Sec. 2
Chung Hsiao E. Road
Taipei   Tel. (02) 391.7396/391.7397
            Telefax: (02) 394.9176

THAILAND – THAÏLANDE
Suksit Siam Co. Ltd.
113, 115 Fuang Nakhon Rd.
Opp. Wat Rajbopith
Bangkok 10200   Tel. (662) 225.9531/2
                   Telefax: (662) 222.5188

TURKEY – TURQUIE
Kültür Yayinlari Is-Türk Ltd. Sti.
Atatürk Bulvari No. 191/Kat 13
Kavaklidere/Ankara   Tel. 428.11.40 Ext. 2458
Dolmabahce Cad. No. 29
Besiktas/Istanbul   Tel. 260.71.88
                       Telex: 43482B

UNITED KINGDOM – ROYAUME-UNI
HMSO
Gen. enquiries   Tel. (071) 873 0011
Postal orders only:
P.O. Box 276, London SW8 5DT
Personal Callers HMSO Bookshop
49 High Holborn, London WC1V 6HB
                    Telefax: (071) 873 8200
Branches at: Belfast, Birmingham, Bristol, Edin-
burgh, Manchester

UNITED STATES – ÉTATS-UNIS
OECD Publications and Information Centre
2001 L Street N.W., Suite 700
Washington, D.C. 20036-4910 Tel. (202) 785.6323
                            Telefax: (202) 785.0350

VENEZUELA
Libreria del Este
Avda F. Miranda 52, Aptdo. 60337
Edificio Galipán
Caracas 106   Tel. 951.1705/951.2307/951.1297
                 Telegram: Libreste Caracas

Subscription to OECD periodicals may also be
placed through main subscription agencies.

Les abonnements aux publications périodiques de
l'OCDE peuvent être souscrits auprès des
principales agences d'abonnement.

Orders and inquiries from countries where Distributors have not yet been appointed should be sent to:
OECD Publications Service, 2 rue André-Pascal,
75775 Paris Cedex 16, France.

Les commandes provenant de pays où l'OCDE n'a
pas encore désigné de distributeur peuvent être
adressées à : OCDE, Service des Publications,
2, rue André-Pascal, 75775 Paris Cedex 16, France.

1-1995

OECD PUBLICATIONS, 2 rue André-Pascal, 75775 PARIS CEDEX 16
PRINTED IN FRANCE
(11 95 01 1) ISBN 92-64-14377-7 - No. 47739 1995